Global Migration and Social Change series

Series Editors: **Nando Sigona**,
University of Birmingham, UK

The *Global Migration and Social Change* series showcases original research that looks at the nexus between migration, citizenship and social change.

Forthcoming in the series:

Postcoloniality and Forced Migration
Mobility, Control, Agency
Edited by **Martin Lemberg-Pedersen, Sharla M. Fett, Lucy Mayblin, Nina Sahraoui** and **Eva Magdalena Stambøl**

Navigating the European Migration Regime
Male Migrants, Interrupted Journeys and Precarious Lives
Anna Wyss

Out now in the sei

Temporality in Mobile Live
Contemporary Asia–Australia Migration and Everyday Time
Shanthi Robertson

Negotiating Migration in the Context of Climate Change
International Policy and Discourse
Sarah Nash

Belonging in Translation
Solidarity and Migrant Activism in Japan
Reiko Shindo

Find out more at

bristoluniversitypress.co.uk/global-migration-and-social-change

Global Migration and Social Change series

Series Editor: **Nando Sigona**,
University of Birmingham, UK

Find out more at
bristoluniversitypress.co.uk/global-migration-and-social-change

VISITING IMMIGRATION DETENTION

Care and Cruelty in Australia's Asylum Seeker Prisons

Michelle Peterie

BRISTOL
UNIVERSITY
PRESS

First published in Great Britain in 2022 by

Bristol University Press
University of Bristol
1–9 Old Park Hill
Bristol
BS2 8BB
UK
t: +44 (0)117 374 6645
e: bup-info@bristol.ac.uk

Details of international sales and distribution partners are available at bristoluniversitypress.co.uk

British Library Cataloguing in Publication Data
A catalogue record for this book is available from the British Library

ISBN 978-1-5292-2660-7 hardcover
ISBN 978-1-5292-2661-4 paperback
ISBN 978-1-5292-2662-1 ePub
ISBN 978-1-5292-2663-8 ePdf

Cover design: Andrew Corbett
Front cover image: Shutterstock/estherpoon
Bristol University Press use environmentally responsible print partners
Printed and bound in Great Britain by CMP, Poole

Contents

List of Abbreviations

ABC	Australian Broadcasting Corporation
ABF	Australian Border Force
AHRC	Australian Human Rights Commission
AITA	Adelaide Immigration Transit Accommodation
APOD	Alternative Place of Detention
BITA	Brisbane Immigration Transit Accommodation
CALD	Culturally and Linguistically Diverse
IDC	Immigration Detention Centre
ITA	Immigration Transit Accommodation
MITA	Melbourne Immigration Detention Centre
NGO	Non-Government Organization
PNG	Papua New Guinea
PTSD	Post-Traumatic Stress Disorder
RCOA	Refugee Council of Australia
UN	United Nations

Acknowledgements

First and foremost, I would like to thank the many people who participated in this study as interviewees. Were it not for their generosity and strength, this book would not have been possible. Particular thanks to those who entrusted me with sensitive or distressing testimonies, and to those who welcomed me into their communities as a friend. I hope that this book does justice to your experiences, and to those of the people you support in detention.

It takes a village to raise a researcher, and I am profoundly grateful for mine. This book began as a PhD project at the University of Sydney (USYD), and was extended, reimagined and refined during Postdoctoral Research Fellowships at the University of Queensland (UQ) and the University of Wollongong (UOW). The fieldwork that informs this book was funded by an Australian Research Training Program Stipend Scholarship, a USYD Travel Grant, and a UQ Small Research Grant. I gratefully acknowledge both this financial support and the institutional backing it represents.

I owe a debt of gratitude to innumerable colleagues within and beyond USYD, UQ and UOW. While it is not possible to thank everyone individually, several people deserve specific acknowledgement. Heartfelt thanks to Dr David Neil, without whose long-term influence and intellectual generosity this book may never have been started, and would certainly not exist in its current form. Deepest gratitude to my PhD supervisors, Dr Susan Banki and Professor Stephen Castles, who provided guidance, oversight and support through the doctoral project that began this research. Sincerest thanks to Professor Gillian Triggs, Professor Scott Poynting and Associate Professor Caroline Fleay, who gave valuable feedback concerning that initial project and galvanized me in my desire to continue this work. Warmest thanks to mentors Professor Greg Marston, Professor Gaby Ramia and Professor Alex Broom – as well as dear friends and writing companions Dr Louise St Guillaume, Dr Derya Ozkul and Dr Dora Anthony – who have provided unwavering encouragement and gentle accountability as this book has taken form. Deepest gratitude to psychologist Dr Carole Carter, who helped me to navigate my own emotions during fieldwork for this project, and to the countless people who – at different times and in different ways – have lent me their wisdom and hope.

Thank you to the team at Bristol University Press/Policy Press who saw the potential in this book and guided me through the publication process. Particular thanks to editor Shannon Kneis, series editors Professor Nando Sigona and Associate Professor Alan Gamlen, and project manager Matt Deacon. Thank you also to Ella Sellwood and the anonymous reviewers who read the manuscript for this book prior to its publication and provided feedback.

Finally, deepest thanks to my family, and to those dear friends who qualify as such. I think in particular of my Mum and Dad; of Luke, Simone, Hayden and Emily; of David; of Jack and Marg; and of my MHS, John Street and contemplative community friends. You have nurtured my dreams, supported my endeavours, celebrated my successes, and been my soft place to land. I appreciate you immensely and love you beyond words.

Series Preface

Michelle Peterie's book is the eighth in the *Global Migration and Social Change* series. *Visiting Immigration Detention* offers a captivating account of Australia's onshore immigration detention system and its negative individual and societal impacts. The aim of our book series is to offer a platform for original, engaged and thought-provoking scholarship in refugee and migration studies, open to different disciplinary perspectives, theoretical frameworks and methodological approaches. Peterie's book fully matches our aim by painting a vivid and worrying portrait of the working and function of Australia's onshore immigration detention facilities, contrasting the care and friendship exchanged between detainees and regular visitors with the institutional violence of the immigration regime.

The book will resonate with students, researchers and everyone keen to understand the impact of immigration detention regimes, offering in-depth insights into one that, since the early 2000s, has attracted extensive international attention and produced highly polarized views – for many the Australian approach institutionally violates the human rights of migrants and refugees and breaches the country's international obligations towards those in need of international protection. For others, like the current UK Home Secretary, it offers a template to follow for the reform of the immigration system. The New Plan for Immigration promoted by the British government under Boris Johnson explicitly refers to Australia as a positive example to follow in its attempt to deter the arrivals of asylum seekers to the UK. The UK has been looking closely in particular to Australia's policy of *offshore* asylum processing, which has removed detainees from public view and reduced accountability by placing detention facilities outside the jurisdiction of its courts. However, as Peterie's book shows, Australia also has an *onshore* detention system which is also opaque. Detainees in this system, Peterie argues, 'are hidden in plain sight – held in prison-like centres', many in remote and hard-to-access locations. The book offers unique insight into detention facilities and the harm produced by immigration detention through the accounts of 70 detainees' friends and loved ones as they enter detention as private visitors. In doing so, the book makes three important contributions to scholarship on immigration detention. First, it exposes everyday carceral practices and their consequences on health, hope and relationships. Second, it expands our understanding of who is harmed by such practices, and how harmful practices reverberate and affect inmates and visitors. Finally, the author makes a compelling case for understanding these harmful practices and effects not as accidental or unintentional, but as epitomising a policy logic that accepts cruelty as a mechanism of control.

Nando Sigona
Oxford, March 2022

Preface

Care-based interventions in situations of injustice attract significant suspicion in the social sciences. Scholars caution that caring responses to social issues often ignore the structural causes of suffering, obscuring systemic problems by focusing on meeting the needs of individuals. Concerns about power discrepancies are also prominent. Seemingly altruistic 'caregivers' are charged with reinforcing social hierarchies, adopting privileged roles as heroes and saviours while 'care recipients' are locked into disempowered positions as helpless victims. The volunteer is characterized as deriving emotional gratification from their privileged role. Such critiques are particularly prominent in research about efforts to assist racial minorities, where colonial patterns of power and domination can endure and thrive under a veil of altruism and good intentions.

But do clear lines always exist between the personal and the political, between care and activism? And what happens to interpersonal power dynamics in institutional spaces characterized by violence and control?

I began this research in 2015, intending to analyse the social, political and emotional contours of asylum seeker support work at the level of personal relationships. My interviews with participants in a range of refugee and asylum seeker support programmes drew my attention to the work of people who visit refugees and asylum seekers in immigration detention facilities. As I listened to their stories, it became apparent that issues of power, privilege and emotion were of critical importance to these people. I also began to understand that these ideas held different meanings and carried different resonances in the carceral spaces of Australia's detention centres.

As I continued my research in different parts of Australia, I saw with growing clarity that detention centre environments distort and to some extent collapse conventional distinctions between empowered caregivers and disempowered care recipients. Within detention environments, visitors are positioned not as privileged benefactors but as quasi-prisoners. The inaccuracy of emotional gratification claims was stark. Interviewees were often reluctant to focus on their own emotional experiences, but when asked acknowledged sleepless nights; feelings of shame, complicity and powerlessness; and even clinical diagnoses of depression and Post-Traumatic

Stress Disorder. Equally, while many visitors did not identify as activists or use the language of resistance, most nonetheless conceptualized the work of being a friend to the stranger as a political act.

The echoes of my original research focus can still be found within this book. My research still engages with fundamental questions of power, privilege and emotion. But this is not the book I initially planned to write. Concerns about power discrepancies at the interpersonal level remain present but have been eclipsed by larger questions regarding state power, institutional affect and policy intent. Concerns about volunteers deriving emotional gratification from their work have at once been challenged and become secondary to questions about how and why detention regimes inflict harm – not only on detainees, but also on their loved ones and supporters. The allegations of apoliticism that have been so central to critiques of care-based volunteer work have been called into question as a more complex picture has emerged regarding the intimate relationship between personal care and political activism.

Drawing on more than 70 in-depth interviews with regular visitors to Australian immigration detention facilities, as well as other corroborating sources, this book paints a unique and vivid picture of these carceral spaces. It tells the story of Australia's onshore immigration detention network as witnessed and experienced by the people who enter these spaces to offer friendship and support. Ultimately, it offers a richer understanding of how detainee isolation and despair is produced and weaponized through the details of institutional life; a deeper recognition of what deterrence looks and feels like in Australia's onshore immigration detention system; and an expanded appreciation of the human costs – both direct and collateral – that this system imposes.

Introduction: Studying Immigration Detention

The veil of secrecy

Asylum seeker deterrence policies are built on cruelty. In practice, deterrence involves the infliction of profound harm so that people in urgent need of refuge will seek safety elsewhere. Deterrence policies are popular with many Australians, and governments on both sides of politics have derived electoral advantage from hardline measures including mandatory detention. Yet these same governments have gone to great lengths to hide or whitewash the violence deterrence entails. This book is about these hidden realities, and about the human and societal costs of intentionally employing cruelty for political ends.

Australia's immigration detention system is shrouded in secrecy. Since 2001, people seeking protection at the border have regularly been imprisoned in Australian-run facilities in the Pacific countries of Papua New Guinea (PNG) and Nauru. Australia's now infamous policy of offshore processing has removed detainees from public view. It has also reduced accountability by placing detention facilities outside the jurisdiction of Australia's courts.

Australia's *onshore* detention system is also opaque. These facilities receive little attention in public debate and are largely invisible to the general community. Detainees in this system are hidden in plain sight – held in prison-like centres, many on the outskirts of major population centres.

One of the reasons Australia's onshore detention facilities have fallen beneath the radar is because the cruelty enacted within them evades easy detection. Australia's offshore processing facilities have attracted widespread condemnation in part because of their overt brutality. At considerable personal risk, detainees and whistle-blowers have ruptured the secrecy of these centres, sharing damning evidence of harsh conditions, inadequate medical treatment, and endemic physical and sexual violence. Given the constraining influence of Australia's courts, open violence and ill-treatment are less prevalent in the onshore system. In comparison to conditions offshore, these centres can seem humane to a casual observer.

Yet rates of self-harm in onshore detention facilities are alarmingly high and indicate that people held within them are under significant strain. A 2019 study by Kyli Hedrick and colleagues, for example, found that the rate of self-harm among people in Australia's onshore detention network is an alarming 214 times higher than the rate of hospital-treated self-harm in the Australian community. In contrast, the rate of self-harm among community-based asylum seekers is four times that of hospital treated self-harm in the Australian community.

This book offers a new and unique window into these onshore facilities, following detainees' friends and loved ones as they enter detention centres as private visitors. In doing so, it makes three main contributions to the existing scholarship on immigration detention. First, it provides a rare qualitative account of *how* harm is enacted through carceral practices in Australian onshore detention centres. It exposes the shifting systems of deprivation and frustration that dictate life in these facilities, corroding health, hope and relationships, and maintaining a debilitating asymmetry of power.

Second, it adds to extant understandings of *who* is harmed by detention regimes. A wealth of evidence already exists concerning the devastating impacts of detention for people who are personally incarcerated (see von Werthern et al, 2018). Bringing together testimonies from detainees' loves ones and supporters around Australia, this book highlights the unacknowledged harm detention imposes beyond the detainee. It also examines the emotional politics of solidarity within these institutions, illuminating both the potentials and pitfalls of care as a form of political resistance.

Finally, in locating visitor testimonies within Australia's overarching programme of asylum seeker deterrence, this book makes a theoretical claim concerning *why* harmful practices endure and replicate in detention environments. Researchers and human rights organizations at times frame the adverse impacts of detention as a government failure or unintentional oversight. This book offers an alternative diagnosis. It demonstrates that the reverberating harms detention imposes are not *failures* of this system but rather evidence of its essentially malign *function*. Cruelty is the point.

Detention as deterrence

Australia's immigration detention policy is driven by a political commitment to asylum seeker deterrence. Deterrence, as conceptualized in this book, can take two forms: general deterrence or specific deterrence. *General deterrence* refers to efforts to discourage would-be asylum seekers from travelling to countries where detention policies are in place. As Ephraim Poertner (2017: 18) explains, 'the politics of [general] deterrence produces geographies of asylum that turn "location marketing" upside down': countries compete with one another to become the *least* attractive destination for people seeking asylum.

Immigration detention is a primary instrument in many general deterrence regimes, but other restrictive or punitive policies can also function as general deterrence measures. Boat turn-backs, offshore processing,[1] limiting access to permanent protection, and withholding social welfare or employment opportunities, for example, can all have deterrent effects if they make destination countries less attractive to asylum seekers (Gammeltoft-Hansen and Tan, 2017; Fitzgerald, 2020).

General deterrence measures are premised on the assumption that 'pull factors' (such as favourable immigration policies) influence migration flows as much, if not more, than the 'push factors' that force some people to flee their countries. It is highly unlikely that this is the case (Nethery, 2019; Bloomfield, 2016). Nonetheless, political leaders persist with policies of this kind – framing them, in Australia's case, as effective strategies to 'stop the boats'.

One of the ethical problems with the general deterrence paradigm, of course, is that many asylum seekers are fleeing violence and persecution in their countries of origin and are thus entitled to protection. The 1951 Refugee Convention recognizes the right of forced migrants to cross national borders without authorization to access safety. In this context, general deterrence policies are often framed by governments as necessary efforts to keep out people who are not really refugees (Kathrani, 2011). The fact remains, however, that the majority of people seeking asylum in Australia do have legitimate refugee claims (McAdam and Chong, 2014).

In addition to general deterrence, immigration detention policies can be understood as forms of *specific deterrence*. Specific deterrence involves efforts to persuade asylum seekers already in a country to abandon their refugee claims and return home (Hassan, 2000; Leerkes and Broeders, 2010). Where general deterrence aims to make coming to a country unattractive to all prospective asylum seekers, specific deterrence makes it untenable for those already in a country to stay. At times, financial and other incentives are also provided to further incentivize repatriation (see Whyte, 2014).

Australian governments have been open in framing immigration detention as an element of the country's general deterrence policy (Coalition, 2013). Stemming the flow of new boats of supposedly 'non-genuine' refugees has been embraced as a core policy objective by Australian governments on both sides of politics. There has been a notable reticence, however, to openly admit that mandatory detention is also designed to harm people who have already come to Australia for help. Despite this, there is clear evidence that Australia has subjected people in detention to intentional cruelty in the service of specific deterrence. For example, documents leaked by a whistle blower in 2017 showed that staff at Australia's PNG facility had been explicitly instructed to make life unpleasant for the asylum seekers detained there, in an effort to pressure them into accepting 'voluntary' repatriations. *The Guardian* reported at the time that,

For more than a year, camp managers and security staff [...] waged a campaign to make Australia's detention centre for refugees and asylum seekers on Manus Island as inhospitable as possible. [...] A plan drafted in early 2016 outlines moves to coerce those recognised as refugees into leaving the detention centre and accepting resettlement in Papua New Guinea, while pushing asylum seekers to abandon their protection claims and return home. (Boochani et al, 2017: np)

The same year, a United Nations (UN) Human Rights Committee report found that harsh conditions offshore had 'reportedly compelled some asylum seekers to return to their country of origin, despite the risks that they face there' (np). While these returns may not have technically breached Australia's non-refoulment obligations,[2] they cannot be characterized as genuinely voluntary (Webber, 2011; Gerver, 2017; Leerkes et al, 2017; Peterie, 2018a).

It is rare for documents to emerge that so clearly demonstrate premeditated cruelty in the service of specific deterrence. So far, comparable evidence has not surfaced concerning Australia's onshore detention system. It is the contention of this book, however, that the onshore network must also be understood in the light of this objective of specific deterrence. Subsequent chapters will show that even the quotidian details of life in detention reveal a tacit intention of specific deterrence.

The study

This book provides a unique account of Australia's onshore immigration detention system by documenting the experiences of people who enter these spaces as visitors. This visitor perspective is partly a pragmatic one – studying secure institutions if far from simple, and researchers in Australia are routinely denied access to detention spaces (Zion et al, 2010). Yet this perspective also underwrites the book's main contributions as visitor testimonies help illuminate both the less-obvious strategies through which isolation and desperation are produced in detention, and the reverberating impacts of this carceral regime.

The empirical research that informs this book took place over five years (2015–20) and involved more than 70 in-depth interviews[3] with regular visitors to Australia's onshore detention facilities. Participants variously described themselves as volunteers, advocates, activists, and/or friends to people in detention, and often saw themselves as fulfilling more than one of these roles simultaneously. The majority of participants came from non-refugee backgrounds and were permanent residents or citizens of Australia. Most had begun visiting detention because they wished to render assistance. The two things all participants had in common were a close connection to at least one person in detention, and regular physical interactions with the detention machine.

Interviewees were invited to share their stories of visiting detention. Participants told me about their original decisions to commence their visits. They explained what visiting involved on a practical level, both physically and emotionally, and reflected on the escalating rules and restrictions that governed their visits. They spoke at length about the friendships they developed within detention; about how the logic of the detention system shaped their (new and existing) relationships; and about their efforts to both offer and receive hospitality and care. Visitors talked about their friends' lives in detention and described – often through tears – the human costs of mandatory detention. They also shared their own struggles to endure the damaging effects of the system.

Participants were asked if any memories stood out to them as highlights or lowlights, or as otherwise representative of what visiting detention entailed. Making room for narratives in qualitative interviews is valuable because it gives participants greater scope – through their selection and curation of stories – to highlight what they consider to be the most salient aspects of their experiences. It also allows participants to reflect on why these stories are of particular significance, and to communicate the complexity of their lives and emotional landscapes. As Jane Elliott writes, narrative-based research affords a unique 'understanding of the social world *from the perspective of the individuals being studied*' (2005: 122; emphasis added).

Interviews were conducted with detention centre visitors in the Australian states of Queensland, New South Wales, Victoria, Western Australia, the Northern Territory and South Australia. While the majority of interviewees visited facilities in Australia's largest cities of Sydney, Brisbane and Melbourne, together the interviewees had visited all of the major facilities in the onshore system as it existed during the research period,[4] as well as numerous Alternative Places of Detention (APODs) (see Figure 1.1).[5]

In addition to these empirical interviews, this book draws on extensive archival research, conducted between 2013 and 2021. Parliamentary Hansard database Parlinfo was used to access ministerial press releases and speeches from recent decades; physical collections at the National Archives of Australia were used to access older materials. This research – which focused on the discursive narratives that have accompanied and justified government policies – informs the historical background provided in Chapter One. The socio-political context this research affords adds something important to our understanding of both why the participants in this study commenced visiting detention, and what these visits mean at the political level. Several Freedom of Information requests were also lodged during the writing of this book and have been used to confirm and contextualize visitor testimonies, particularly where they describe official institutional rules and

Figure 1.1: Facilities in Australia's onshore immigration detention network 2015–20.

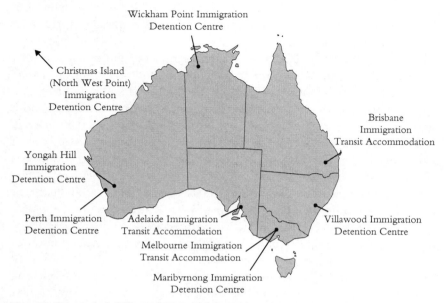

Wickham Point Immigration Detention Centre

Christmas Island (North West Point) Immigration Detention Centre

Brisbane Immigration Transit Accommodation

Yongah Hill Immigration Detention Centre

Perth Immigration Detention Centre

Adelaide Immigration Transit Accommodation

Melbourne Immigration Transit Accommodation

Villawood Immigration Detention Centre

Maribyrnong Immigration Detention Centre

Note: Facilities include Villawood IDC, Sydney; Brisbane Immigration Transit Accommodation (BITA), Brisbane; Maribyrnong IDC, Melbourne; Melbourne Immigration Transit Accommodation (MITA), Melbourne; Adelaide Immigration Transit Accommodation (AITA), Adelaide; Perth IDC, Perth; Wickham Point IDC, Darwin; Yongah Hill IDC, Yongah Hill; and North West Point or Christmas Island IDC, Christmas Island. The network also includes numerous APODs.

Source: Adapted from Creative Commons, derivative work of File:Oceania98.svg by User:Brianski

policies. Wherever possible, detainees' own words – carefully gathered from public social media posts, media interviews and Australian Human Rights Commission (AHRC) inspection reports – have been included to provide a first-hand perspective concerning the realities of detention centre life and the significance of centre visitors.

Outline of the book

This book tells the story of Australia's onshore immigration detention system across eight chapters. Chapter One locates the system in its political and historical context and, in doing so, explains why the participants in this study felt a moral imperative to visit the people Australia detains. It describes the vilification and politicization of asylum seekers in Australia, and the evolution of Australia's controversial policy of indefinite mandatory detention. The specific policy backdrop for this book – Operation Sovereign Borders – is described in detail.

Chapter Two provides a theoretical scaffolding for understanding the functions of Australia's immigration detention facilities, and how violence is enacted w ithin this system. Drawing on research concerning the production of psychological pain in civilian prisons, it highlights the clandestine mechanisms through which carceral institutions inflict pain in socio-legal contexts where overt violence is not socially or legally tenable.

Chapter Three describes the process individuals must go through to gain entrance to detention facilities in Australian, demonstrating that these centres largely operate as prisons. It shows that visitor application and entrance processes have become complex and intimidating in recent year as centres have taken an increasingly securitized approach to visitor admission. In describing these processes and their escalation, this chapter begins to reveal the mechanisms of bureaucratic control that characterize Australia's onshore detention system. It also shows how visitors are targeted as part of this system.

Chapter Four explores the daily realities of life in detention, as witnessed and experienced by centre visitors. The chapter paints a detailed picture of immigration detention facilities as prison-like environments in which detainees are made to feel their vulnerability in the small details of institutional life. Rules are regularly changed and erratically enforced, and micro-level controls function to infantilize and disempower. This elaborate system of deprivations and frustrations keeps detainees in a state of anxious vigilance. It also extends to target visitors, positioning them as quasi-inmates and frustrating their efforts to provide meaningful help.

Chapter Five examines the relationships that develop between detainees and visitors, and considers the political significance of these friendships. It shows that in an institutional context where deterrence is enacted through the micro-level production of isolation and despair, visitors' efforts to disrupt the socio-emotional conditions of detention can constitute a meaningful (if imperfect) form of political resistance. It also demonstrates that visitor-detainee relationships can be a basis for more recognisable forms of political action as visitors advocate for detainees and bear public witness to institutional violence.

Chapter Six concerns the use of involuntary movement within the detention network. Against the backdrop of the previous chapter, it shows that the practice of regularly relocating detainees within the detention system attacks their networks of care and resistance. While detention facilities are often envisaged as places of confinement, forced movement is an important aspect of how these institutions enact power. Instability, despair and compliance are produced not only through the bleakness of institutional life, but also through the forced relocation of detainees between detention facilities and away from the visitors who provide social, emotional and instrumental support.

Chapter Seven documents the impacts of immigration detention on centre visitors. It acknowledges the benefits visitors derive from their relationships, but also highlights the traumatizing dimensions of the visitation experience. Visiting detention, this chapter shows, involves witnessing trauma. It also involves a painful experience of secondary prisonization as visitors are targeted by a broader scheme of deprivation and frustration within the centres. The visitation experience is thus characterized by feelings of powerlessness and ontological disruption that at times feed into visitor attrition – thus serving to isolate detainees and further breed despair.

The book concludes with a brief review of the study's main findings, emphasizing the importance of recognizing the multiple forms of violence that immigration detention centres employ and the tacit intent that underlies them. The harms documented in this book are not accidental but reflect a policy logic that accepts and even requires cruelty as a mechanism of control. In practice, deterrence involves the strategic production of despair as detainees and their supporters are pushed to breaking point to achieve crude political objectives.

In telling the stories of detention centre visitors, this book sheds light on the best and worst of Australian society. It relates stories of friendship, humanity, solidarity and resistance. Its ultimate conclusions, however, are stark. Australia's onshore detention system inflicts predictable and preventable harm. It harms detainees, and it harms the people who endeavour to support them. It does so by design.

1

Immigration Detention in Australia

Hannah's story

It's a windy day in Melbourne. Hannah, a dark-haired woman with a warm, open demeanour, smiles at me across the table at the Docklands library. It is 2019 and Hannah has been visiting people in detention for almost 17 years. For most of that time she has visited detention at least once a week, but in recent months she has pulled back slightly. "I'm really tired", Hannah tells me. "I feel really traumatized."

It was 2002 when Hannah first learnt that asylum seekers were being imprisoned in her city. She was already involved in social justice work, and news of the detention situation arrived via her activist networks.

> 'We heard from friends in those kinds of networks that they were imprisoning refugees in the Maribyrnong Detention Centre. We were just horrified – a small group of us – so we contacted quite a well-known advocate [...] who was visiting, and we said, "how do we do this? We can't believe this is happening. Can we come in and offer some kind of support?"'

Her desire to act, Hannah explains, was deep and instinctive.

> 'I feel naïve saying it now, but I think it was just about this shock of imprisoning people, and thinking, this is outrageous and we need to let these people know that there are people out here who think that. And that they're not alone. And that we would actively try to assist in whatever way, shape or form we could. For me, it's just about being a human being. [...] To go and visit was the first thing for us to do – to say, "oh my God. Sorry! What do you need?"'

In deciding to visit detention, Hannah and her friends – like many of the participants in this study – were acting on a basic human impulse to reach out to the suffering other. Yet in extending the hand of friendship, they were also taking a stance on what had become one of Australia's most polarizing political issues.

2001 had brought so-called 'illegal immigrants' to the forefront of Australia's political debate. In the aftermath of the September 11 terrorist attacks in the US, Australian Prime Minister John Howard had campaigned for re-election on a platform of border protection and national security. Refugees and asylum seekers, travelling to Australia by boat in search of safety, were portrayed by politicians and the media as criminals and potential terrorists. For Hannah and others like her, this rhetoric obscured a more fundamental truth. These vilified strangers were people *who had come to Australia for help and were instead being punished.*

Despite the hundreds of detainees who have come in and out of Hannah's life since 2002, she still recalls her first visit to Maribyrnong IDC.

'*I went with a friend who also still visits today – 17 years later – and we're friends with the two men that we met on that first day. One of our friends is married to one and we still see those two men. They were strong men. They were activists from their countries. One was a journalist and one was a human rights activist in his country as well, and they were doing work inside the centre – lots of casework for the more vulnerable people in there.*'

The stereotypes and political tropes that are so often applied to refugees and asylum seekers, Hannah stresses, are far from accurate. Refugees and asylum seekers are not 'illegals' or criminals, but neither are they helpless victims or "some kind of innocent perfect people". They are fellow human beings. And the conditions Australia has subjected them to have been nothing short of torturous.

★★★

The imperative to act

Australia is by no means alone in imprisoning asylum seekers. In the last two decades, wealthy countries across the globe have adopted immigration detention policies to deter forced migrants from seeking their help (Nethery and Silverman, 2015). The detention of unauthorized immigrants, including people seeking asylum, is now the norm in the US, the UK and most of Europe (The Migration Observatory, 2020). Between 2009 and 2019, the number of people in held detention in the UK fluctuated between 24,000 and 32,000 per year (The Migration Observatory, 2020). France alone has 22 Administrative Detention Centres which in 2017 held 46,800 people, including 2,797 minors (Global Detention Project, 2018). In 2016 the US detained 44,270 asylum seekers as part of a larger cohort of 300,000 immigration detainees (Global Detention Project, 2016).

Despite this ubiquity, Australia's detention policies are harsh by international standards. Australia is the only country in the world with a policy of indefinite mandatory detention, meaning all non-citizens in the country without a valid visa are automatically detained for an indefinite duration – until they are removed from the country or granted a visa (AHRC, 2017a). Australia's policies have regularly been condemned by international human rights organizations. Notable critics of Australia's regime include the UN High Commissioner for Refugees (Al Hussein, 2014), the UN Committee against Torture (2014), the UN Human Rights Council (2016) and the International Criminal Court (Stayner, 2020).

Nonetheless, Australia has maintained its commitment to indefinite mandatory detention for over three decades. Successive governments have been willing to accept considerable reputational damage – as well as staggering financial costs – to maintain the controversial policy. Between 2008 and 2020, the Australian government spent an estimated 20 billion dollars on immigration detention (Essex, 2020), paying over $573,000 per person per year to detain asylum seekers offshore and $346,000 per person per year to detain asylum seekers in the onshore system (Asylum Seeker Resource Centre et al, 2019).

For the most part, the Australian public has supported this course, rewarding governments that take a hardline approach to the issue of 'the boats'. As political leaders on both sides of politics have engaged in a race to the bottom to repel asylum seekers, however, a growing number of Australians have been troubled by the cruelty being enacted in their name.

This chapter provides a backdrop to this book by offering a detailed description of Australia's response to people seeking asylum. It begins with a historical outline of Australia's detention policies, documenting their development over time. It then provides an overview of Operation Sovereign Borders – the specific policy that was in place when fieldwork for this study was undertaken. Ultimately, this chapter maps the escalation and securitization of Australia's detention regime, explaining why visitors like Hannah felt such a strong moral compulsion to *do* something to support people in detention.

The evolution of Australia's asylum seeker policies

From White Australia to multiculturalism

Xenophobia or 'fear of the stranger' has been part of Australian society since colonization. Australia's 'settlement' by British colonizers involved the violent invasion of Indigenous lands. Throughout the colonial eras, Indigenous Australians were viewed as a primitive people and 'dying race', and colonizers understood the nation to be fundamentally British. Immigrants from other countries – including Chinese who had come to Australia to work on the goldfields – were also viewed with some hostility. In the late nineteenth century, in an environment of 'extreme economic competition' (McMaster, 2002b: 281), colonists decided that excluding the non-British 'Other' was the only way to protect their prosperity and that of the burgeoning nation. At

Federation, these protectionist impulses were formalized in the *Immigration Restriction Act 1901,* which enshrined the ideal of a white Australia by limiting non-white (particularly Asian) immigration to the country.

This preoccupation with keeping Australia white reflected deeper anxieties regarding invasion and usurpation (McMaster, 2002b; Papastergiadis, 2004). In seeking to control who entered Australia, settlers recognized not only their own geographic isolation and (by extension) vulnerability in Asia, but also the precariousness of their claims to belonging.

The White Australia policy remained in place until after World War II, when it was relaxed to increase Australia's working-age population and thus ensure the country's economic recovery and military security. This change saw an influx of post-war refugees and immigrants from across Europe. Non-European immigration, however, was still discouraged. Over the following decades, immigration restrictions continued to ease. In 1973, the final tenets of the White Australia policy were officially dismantled when the (centre Left) Labor government, led by Prime Minister Gough Whitlam, removed the racially discriminatory aspects of Australia's immigration laws and adopted a new policy of multiculturalism. The change, however, coincided with a reduction to Australia's overall immigration rate to protect job opportunities for citizens during a period of rising domestic unemployment (Jupp, 2002). It was thus not until immigration quotas were increased after the election of (centre Right) Liberal Prime Minister Malcolm Fraser in 1975 that this new immigration policy really took effect. When the first maritime asylum seekers arrived in Australia the following year, multiculturalism faced its first big test.

The first recorded asylum seeker vessel arrived in Australia in 1976, carrying five Indochinese refugees. It was to be the first of a wave of boats fleeing Vietnam at the end of the Vietnam War. The Fraser government reaffirmed its overlapping commitments to protecting Australia's allies in the Vietnam War, enacting a non-discriminatory immigration policy, and honouring Australia's human rights obligations under international law. As Immigration Minister Michael MacKellar (1977) asserted at the time, "[w]e are duty bound to assess [asylum claims] and if [refugee status] can be demonstrated, provide assistance". Holding these commitments alongside its desire to retain control at the border, the Fraser government devised a new asylum seeker policy with support from neighbouring countries. The government asked regional transit countries to prevent asylum seeker boats from embarking for Australia. At the same time, it sent teams of immigration officials to interview those on route to Australia and accepted qualifying refugees directly into the country. Between 1977 and 1982, Australia accepted more than 54,000 Indochinese refugees from countries in the region, thus minimizing the need for displaced individuals to make dangerous boat voyages to Australia. It also resettled more than 2,000 asylum seekers who reached Australia directly by boat (Stevens, 2012).

During this period, Australia had three immigration detention facilities, located in Sydney, Perth and Melbourne. These centres were used only on a discretionary and short-term basis, often to hold people who had overstayed or otherwise breached the conditions of their visas. Only the Sydney facility was suitably equipped to accommodate new arrivals. As such, asylum seekers who reached Australia by boat were processed at the Westbridge Migrant Centre in Sydney alongside newly arrived entrants from Australia's formal refugee and humanitarian programmes. In contrast to the prison-like facilities that would succeed it, the centre was open and unfenced, although new entrants were required to stay within the facility and attend a daily rollcall (Phillips and Spinks, 2013).

In the years that followed, Australia's response to people seeking asylum – as well as the discourses that accompanied government policies – would become increasingly hostile. Indeed, key Fraser government innovations such as preventing asylum seekers from travelling to Australia would ultimately be abstracted away from any human rights imperative and used not to facilitate safe and orderly access to protection, but to exclude the unwanted stranger. Equally, immigration detention centres, including the original Westbridge Migrant Centre, would be reimagined as prisons as new arrivals were discursively transformed from refugees into 'illegal immigrants'.

The introduction of indefinite mandatory detention

In November 1989, several years after the initial influx of Vietnamese asylum seekers had been resettled in Australia, an asylum seeker boat arrived in Western Australia's Pender Bay. It was to be the first in a new wave of asylum seeker vessels, this time coming mainly from Cambodia. These asylum seekers would not be afforded the welcome that Fraser's government offered. Under the Hawke and Keating Labor governments, the new arrivals were held first in Broome, before being sent to the Westbridge facility in Sydney. In 1991, a new centre in Port Hedland – a disused mining camp in remote Western Australia – was created, and many of the detainees were transferred there (Phillips and Spinks, 2013). Access to legal representation and community support at this new facility was limited, and asylum seekers were kept out of sight, out of mind (Manne, 2013; McMaster, 2002a, 2002b). As Don McMaster (2002b: 285) notes, physical isolation meant that asylum seekers could be 'denied adequate social rights and made vulnerable to intimidation'.

In 1992, in response to challenges in the courts (McMaster, 2002a), the Keating government acted to provide a retrospective legal basis for its growing detention regime. The legislation – which required asylum seekers arriving in Australia without a visa to be detained for up to 273 days (Human Rights and Equal Opportunity Commission, 2004) – was envisaged as a short-term response to this specific cohort of asylum seekers, but also spoke to broader concerns regarding the integrity of Australia's borders. As Minister for Immigration Gerry Hand (1992: np) stated at the time,

> The Government is determined that a clear signal be sent that migration to Australia may not be achieved by simply arriving in this country and expecting to be allowed into the community [...] this legislation is only intended to be an interim measure. The present proposal refers principally to a detention regime for a specific class of persons. As such it is designed to address only the pressing requirements of the current situation. However, I acknowledge that it is necessary for wider consideration to be given to such basic issues as entry, detention and removal of certain non-citizens.

In 1994, the government extended the policy, removing the 273-day limit from the *Migration Act* and instead providing that unauthorized arrivals could only be released from detention if they were granted a visa or removed from the country. Australia thus became the only country in the world with an official policy of indefinite mandatory detention (Phillips and Spinks, 2013).

In the years that followed, Australia's onshore immigration detention system continued to expand with new facilities established in difficult-to-access parts of Australia, including on Christmas Island[1] and at remote mainland sites like Baxter, Curtin and Woomera. Conditions at these facilities were far from hospitable. A 2002 Lancet article noted that families at the Woomera facility lived in small rooms or dormitories up to 500m from toilet facilities. Many had no air-conditioning or running water, and temperatures reached up to 50 degrees C during the day. There were minimal recreational or educational facilities and children had few cool spaces in which to play (Loff et al, 2002). The Woomera centre was originally intended to hold 400 people, but soon became severely overcrowded. Just eight weeks after the centre's opening, 936 detainees were held within it; by April 2000, this figure had risen to 1,500 (Fiske, 2016).

In these trying conditions, incidents of self-harm proliferated. Australia's detention regime had received negligible media attention in the early years of its operation, but Australian media outlets now began reporting shocking stories of detainees sewing their lips together, engaging in hunger strikes and suicide attempts, and rioting in the desert (Fiske, 2016; Tazreiter, 2010). Detainees, hidden from the public in these remote facilities, wanted Australians to know that they were there and they were suffering (Fiske, 2016). As community awareness grew, so too did Australia's asylum seeker support movement. As Claudia Tazreiter (2010: 207) writes, 'Australian citizens became increasingly outraged and willing to act on behalf of others – even of strangers – as overwhelming evidence of injustice was revealed'.

Howard's Pacific Solution

The next major escalation in Australia's response to people seeking asylum came in 2001. After years of simmering anti-migration sentiment, the events of September 11 brought a new level of vitriol to the surface of Australia's asylum seeker debate, and a new level of cruelty to Australia's detention policy.

In the mid-1990s, Independent MP Pauline Hanson had been elected to parliament on a fierce anti-multiculturalism platform and had subsequently formed a right-wing political party called One Nation. One Nation had presented itself as a party that was bold enough to say what 'ordinary Australians' were thinking, even if this wasn't politically correct. Hanson blamed immigrants for increases in crime, opposed immigration from 'non-Christian' countries, and denounced new Australians who failed to assimilate into Australian society (Poynting, 2002). At this time, most arriving asylum seekers were fleeing politically volatile areas of the Middle East. Some came from Islamic backgrounds. As fears mounted regarding the perceived cultural incompatibility of this new influx of immigrants, the Middle Eastern Other was blamed for myriad social problems within Australia. As Scott Poynting and colleagues (2004: 49) observe, the logic of racialization saw Middle Eastern 'conflated with Arab, Arab with Muslim, Muslim with rapist, rapist with gang, gang with terrorist, terrorist with "boat people", "boat people" with barbaric, and so on in interminable permutations'. By 2001, the Middle Eastern immigrant had been transformed into a national villain onto whom the country's fears could be projected.

In 2001 – a federal election year – the (centre Right) Howard government made the decision to exploit and amplify these fears for political gain. A month before the federal election campaign commenced, a Norwegian freighter, the *Tampa*, rescued 433 asylum seekers from a sinking boat in international waters (Mares, 2002). The *Tampa*'s captain requested permission to bring the rescued passengers to Australia's Christmas Island, which was close by. The Howard government seized its opportunity. In a highly publicized and politicized decision, the *Tampa* was refused permission to enter Australian waters and armed Special Air Service troops were deployed to enforce the decision (Lynch and O'Brien, 2001). With Australia and the world watching, Howard (in Rundle, 2001: 3) declared that the *Tampa* asylum seekers would "never set foot on Australian soil". The government negotiated with two small Pacific nations – both in serious financial difficulties (Nethery, 2019) – and convinced them to take the passengers in exchange for remuneration. As Glenn Banks and Andrew McGregor (2011: 233) explain,

The former Australian colonial territory of Papua New Guinea, which allowed Manus Island to be used as a 'human processing zone', and the tiny island state of Nauru (whose once bountiful supplies of phosphate had long since been diminished by Australian mining companies and used to enhance the New Zealand and Australian agricultural economies) became sites to 'outsource' and 'offshore' humanitarian responsibilities.

A new militarized border protection policy – the 'Pacific Solution' – was born (Spinks and Phillips, 2011).

Under the Pacific Solution, Australia's migration zone was reduced to prevent asylum seekers from lodging refugee claims at almost 5,000 newly excised Australian islands, including Christmas, Ashmore, Cocos and Cartier Islands (Phillips and Spinks, 2013). The government also legislated to send any asylum seekers who reached Australia to offshore detention camps in PNG or Nauru. A new policy of intercepting and turning back asylum seeker boats in international waters was also introduced. The focus throughout was on asserting Australia's sovereignty and regaining control of the country's borders. As Howard (2001b) declared at the time, "*we* will decide who comes to this country and the circumstances in which they come". Like Fraser, Howard saw the importance of a firm border and an orderly immigration programme. Unlike Fraser, however, he did not provide safe resettlement pathways for would-be asylum seekers.

The purported threat posed by Middle Eastern immigration was already looming in the national imagination when, on 11 September 2001, catastrophic terrorist attacks took place in the US. The Australian government rallied behind its wartime ally, committing troops to America's subsequent 'War on Terrorism'. Closer to home, the government also prepared to fight this war on its own doorstep (Marr and Wilkinson, 2003). Ignoring the reality that many of the asylum seekers arriving in Australian waters were fleeing the very regimes the US coalition opposed (Martin, 2015), the government framed irregular migration as a defence issue and conflated asylum seekers with the 'enemy' of September 11. Insofar as asylum seekers were entering Australian waters without authorization, Howard insisted (2001c), there was "no way" of knowing whether they were terrorists. Defence Minister Peter Reith warned that asylum seeker boats could be "a pipeline for terrorists to come in and use your country as a staging post for terrorist activities" (in Albanese, 2005). Framing the forthcoming election as a referendum on national security and himself as a tough and decisive leader, Howard streaked ahead in the polls.

Just a month after the *Tampa* incident and two days into Howard's official re-election campaign, Australia's HMAS *Adelaide* intercepted an asylum seeker boat as it entered Australia's contiguous zone. When attempts to deter the vessel were unsuccessful, a boarding party took control of the boat and redirected it to Indonesia. Amid the confused telephone conversations that followed, Australia's Northern Command commander – and, soon after, Immigration Minister, Philip Ruddock – came to believe that asylum seekers had thrown their children into the water. This was not correct. Nonetheless, Ruddock briefed the media.

> Disturbingly a number of children have been thrown overboard, again with the intention of putting us under duress. [It was] clearly planned and premeditated. People wouldn't have come wearing life jackets unless they intended some action of this sort. (Ruddock in *The Sydney Morning Herald*: np)

Almost immediately, doubts emerged regarding the veracity of these claims, but the government doubled down on its story. "I certainly don't want people of that type in Australia, I really don't", Howard (2001a) declared.

At best, asylum seekers were now portrayed as manipulative 'illegal immigrants' who had 'jumped the queue' by coming to Australia without authorization (Pickering, 2001; Klocker and Dunn, 2003; Gelber, 2003). At worst, they were child abusers, criminals and 'Islamic terrorists' – the antithesis of the (nominally Christian) Australian Us (Poynting et al, 2004; Marr and Wilkinson 2003). Howard's ultimate electoral win would change the shape of domestic politics, bringing the issue of 'the boats' to the forefront of the public consciousness and setting the tone of federal election campaigns for decades to come.

There is debate among migration experts as to whether the Pacific Solution was effective in deterring asylum seekers from travelling to Australia, or whether the marked reduction in asylum seeker numbers following the policy's introduction was the result of international developments including the fall of the Taliban in Afghanistan and of Saddam Hussein in Iraq (Nethery, 2019). What is clear is that in the early years of the Pacific Solution asylum seeker boats all but ceased (Hatton and Lim, 2005). In 2001, 5,516 asylum seekers arrived in Australia by boat; by 2002, this number had fallen to one (Phillips, 2017).[2]

Labor's new politics of 'compassion'

With new boat arrivals no longer dominating the news, community apprehensions appeared to recede. By 2007, growing segments of the Australian population were awakening to the human and reputational costs of Australia's hardline deterrence policies. Other threats – including the potentially catastrophic consequences of human-induced climate change – were also taking a more prominent place on the national agenda. After 11 years in government, Howard was defeated in the 2007 federal election and a Labor government was elected. The following year, Prime Minister

Kevin Rudd officially closed Australia's offshore processing facilities in PNG and Nauru (Phillips and Spinks, 2013). He did not, however, alter Australia's policy of indefinite mandatory detention, amend the legislation that had made offshore processing possible or cease work on the high-security detention facility under construction on Australia's Christmas Island (Nethery and Holman, 2016).

New asylum seekers arriving in Australia at this time were detained indefinitely within the extant onshore immigration detention network. The network had been through various changes in the preceding decade, but now consisted of seven secure detention facilities (Villawood IDC, Perth IDC, Maribyrnong IDC, Northern IDC, Christmas Island IDC, BITA and MITA), as well as several APODS (AHRC, 2008). These facilities were, in most instances, significantly less isolated than both Australia's offshore processing facilities and the remote onshore centres that Australians had seen on their television screens in the late 1990s and early 2000s. They were also, however, a far cry from the open and unfenced facilities that had originally been utilized. Australia had essentially moved to a network of prison-like centres mainly located on the outskirts of its capital cities. In 2008 (p. 22), the AHRC described the centres as follows:

> Put simply, most of the centres feel like prisons. High wire fences, lack of open green space, walled-in courtyards, ageing buildings, pervasive security features, cramped conditions and lack of privacy combine to create an oppressive atmosphere.

Despite these enduring concerns, Labor's decision to end offshore processing was broadly welcomed as a humane development in Australia's response to people seeking asylum. Indeed, Labor actively encouraged this reading, adopting a new discourse of 'compassion'.

Under Howard, people seeking asylum had been discursively constructed as a threatening enemy and cultural Other. They had become a screen onto which historical and contemporary anxieties could be projected for political gain. In an effort to redeem the figure of the asylum seeker, the Rudd government represented people seeking asylum in a markedly different way – not as dangerous criminals, but as helpless victims. The real enemies, the government insisted, were not desperate asylum seekers but the people smugglers who exploited their misery. As Minister for Immigration and Citizenship Chris Evans (2008) stated, "[w]e recognise that tackling people-smuggling, rather than vilifying its exploited clients, should be the focus of government policy". Where Howard had suggested that asylum seekers were the antithesis of the Australian (Christian) Us, Rudd (2006, np) evoked Biblical imagery in this call for compassion.

> The biblical injunction to care for the stranger in our midst is clear. The parable of the Good Samaritan is but one of the many which deal with the matter of how we should respond to the vulnerable stranger in our midst.

Rudd was trying to reverse the polarity of political rhetoric and bring the asylum seeker back into Australia's circle of care.

This notion of vulnerability was key to Labor's rhetoric and posed a direct challenge to Howard's discourse of danger and threat. It also, however, stripped asylum seekers of their agency. Maritime arrivals were not portrayed as complete individuals, capable of the full breadth of human emotions and desires. Neither were they recognized as autonomous people who had made difficult decisions to protect themselves and their families in a regional context where safe pathways to resettlement had been cut off or restricted (Essex, 2020). Rather, asylum seekers were transformed into passive victims in need of rescue, and Australia was positioned as their would-be saviour. This construction located Australia's response to people seeking asylum within the domain of generosity, not human rights. It also afforded Australia a position of power and control in relation to people seeking asylum, just as the Howard government's more punitive discourse had (Peterie, 2017; see also Silverstein, 2020). In this way, Rudd's discourse of compassion lay the foundation for his party's later reinstatement of offshore processing – this time in the name of tough love.

Where only 161 asylum seekers had arrived in Australia by boat in 2008, this number had risen to 17,204 by 2012 (Phillips, 2017). Australia's stretched onshore detention network had grown from seven facilities to twelve. Under fierce attack from the opposition, the government experimented with a range of ultimately unsuccessful policy solutions (including a 2011 refugee-swap deal with Malaysia which did not survive a High Court challenge) in a bid to curb the flow of boats and appease community concern. In 2012, with an election looming, the Labor government reinstated offshore processing in a desperate effort to regain the public's confidence and avoid political disaster. Yet the government did not entirely abandon its discourse of compassion. These harsher policies, Labor insisted, were needed to protect asylum seekers from people smugglers and save lives at sea. "There is nothing humane about a voyage across dangerous seas with the ever-present risk of death in leaky boats captained by people smugglers", Prime Minister Julia Gillard (2010) said. Humanitarian and border protection concerns were thus brought together in a discourse of paternalistic compassion, calculated to appeal to all (Peterie, 2017).

Despite this discursive maneuvering and the government's revival of hardline deterrence policies to regain the public's confidence, the Labor government would not survive the next election. The year 2013 saw the

Liberal–National Coalition elected to government after a campaign in which border protection policies again featured prominently. Following in Howard's footsteps, the government, under Prime Minister Tony Abbott's leadership, introduced a militarized border protection programme called Operation Sovereign Borders. A new law enforcement agency – tellingly titled Australian Border Force (ABF) – was created to oversee the programme. The government asserted that asylum seekers arriving in Australia without authorization would *never* be resettled in the country, regardless of whether they were found to be refugees. Under the Coalition government, Australia returned to the lexis and logic of the Pacific Solution. "[T]his is our country and we determine who comes here", Abbott (2013) declared.

Operation Sovereign Borders
The anguish offshore

The empirical research that informs this book was undertaken between 2015 and 2020. That is, at a time when people seeking asylum in Australia were deterred and detained under Operation Sovereign Borders. While some interviewees had been visiting detention since the turn of the century, most commenced their visits in the early or mid-2010s, around the time that Operation Sovereign Borders commenced. Hardening government policies and discourses, together with horror stories from offshore, were key catalysts in many visitors' decisions.

The harms associated with offshore processing were apparent during the Howard years, but under Operation Sovereign Borders, evidence of atrocious conditions at these centres mounted. In one widely reported incident in February 2014, dozens of men detained by Australia on PNG's Manus Island were assaulted by police, security guards and facility employees after protests turned violent. Some asylum seekers 'taking shelter in their bedrooms were dragged outside to be beaten' (AHRC, 2017a: 36). Seventy detainees sustained injuries during the attacks, and Iranian asylum seeker Reza Berati was beaten to death (Essex, 2020). Two centre employees were subsequently convicted for Berati's murder, although the judge in the case intimated that other culprits may have escaped without charge (Tlozek, 2016).

A 2015 inquiry added to this picture of violence and abuse. It substantiated several specific allegations of rape at Australia's Nauru processing centre and found that instances of sexual abuse at the facility were underreported (Moss, 2015). The following year, a leaked cache of more than 2,000 incident reports revealed the true extent of the problem. These 'Nauru Files' highlighted widespread self-harm and trauma at the Nauru facility, as well as endemic levels of sexual assault, particularly against young asylum seeker women. Perhaps most alarmingly, over half of the reported incidents involved children. There were seven reports of sexual assaults on children,

59 reports of other assaults on children and 30 reports of self-harm involving children (Farrell et al,, 2016).

As rates of physical and psychological illness at the Nauru and PNG centres rose, there was also concern that Australian authorities were overriding clinical recommendations to deny sick detainees access to emergency medical treatment in Australia (Neil and Peterie Forthcoming). Several detainees died after being denied emergency transfers to Australia. In 2014, for example, Hamid Kehazaei – a 24-year-old Iranian asylum seeker at the Manus Island facility – sought treatment for a small skin lesion and flu-like symptoms, both caused by a common tropical infection. The Manus Island facility clinic did not have the necessary antibiotics to treat the infection and Mr Kehazaei's condition deteriorated. Treating doctors sought permission to transfer their patient to Australia, but the Immigration Department[3] rejected the request. Two days after the original request was made, Mr Kehazaei – now septic and semi-conscious – was moved to a hospital in PNG's Port Moresby. Mr Kehazaei's condition was misdiagnosed and mistreated and he suffered a series of major heart attacks. By the time he was granted transfer to Australia, Mr Kehazaei was severely brain damaged with multiple organ failure (Doherty, 2018a; 2018b). The coroner who investigated Mr Kehazaei's death found the Australian government responsible, noting that 'multiple errors' and 'systemic failures' had led to his entirely preventable death (Ryan in Doherty, 2018a).

In another incident in 2016, Iranian refugee Omid Masoumali died after self-immolating on Nauru. An inquest into the 23-year-old's death found that Mr Masoumali would have had a 90 to 95 per cent chance of surviving if he had been immediately transferred to Australia for medical treatment. Instead, he was not evacuated to Brisbane until 30 hours later, where he died from his injuries (Vujkovic, 2019). As the UN Human Rights Committee summarized in late 2017, the PNG and Nauru facilities were characterized by 'inadequate mental health services, [...] serious safety issues and instances of assault, sexual abuse, self-harm and suspicious deaths'. Detained refugees and asylum seekers were simultaneously being harmed and being denied appropriate health care to treat their physical and psychological injuries.

The onshore system

Given the horrors occurring offshore, it is unsurprising that – insofar as immigration detention was discussed in Australia – media and community attention during this time overwhelmingly focused on the situation offshore. Nonetheless, Australia's onshore immigration detention system continued to operate, albeit accommodating significantly fewer asylum seekers than it had in the past. In January 2013, some 5,697 people were detained onshore in Australia; around 96 per cent of this cohort were asylum seekers (Department of Immigration and Citizenship, 2013). Five years later, in January 2018, the onshore detention population had fallen to 1,287 people, of whom only 25.9 per cent were asylum seekers (Department of Home Affairs, 2018a).[4] These changes were largely a consequence of new maritime asylum seekers (insofar as boats were still arriving in Australia) being sent offshore to PNG or Nauru for processing. It also, however, reflected government efforts to release children and their families from secure detention facilities in the face of mounting public concern regarding the physical and psychological suffering experienced by children at these centres.

Given this reduced demand, numerous onshore detention centres were closed during this period. When Operation Sovereign Borders commenced, twelve immigration detention facilities were in operation in Australia: Christmas Island IDC, Curtin IDC, Maribyrnong IDC, Northern IDC, Perth IDC, Scherger IDC, Villawood IDC, Wickham Point IDC, Yongah Hill IDC, AITA, BITA and MITA. This fell to between six and nine facilities during the years that this study was undertaken: Christmas Island IDC, Perth IDC, Villawood IDC, Wickham Point IDC, Yongah Hill IDC, Maribyrnong IDC, AITA, BITA and MITA. Wickham Point IDC ceased operation in 2016, while Maribyrnong IDC, which had been recognized as one of the most violent in Australia (Hashman et al, 2016), was officially closed at the end of 2018. Christmas Island IDC, the most isolated facility in the onshore network, was closed in October 2018 but reopened the following year, purportedly to discourage offshore detainees who viewed the onshore system as comparatively comfortable from seeking unnecessary medical transfers to Australia (Ryan, 2020). Various APODs were also used throughout this period, including Kangaroo Point Central Hotel and Apartments in Brisbane and the Mantra Bell City Hotel in Melbourne.

While the number of asylum seekers detained onshore fell dramatically under Operation Sovereign Borders, new detainees were still entering the network during this time. Many of these individuals entered detention after having spent months or years living in the Australian community. They were detained following adverse legal decisions surrounding their refugee claims, or because they had breached a condition of their visas or community detention. In one case, which received widespread media attention, a Sri Lankan Tamil couple with two young Australian-born daughters were detained after four years living in the small Queensland town of Biloela. 'The Biloela family' as they became known, had become valued members of the Biloela community, with husband Nades working at the local abattoir, wife Priya cooking curries for staff at the town's hospital, and daughters Kopika and Tharunicaa forming friendships with local children. In March 2018, the family was re-detained in a dawn house raid. Their refugee claims had been rejected. A last-minute legal injunction prevented their deportation, and the family spent years in secure detention facilities – first in Melbourne and later on Christmas Island – as they fought their deportation.

Medical evacuations

In addition to housing people like Nades and Priya, Australia's onshore detention facilities were used to accommodate offshore detainees who had been brought to Australia for medical treatment, as well as any family members who accompanied them. As noted above, the process of gaining medical transfer to Australia was deeply flawed, and many detainees were irrevocably harmed because of their inability to access adequate and timely health care. Treating doctors in PNG and Nauru regularly requested their patients' medical transfer to Australia, but transfer decisions were made by bureaucrats within the Immigration Department who had no obligation to heed medical advice. Nonetheless, between November 2012 and June 2018, some 126 detainees from PNG and 376 detainees from Nauru were transferred to Australia for medical care, in some cases as a direct result of legal challenges (Refugee Council of Australia (RCOA), 2019).

At this time, medical transferees were typically accommodated in immigration detention facilities or treated at nearby hospitals which had been designated as APODs. Numerous community visitors to facilities like BITA visited sick detainees at their local hospitals or supported transferees' accompanying family members at the detention centres themselves. In theory, these medical evacuees would be returned offshore at the conclusion of their treatment, and in some cases this did occur. In 2015, for instance, 245 people were transferred to Australia and 176 were returned offshore; by 2016, however, rates of returns were decreasing (Department of Home Affairs, 2020). In one harrowing incident in 2016, a 21-year-old Somali woman self-immolated after she was returned to Nauru following medical treatment in Brisbane (Doherty and Davidson, 2016). In another case earlier the same year, doctors at a Brisbane hospital refused to discharge a 12-month-old asylum seeker baby amidst fears she would be returned to Nauru upon her release. "As is the case with every child who presents at the hospital, this patient will only be discharged once a suitable home environment is identified", a hospital spokesperson explained at the time (in Doherty, 2016). As the years progressed, lawyers sought legal injunctions to prevent their clients being expelled from Australia and returns became rare. In 2018, 420 people were transferred to Australia for medical treatment but fewer than five were returned.

In 2019, the medical transfer process underwent a significant change. A 2018 by-election in the conservative federal electorate of Wentworth had seen former president of the Australian Medical Association Professor Kerryn Phelps elected as an independent MP, tipping the balance of power in parliament. Phelps had run for office on a platform of economic conservatism and social justice, including climate action and refugee rights.

Soon after her election, the *Home Affairs Legislation Amendment (Miscellaneous Measures) Act 2019* or 'medevac' bill was passed into law with Phelps' support. The law fundamentally altered the medical transfer process for refugees and asylum seekers in PNG and Nauru, ensuring that medical advice was prioritized over political considerations in all decisions. As the Senate Legal and Constitutional Affairs Legislation Committee (2019: 5) reported at the time, the law required that before a detainee and any accompanying family members could be transferred to Australia, two treating doctors had to advise the Immigration Department that:

> a transitory person requires medical or psychiatric assessment or treatment, and; they are not receiving such treatment in the relevant regional processing country; and it is necessary for them to be transferred to Australia for such assessment or treatment.

Once the treating doctors had made this recommendation, the minister had 72 hours to approve or refuse this recommendation. Refusals could only be made if the minister reasonably believed a transfer was not medically necessary, in which case the decision would be referred to a panel of medical experts for independent judgement; or because of a security threat posed by the specific individual in question. 192 people were transferred to Australia under the law's provisions, before the government – having made a secret deal with an independent senator – repealed the law in December 2019.

Medevac's repeal was fiercely opposed by Australia's medical bodies, who lodged submissions in support of the legislation, as well as by Australian and international human rights organizations (Essex, 2020; Neil and Peterie, Forthcoming). It was devastating news for the refugees and asylum seekers still held offshore. For the 192 people who had made it to the mainland under medevac, however, Australia would now – at least for the time being – be home. As the Secretary of the Immigration Department, Michael Pezzullo, told a medevac senate inquiry in August 2019,

> There are currently over 320 matters before the courts which have been commenced by transitory persons in Australia — those here for medical and associated purposes — involving just under 1,000 individuals. Approximately 500 of these persons are now considered to have an effective barrier to their return, and it's anticipated that any attempts to return the remainder would result in the initiation of legal proceedings. What has commenced as medical transfer actions under various sections of the act has, over time, been transformed into legal blocking actions to keep these persons in Australia, irrespective

of their medical status. (Pezzullo in Commonwealth of Australia, 2019: 14)

Australia's various medical transfer processes thus saw hundreds of refugees and asylum seekers absorbed into the onshore system. While families with children were generally offered community alternatives to detention, many single men – including those who had already been found to be refugees – faced the prospect of indefinite mandatory detention in Australia's onshore detention system. This occurred despite these individuals having passed security checks prior to their transfer to Australia, which meant they posed no specific threat to the community.

Support for people seeking asylum

Australia's asylum seeker support movement has generally grown during periods of policy escalation, when government politicking has brought Australia's hardline asylum policies to the public's attention. This was true throughout the Howard era (Tazreiter, 2010), but also continued under Operation Sovereign Borders.

During this period, a number of detainees overcame the veil of secrecy shrouding Australia's detention system and shared their stories through media articles, social media posts, documentary films, books and other creative projects (Tazreiter, 2020; Rae et al, 2018; Rae et al, 2019). Most notably, Iranian journalist Behrouz Boochani, who was detained in PNG from 2013 to 2017, gained a large public following publishing regular articles in *The Guardian* and on other media platforms. During his detention, Boochani used his mobile phone to surreptitiously film a documentary (*Chauka, Please Tell Us the Time, 2017*), and to write a personal memoir that went on to receive widespread critical acclaim (Boochani, 2018a). Onshore, refugees and medevac transferees Mostafa ('Moz') Azimitabar and Farhad Bandesh, among others, also shared their experiences.

Detainees' activism was supported by a growing body of concerned Australians. An eclectic coalition of actors – lawyers, academics, public figures, health professionals, faith groups, journalists, human rights organizations and third sector representatives – came together with detainees, their families and members of the broader public to condemn Australia's policies. Doctors and other healthcare workers proved to be particularly powerful allies as they used their respected status in the community to lobby for policy change (Essex, 2020).

Like many members of this growing movement, the participants in this study felt a moral compulsion to do something in response to this evolving situation. Specific triggers and intensions varied from individual to individual, and some visitors had pre-existing relationships with the people they visited.

Nonetheless, two main aims recurred in visitors' discussions of why they began visiting detention. First, visitors wanted to take a stand against the government's policies. To assert – publicly and unequivocally – that they did not condone what was being done, often in their name. Entering institutional spaces to extend the hand of friendship was about contesting the assumptions that upheld the detention system to begin with. Where Australia's policies treated asylum seekers as criminals who deserved incarceration, visitors wished to assert, though their actions, that asylum seekers were fellow human beings and (actual or potential) friends.

In using their bodies to send these messages, visitors had several audiences in mind. If Australia's current policies were in place because politicians believed they were electorally popular, visitors hoped their actions might cause policymakers to reconsider their views.

> '[T]he only way that change of this type will happen is if the government realizes – or believes, ultimately – that they'll lose votes. And so it has to come from the people. The pressure has to come from the people.' (Robyn, Brisbane)

Equally, visitors wanted to influence their broader communities by showing their friends, family members and acquaintances that people in detention were humans too. They hoped to cast a vision of a kinder Australia.

Another audience for these statements was the people Australia detained. In this sense, the desire to take a stand came together with a second aim – one of alleviating suffering. Visitors with loved ones in detention wanted to show them that they were loved and remembered. People entering detention without pre-existing relationships wanted detainees to know "that some Australian people feel for them and are mad about the system" (Claire, Melbourne). As Roberta in Perth explained,

> 'The people in detention – it just struck me that it must be an incredibly difficult situation for them without any support networks. And even if all I could do was to offer social support it's probably worthwhile to have the detainees realize the government policy does not reflect the way normal Australians see them.' (Roberta, Perth)

Some visitors had particular skill sets that they wished to offer in the service of this aim. Several interviewees came from social work or psychology backgrounds and wanted to use this expertise to provide emotional support. Other participants had worked with refugees or other disadvantaged groups in careers as doctors, teachers or aid workers and imagined their professional skills might be useful in detention. But in many cases, visitors had only a vague sense of how they might help. The main thing, at least initially, was simply being there and offering what they had.

Conclusion

For decades now, Australian governments on both sides of politics have worked to deter and expel maritime asylum seekers. Australia has externalized its borders, preventing asylum seekers from reaching the country by intercepting their vessels in international waters or processing their refugee claims offshore. At the same time, Australia has maintained a system of prison-like detention facilities onshore. The detention system today is markedly different to that which was in place under Fraser, or even under the Keating government. The general trajectory has been one of escalation, driven by political calculation. Detention policies have become militant and detention centres have been securitized. The financial, reputational and human costs have ballooned.

In spite or perhaps because of these strategies of exclusion and harm, a broad asylum seeker support movement has emerged in Australia. Members differ in their philosophies, backgrounds, faiths and affiliations and thus reflect the diversity of Australian society. Within this movement, hundreds of community members do the day-to-day work of visiting people detained in the onshore system. Some visitors come from refugee backgrounds or have pre-existing relationships with the people they visit. Many do not. What visitors have in common in a desire to stand against Australia's policies by supporting people in detention through personal relationships and associated acts of solidarity. Visitors' experiences in detention – as witnesses, friends and human collateral of this system – are the focus of this book.

2

Theorizing Detention Centres
as Prisons

Elizabeth's story

It's an autumn morning in 2016, and I have come to the inner west of Sydney to meet refugee advocate Elizabeth. Elizabeth is in her late seventies and is something of an institution in Sydney's asylum seeker support movement. She visits Villawood IDC regularly and is the co-founder of an organization that raises money to support asylum seekers living in the community. In recent years, Elizabeth has been in and out of hospital, and she uses a walking stick to get around. Her mind, however, is as sharp as ever.

Elizabeth first became involved in asylum seeker advocacy work in the early 2000s. As an enthusiastic traveller and lifelong learner, she understood the factors that pushed asylum seekers to flee their homelands. Like many of my interviewees, she was deeply uncomfortable with the government's policies. "I understand why there are refugees", Elizabeth explains. "I thought, 'what can I do? I must be able to do something.'"

Elizabeth had been reluctant to visit detention at first. She instead focused on writing to detainees at Australia's remote Curtin and Port Hedland detention facilities, and made the spare bedroom of her apartment available to people leaving detention. Elizabeth had recently retired from a long career in corrective services and was unsure whether she wanted to visit another correctional setting. During her career, Elizabeth sat on various committees and prison taskforces, as well as the parole board. She also visited carceral institutions regularly.

> *'I was in and out of the gaols a fair bit for work, but I was also looking after the half-way houses and accommodation for when they came out and giving support to various organizations to provide support for the prisoners when they came out. So I had a very varied job in corrective services.'*

When Elizabeth finally decided to go to Villawood IDC, her fears were confirmed. "I thought, 'shit! This is like another bleeding gaol'", she recalls. But once there, there was no turning back.

In the years since that first visit, Elizabeth's view of detention has not changed. In addition to her regular Villawood IDC visits, she has been to Maribyrnong IDC in Melbourne, and has supported innumerable people upon their release from facilities around Australia. Her view of immigration detention facilities is that they are essentially prisons. "Nothing is easy", she explains. "It's a gaol. Villawood is a gaol. The other place is a gaol. They are all gaols".

★★★

Immigration prisons

In 2014, at a Human Rights Commission hearing into the detention of children in Australia, Commission President Professor Gillian Triggs likened detention centres to prisons. Immigration Minister Scott Morrison, who would later serve as Australia's Prime Minister, took umbrage with the comparison. "[A]re you suggesting the Long Bay jail is the same as the pool-fenced Alternative Place of Detention at Phosphate Hill on Christmas Island?" he asked. Professor Triggs defended her statement. "I've been a practising lawyer since I was 22-years-old and I've been to many prisons", she said. "I know a prison when I see it. These are prisons." (in Yaxley, 2015).

Morrison is one of a plethora of Australian politicians who have pushed back against comparisons of this kind. The Australian government has been at pains to insist that detention centres are not prisons and that detainees are not being punished (Hurst, 2014). Such assertions are not surprising. To punish asylum seekers for seeking safety, after all, would be a violation of international law (McAdam and Chong, 2014). People in immigration detention are held without charge or trial, purportedly for administrative purposes only.

Irrespective of these official denials, however, the similarities between detention centres and prisons are stark. Professor Triggs is one of innumerable international experts – including carceral scholars from across the world (for example, Moran et al, 2013; Moran, 2013; Longazel et al, 2016; Pugliese, 2008; Bull et al, 2012) – to argue that detention centres are best understood of prisons. People with direct experience of incarceration in these facilities also embrace this language (Tofighian, 2020).

The most obvious similarity between detention centres and prisons concerns the security measures they employ. Detention facilities in Australia's onshore network were once 'open', allowing detainees some freedom of movement (see Chapter One), but are now highly secure. Detainees are held in locked facilities that they cannot leave of their own volition and are subject to constant surveillance by centre guards. In many cases, the design aspects of these centres 'are indistinguishable from, as they have been modelled on, Supermax high security prisons' (Pugliese, 2008: 208).

There are also important overlaps in who is subject to incarceration (Bull et al, 2012). Around the world, young men are overrepresented in carceral populations, and people of colour are imprisoned at significantly higher rates than white people (see, for example, ABS, 2021; Australian Law Reform Commission, 2017; Golash-Boza and Hondagneu-Sotelo, 2013; Billings, 2019). Carceral scholars point to the influence of societal factors on these demographic trends, stressing that underlying issues of poverty and deprivation – together with the criminalization and disproportionate policing of particular activities and communities – mean that already marginalized people are more likely to end up in a carceral institution (for example, Ortiz and Jackey, 2019). In essence, entrenched racial inequalities mean that young men of colour are at greater risk of incarceration.

This trend is reproduced through Australia's detention policies. In Australia, people arriving by boat in search of asylum are routinely incarcerated, whereas asylum seekers who arrive by air typically are not. The mediating factor, here, is that air arrivals generally have visas, but this discrepancy is largely a consequence of government policy rather than any failure on the part of the asylum seekers themselves. People who arrive in Australia by boat generally do so because safer air routes have been closed off to them; they come from countries in the Global South where it is hard, if not impossible, to secure a visa to Australia. Detention systems thus exist within a broader context of inequality. They reflect and reinforce a deeply colonial international system in which an individual's country of birth significantly influences their life prospects (Badiou, 2015; Smith, 2016).[1] As Mary Bosworth and Sarah Turnbull (2014: 93) argue, the disproportionate incarceration of non-white bodies functions to reproduce 'the "whiteness" of the citizenry and the state, while naturalizing the illegality of non-white, non-citizen others'. From this viewpoint, carceral regimes function to create and recreate hierarchies of belonging along racial lines (Bashford and Strange, 2002).

A third similarity between detention centres and prisons that is regularly remarked upon by carceral scholars concerns the private management of these facilities. The privatization of incarceration is a growing trend internationally, such that many prisons are now run by private contractors on a for-profit basis (Byrne et al, 2019). The intersection of racism and privatization in corrective settings means that private companies essentially derive profit from the incarceration of people of colour. Significantly, it is not only prison contractors who benefit from the prison industrial complex. Daniel Eisenkraft Klein and Joana Madureira Lima (2021: 1751) explain that the prison industrial complex includes a raft of commercial actors including those involved in 'bail programs, community surveillance, prison construction, corrections data systems, security equipment, prison food and vending machines, transportation, health services, communications, and prison labor'. While Australia's prison population is small by international standards, almost 20 per cent of prisoners in this system are held in private prisons. This is the largest proportion of prisoners in privately operated prisons in the world (Byrne et al, 2019; Sands et al, 2019).

The privatization of immigration detention in Australia means that this system is beholden to the same economic imperatives that inform private prisons. It again allows profit to be derived from the racialized, marginalized, criminalized and ultimately *commodified* bodies of people of colour. All of Australia's immigration detention centres are managed by private contractors. The onshore network is run by Serco – a company with extensive experience in prison management (Bull et al, 2012). Across the globe, immigration detention and deportation, like incarceration more broadly (Schlosser, 1998), has become a profitable industry (Asylum Seeker Resource Centre et al, 2019).

These similarities support the claim that immigration detention centres are effectively prisons, but it is important to extend this analysis further. Detention centres look like prisons and are run by prison contractors as part of a broader system of colonial exploitation. But they also *operate* like prisons in the fine details of institutional life. This equivalence of practice and outcome is the focus of this chapter, and the theoretical foundation on which this book is built.

The pains of imprisonment

In most of the Western world, imprisonment is the default punishment for serious crimes (Martin and Mitchelson, 2009). This has not always been the case. In earlier eras, physical violence was the main form of state punishment. During the Enlightenment, however, reformers advocated for more humane alternatives to corporal punishment and the prison rose to prominence. A key claim in the prisons literature is that this historical transition away from the brutalization of prisoners was not a transition to a more benign system, but rather a transition to a system that replaced overt physical harm with psychological means of breaking and controlling people (Foucault, 1995 [1975]).

In his 1958 book *The Society of Captives*, American sociologist Gresham Sykes (2007 [1958]) showed that prisoners are subject to an interlocking system of deprivations and frustrations. While these techniques might appear benign to the casual observer, they in fact inflict deep psychological pain with remarkable precision. The deprivation of liberty – the fact of being physically contained – is undoubtedly a foundation on which other deprivations and frustrations are built in carceral systems. But imprisonment is more than just physical containment. There are also subtler mechanisms at play through which harm is inflicted. Five deprivations received particular attention in Sykes' research, as key technologies in the production of carceral pain. In addition to the deprivation of liberty, he identified the deprivation of autonomy, the deprivation of goods and services, the deprivation of intimate relationships, and the deprivation of security as key pains experienced by prisoners.

In the years since its publication, Sykes' (2007 [1958]) *The Society of Captives* has been debated, cited and extended by scholars in sociology, criminology and allied disciplines. Some scholars have suggested that late-modern prisons entail additional pains to those described by Sykes and have sought to update his model accordingly. Eminent penal scholar Ben Crewe (2011), for example, has written at length about pain associated with the deprivation of certainty in civilian prisons. The invention of the 'indeterminate sentence', he notes, means convicted criminals are often sentenced for a loosely defined period of time – for example, 'two to five years' – and given little guidance regarding what they must do to ensure the earliest possible release. The instability this creates is a source of distress. Other scholars have described additional deprivations and frustrations as they have applied Sykes' work to specific prison cohorts – for example, long-term inmates (Flanagan 1980; Richards 1978), youth offenders (Cox, 2011), female inmates (Crewe et al, 2017) and foreign nationals (Warr, 2016) who have unique needs and thus find different aspects of incarceration painful.

Sykes' work has also been brought into dialogue with that of other influential theorists, most notably Erving Goffman (1961) and Michel Foucault (1995 [1975]), whose work overlaps with Sykes' in important ways. Goffman, for example, observed that 'total institutions' (as he termed them) subject residents to humiliations and degradations that erase inmates' prior identities. This 'mortification of self' sees even basic bodily functions brought under the control of the institution. Official systems micro-manage even the smallest details of inmates' lives. From a Foucauldian disciplinary perspective, these methods are painful, but also more efficient than any brute use of physical force as they function to remodel the subject's psyche (1995 [1975]).

As Crewe (2011: 512) observes, this work remains highly relevant today.

> Prisoners continue to cite such things as the deprivation of liberty, the misuse of staff authority, the threatening company of other prisoners, being cut off from family and friends, 'unremitting loneliness', the crushing of emotional existence and 'institutional thoughtlessness' as among their primary sorrows.

The main point here – developed and refined through decades of research in civilian prisons and other total institutions – is that prisons are intended systems of deprivation and mortification that attack inmates at the deepest levels of the self (Goffman 1961; Cohen and Taylor 1972). Prisons use a plethora of (often micro-level) rules and practices to inflict pain. Prisoners generally have their basic physical needs met while incarcerated, but they are systematically stripped of agency and autonomy, and denied the pleasures and relationships that help make life meaningful. In imposing these deprivations, prisons assert control and shape inmates' subjectivities, with the effect of corroding their mental health (Edgemon and Clay-Warner, 2019). As Thomas Ugelvik and Dorina Damsa (2018: 1039) summarize, 'pain and frustration are intrinsic to imprisonment. [...] Simply put, any prison will represent a specific configuration of pains and frustrations experienced by its prisoners'.

The deeper political function of prison technologies as revealed in this literature lies in their ability *to obscure* the violence necessitated by policy objectives and maintain an outward appearance of banality. Prisons facilitate a form of plausible denial, making it possible for authorities to maintain that inmates' rights are being respected even as they are systematically violated.

Referred pains

In the context of this book's focus on detention centre visitors, research on the anguish experienced by prisoners' loved ones is also relevant here. It is well established in the prisons literature that an individual's incarceration can cause their dependents significant hardship. Part of this strain is financial, as family members struggle to make ends meet without the income the prisoner previously provided (Braman, 2007; Flynn, 2014; Gonzalez and Patler, 2020). Emotional anguish is also common as family members worry about the prisoner (Braman, 2007), struggle to sustain visits and other forms of contact (Patler and Branic, 2017; Christian, 2005; Christian et al, 2006; Tewksbury and DeMichele, 2005; Golash-Boza, 2019; Tasca, 2018), negotiate the stigma associated with a loved one's incarceration (Benisty et al, 2020; Gonzalez and Patler, 2020), and experience significant changes in their relationship dynamics (Dreby, 2012; Lanskey et al, 2018). A recurring theme in this research is that the collateral impacts of incarceration 'are long lasting, expressing themselves psychologically, socially, economically, and in other forms' (Martinez and Debora Ortega, 2019: 124).

Beyond these indirect impacts, several studies suggest that prisoners' friends and family members also experience something akin to the pains of imprisonment in their interactions with the penal system. In an important ethnographic study of California's San Quentin State Prison, Megan Comfort (2003; 2008) found that prisoner's family members experienced a form of secondary prisonization during visits. Despite their status as free citizens, the institution treated family members as 'quasi-inmates, people at once legally free and palpably bound' (Comfort, 2003: 103). Participants in Moran Benisty and colleagues', 2020 study of the experiences of prisoners' parents and siblings reported a similar phenomenon. They 'described their consistent struggle to relieve aversive psychological "pains" and regain some sense of control, as an experience of "incarceration" that is parallel to that off their offspring' (Benisty et al, 2020: 12–13). Indeed, 'the entire criminal justice system' was experienced by these participants as "painful" (2020: 12).

It is important to stress here that, for Sykes, the deprivations and frustrations of imprisonment are *intended* aspects of the punishment prisoners endure. With respect to the deprivation of autonomy, for example, Sykes argued that prisoners are often denied information and explanation *as a matter of policy*.

> [E]xplanations are often withheld as a matter of calculated policy. Providing explanations carries an implication that those who are ruled have a right to know – and this in turn suggests that if the explanations are not satisfactory, the rule or order will be changed. But this is in direct contradiction to the theoretical power relationship of the inmates and the prison officials. Imprisoned criminals are individuals who are being punished by society and they must be brought to their knees. (Sykes, 2007 [1958]: 74–5)

For Comfort, the deprivations and frustrations that prison visitors experience are also elements of institutional design. The feelings of disempowerment and disorientation that her study participants experienced in prison reflected and served a broader institutional purpose of maintaining power and control. As the coming chapters will show, comparable strategies of visitor subjectification are routinely employed in Australian immigration detention facilities but have received minimal focused attention to date.

Conclusion

There are numerous similarities between detention centres and prisons that invite comparison. A close reading of the existing literature on prisons reveals that prisons are technologies of subjectification that have developed in a context where brute violence is no longer accepted as an appropriate form of punishment. Prisons have political value not because they avoid violence, but because they are able to *obscure* the more clandestine violence they entail (see also Galtung 1969; Dilts, 2012). Prisons employ subtle strategies of deprivation and frustration that inflict harm on inmates and, at times, on the people they love.

Reading Australia's detention system through the lens of this literature means underlining the often subtle mechanisms detention centres employ to inflict harm. In Australia's offshore processing facilities in PNG and Nauru, violence has frequently taken stark and shocking form. These facilities are deliberately located outside Australian territory; people within them are denied access to substantive legal rights, making abuse more likely (Nethery and Holman, 2016; McAdam and Chong, 2014). Australia's onshore detention facilities, however, are located within the jurisdiction of Australia's courts and must contend with significantly more constraints. The onshore network faces the challenge of reconciling its overarching objective of asylum seeker deterrence with the need to maintain a semblance of respect for human rights. In this context, the appropriation of prison practices has become the norm.

Over the coming chapters, this book will present a detailed picture of immigration detention facilities as asylum seeker prisons. Drawing on witness testimony from centre visitors – as well as available statements from centre authorities, politicians and past and present detainees – it will show that these facilities use carceral techniques to impose acute psychological suffering while maintaining an official fiction of banality.

Bureaucratic Violence

Moina's story

It's 2019 and I am in Melbourne interviewing Moina – a kind, down-to-earth woman in her late 60s. From 2002 until 2012, Moina was volunteer kitchen manager at a Non-Government Organization (NGO) that provides daily meals to asylum seekers in her local area. She coordinated the other kitchen volunteers, managed a pantry of donated food, and was personally involved in preparing meals. Moina can't remember when she started visiting MITA, but imagines she's been visiting for almost 13 years. Certainly, she tells me, it's been well over a decade.

In those early days at MITA, Moina recalls, the visitation process was comparatively simple.

> *'I can't even remember when I went the first time. It was a bit of a non-event then because you could go in pretty-much any time after two in the afternoon – stay as long as you like, take in pretty-much anything. You'd whip up a bit of food if you knew somebody liked that. And there was a big common room. You'd sit in the big common room and watch tellie together and [read] the papers. Play games. There were young people there and some that were trying to do a bit of maths and you could go up and work with them on things. So it wasn't a big event. You could literally nick up there for half-an-hour or an hour or stay longer and chat.'*

The process today is very different. Visits must be booked five business days in advance, and special permission must be secured for group visit; visitors must submit to a security inspection as they enter the centres, including walk-through screenings, x-rays and drug tests; and visiting hours are clearly defined and strictly enforced. What was once simple and spontaneous has become complicated, intimidating and time-consuming.

Restrictions surrounding the admission of food are particularly distressing to Moina, who – as her volunteer history attests – sees the provision of food as both a practical form of support and a means of forming human connections.

'For somebody's birthday, I could find a recipe from Iran and I'd cook my Iranian food and take it up and share it. That all went completely. Now you can't take any food you cook yourself. [...] You'd take pomegranates to people who loved that in their country. A lot of them have been through hell and are terribly homesick. People sometimes think they come Australia because they don't like it at home. They love their homeland, but they're forced to come through real fear, so any food from home they're nostalgic for. [...] I used to be able to acknowledge, "I know who you are as an individual". But now they've made it you can [only] take in a pile of junk food.'

Restrictions regarding the admission of gifts and other possessions have had similar effects. Not long ago, Moina would take birdseed into MITA for a young family. Using the seed she provided, the family would go outside, where there was a large gumtree, and feed the birds. These moments of joy and distraction had been treasured by the detained children, but ceased when the centre banned the admission of birdseed. "They said, 'oh no, if they eat the seeds, they could get sick", Moina recalls.

Rummaging in her bag for a brightly coloured children's book, Moina shares another example of these escalating rules and the painful deprivation they produce. One of the detainees she visits is an adult man who was forced to flee his village when he converted to Christianity. Where some of the detainees at MITA have tertiary qualifications and excellent English skills, this man has worked from a young age to support his extended family and has never attended school. Struggling to keep up with the detention centre English classes, he recently asked Moina for a book to help him. "He wanted just to do the letters", she explains, passing me the book.

'I took [the book] in and [the Serco staff] said, "no, he's got to ask for it". They said, "no, he's got to [request the book] not near the visiting centre, but out the back". He went there, but he couldn't write − he had to fill in a request form. [...] The next time [I asked the Serco staff], "could you tell me what's on the form and I'll write that for him and he can go and do it?"' [They said], "no, he's not allowed to take stuff". This went on week after week. [...] He never got it filled in. After about six weeks he said, "I don't care if I never learn to write". And that was the end of it.'

Moina, like so many of my interviewees, has numerous examples of these bureaucratic restrictions and the harms they inflict. But in this moment, it is all that I can do to read the innocent words on the page in front of me. 'L is for lion'.

★★★

The totality of the institution

In his book *Asylums*, Erving Goffman (1961: 11) drew attention to a range of institutions where large numbers of individuals live and work, 'cut off from the wider society for an appreciable length of time'. Within these 'total institutions', as he termed them, residents lead 'an enclosed, formally administered round of life'.

As total institutions, carceral facilities like detention centres enforce a painful separation between detainees and the broader society. This separation is literal, as the detainee is physically contained, but it is also symbolic. As Sykes (2007 [1958]: 67) observes, incarceration is painful in part because it denotes social exclusion and rejection: 'the wall which seals off the criminal, the contaminated man, is a constant threat to the prisoner's self-conception and the threat is continually repeated in the many daily reminders that he must be kept apart from "decent" men'.

For people detained in Australian immigration detention facilities, this sense of social rejection is compounded by the perceived injustice of their social exclusion. Seeking asylum is permissible under international law but Australia routinely incarcerates asylum seekers without charge or trial. Iranian refugee Medhi Ali expressed the pain of this undeserved ostracization in a tweet in 2021. He had come to Australia seeking safety as a 15-year-old and had been detained for over eight years,

> I didn't commit any crimes. All I did was ask for safety when I was a child and I did the time for that by spending almost a decade in detention. What's sadder than this cruel policy is the significant support it has from the Australian community. I wish I'd never asked you for safety. (Ali, 2021a: np)

"[I]t is hard to still be here," he told *The Guardian*, "left behind" (in Doherty, 2021).

While carceral institutions like detention centres maintain a painful separation between inmates and society, the 'totality' of these facilities is not complete (Farrington, 1992). Like other borders, detention centre walls are technologies for managing differential flows of people and resources. They are not impenetrable so much as they are *selectively porous*, allowing centre staff, for example, to cross with ease, while preventing some people or items from being admitted. As sociologist Keith Farrington (1992: 7) puts it, carceral institutions are best understood as enclosed within a permeable membrane of 'structures, mechanisms and policies' which maintain a 'selective and imperfect degree of separation between what exists inside of and what lies beyond prison walls' (see also Baumer et al, 2009; Moran, 2013).

This chapter concerns the selective permeability of Australia's onshore immigration detention facilities, and the subtle yet elaborate mechanisms they use to maintain a degree of totality. Through a close examination of visitation application and entrance processes, it highlights the walls of bureaucracy that maintain painful conditions within these centres. Bureaucracy, this chapter shows, is an important part of how the isolation and deprivation of detention spaces is maintained.

Visitor application processes

Bureaucratic processes – and paperwork in particular – play an ambivalent role in the lives of people seeking asylum. The right documents presented in the right manner can open up new lives and opportunities. But bureaucracy is also central to the enactment of violence (Nare, 2020; Eldridge and Reinke, 2018; Reinke, 2018; Beaugrand, 2011). Bureaucracy is often utilized in state efforts to prevent transient people from accessing protection. Destination countries, for example, control access to their territories in part through visa application processes that favour some immigrants over others. Bureaucracy is not accidental in these systems of withholding. Rather, it is an ideal mechanism for imposing what anthropologist Rallie Murray (2019: 72) refers to as 'trivial evil'. By simultaneously erasing the individual and the unique circumstances of their lives, and making violence seem banal (Arendt 1963) and unexceptional, bureaucracy creates conditions where frontline decision-makers will enact the harmful policies they are charged with enforcing.

Bureaucracy is an under-recognized tool in government efforts to isolate asylum seekers in Australia's onshore immigration detention system. While various rules and regulations ensure detainees cannot leave these centres, walls of paperwork also make it difficult for visitors to enter. When interviewees like Moina began visiting detention in the first decade of the 21st century, most Australian detention facilities had no formal visitor application process in place.[1] As Claire (Melbourne) recalled with respect to her early visits to Maribyrnong IDC,

'At that stage as long as you had a [detainee's] name [you could visit]. Nothing else. I don't think you even needed to have a date-of-birth. And you just rocked up. You didn't ask beforehand. You just rocked up. And the only thing that stopped you going in was in Maribyrnong they had a magical figure of 60 inside the room, counting everybody. So we would be going around counting everybody when we were in there to find out if our friends outside could come in.'

Deb (Melbourne) had a similar recollection of the entrance process at this time.

'The only time you applied in advance in those days was to Baxter. [...] You couldn't just rock up to Baxter. [...] And they weren't too fussed. If you had the name written on a bit of paper and it wasn't spelt properly, they didn't really care.'

By the early 2010s, however, a formal visitor application process had been introduced to most centres. People wishing to visit detention were now 'encouraged' to submit simple physical application form 24 hours before each visit (Immigration National Office, 2013: 7).

When I commenced this research in 2015, the application process was continuing to tighten. Applications were now required 24 hours in advance (Department of Immigration and Border Protection, 2015a), and visitors had to provide their driver's licence or passport details for identification purposes. A degree of flexibility remained in the system, however, particularly when a visitor encountered a friendly Serco officer. In Darwin, Ronelle reflected that completing the application form

'was a bit of a nuisance, but there was a guy who was actually quite helpful – one of the Serco guys. If you'd made a mistake [...] he'd usually ring so you could still fix whatever the problem was and you could still visit. He was actually quite good.'

Oliver in Melbourne described the process in a comparable way.

'There was just a phone number you could call and if I wanted to visit on a Wednesday you could ring up on Monday or even Tuesday and do it over the phone and say, "these are the people I'd like to visit". And they had a friendly enough system that they would tell you, "you can't actually see those three people because someone else is seeing those three people. Would you like to visit a couple more people?" And you actually could have some sort of rapport with the particular person at Serco who was in charge of bookings and they got to know you and you got to know them and you might have both thought it was a silly system but that was all fine.'

Over the next five years, this element of human contact was slowly eliminated. By 2019, visitors had to submit their applications through an online portal at least *five business days* (one week) before each visit (ABF, 2020).

The problems with the new online application were many and varied. A key issue was the increased rate at which visitor applications were rejected – typically because a detainee was already booked to receive another visitor during the requested timeslot, or because the visiting room was already fully booked. The application website also regularly crashed, preventing prospective visitors from lodging the requisite visitation requests the required five business days before their visits.

The application itself had also become long and complex, requiring visitors to submit a privacy acknowledgement; provide their personal details, including 100 points of identification[2] and the details of any accompanying visitors; disclose any controlled items they wished to bring into the facilities; give details of the person they wished to visit, including their date-of-birth; nominate their proposed visiting time; complete several declarations and agree to the conditions of entry; and attach supporting documents as necessary (ABF, 2020). Where other online forms might automatically populate with details from previous submissions, this application required visitors to start the form from scratch each time they visited detention – in some cases multiple times each week.

For visitors who wanted to see more than one detainee during a single visit, the process was even more time-consuming as an additional request form was required (ABF, 2018a).

'It takes three weeks to book a table of five detainees because [...] if you want to apply to visit more than one person there's a special form that you have to fill out for ABF to approve. And so that has to be filled out with the names of the five people. You have to write an explanation of why you should be allowed to visit more than one person. And what is the purpose of your visit. What organization you belong to. And you have to submit that and waste probably a week-and-a-half and often chase it up before ABF approve it. [...] When you receive that back you then have to put in individual applications online to visit each of the people. [...] And then you have to wait another week for that to be processed to know whether you can go and see people or not.' (Oliver, Melbourne)

Visitors without these necessary approvals were turned away.

As Lars (Melbourne) reflected, "[i]t doesn't sound like it should be terribly much – it's just a series of administrative hoops". Yet the challenges presented by these bureaucratic hurdles were significant. Community members with irregular schedules (for example, those employed on casual contracts) found the new system particularly challenging as they couldn't reliably predict their availability.

'[Y]ou have to give them five business days' notice when you apply for a visit and so that's a bit tricky because I work full-time. So then I've got to think, "do I have an afternoon off" or 'can I fit in", or sometimes I'll have an afternoon off just unexpectedly and I think, "oh, if I'd known I would have been able to just drop in", [but] you can't do that. You have to apply ahead of time.' (Beth, Brisbane)

Short visiting hours at some facilities compounded these issues, making it harder to find and book an appropriate visiting slot.

The application's online format was also a problem for people with poor digital literacy or limited internet access. Several participants had noticed a drop in visitor numbers when the application moved to this format and attributed this to some visitors struggling to manage the technology or feeling uncomfortable lodging their personal details online. Visitors from lower socio-economic backgrounds – including some detainees' family members who had few financial resources or connections in Australia – faced additional challenges due to unreliable computer or internet access.

Visitors from culturally and linguistically diverse (CALD) backgrounds also struggled with the length and complexity of the application. Officially, the application was only supposed to be completed by the individual who wished to visit detention (Department of Home Affairs, 2018b), but it was prohibitively complicated for non-English speakers to complete. English-speaking visitors provided assistance where they could, but this again increased the time commitment for all involved.

> '[I]t's not easy for anyone to do, let alone people who really struggle with the language. And it's the liming factor too. If you get your application in too late there is no leniency around that at all. It's just, "no you've missed the deadline, you have to choose a new date".'
> (Roberta, Perth)

The requirement that visitors provide 100 points of identification as part of their application (ABF, 2020) was also an issue for some community-based asylum seekers. Many of these individuals simply didn't "have the appropriate amount of ID to upload to be able to visit. You've got to upload passports, license, photo ID, and a lot of people don't have that amount of points" (Hannah, Melbourne).

The new visitor application process thus created latent forms of visitor exclusion without compromising the official discourse vis-à-vis the humanity and accessibility of these facilities. Spaces that were purportedly open to detainees' friends and loved ones were made *functionally* inaccessible to (some) visitors, reducing visitor numbers and thus increasing detainee isolation. This capacity of bureaucracy to enact exclusion – often disproportionately disadvantaging people in positions of structural vulnerability – is well recognized in the social policy literature. As Evelyn Brodkin and Malay Majmundar (2010: 827) explain, institutions that make access to benefits, services or spaces contingent on 'complicated, confusing, or cumbersome' processes impose costs that may be beyond some individual's capacity to 'pay' (see also Heckert, 2020).

Visitor entrance procedures

Approaching the facilities

The architecture of Australia's onshore detention facilities differs from centre to centre. In recalling their initial detention visits, however, participants across Australia described the intimidating nature of many detention buildings and recalled a burgeoning recognition that they were entering a prison. Visitors to Yongah Hill IDC in Western Australia were particularly emphatic regarding the role that the facility's physical features and surroundings played in creating an atmosphere of threat. These participants described Yongah Hill IDC's remoteness and the surreal views that greeted them as they approached the centre through the Western Australian dessert.

> 'It's about an hour-and-a-half drive out there [from Perth]. Which is strange because it's this very vast open bush landscape that you go through to get there. Then you get around this bend and you see all this steel mesh and stuff poking out of the landscape and that's the detention centre – all these fences.' (Samantha, Perth)

This sensory emersion in a stark landscape afforded visitors a visceral appreciation of the isolation and deprivation their friends endured within the facility.

Visitors to facilities in Australia's largest cities described a similar experience of realization, although these facilities were not as immediately shocking as the Yongah Hill centre. While visitors like Carole (Brisbane) felt afraid when they "looked around and [saw] the barbed wire everywhere", others were startled to realize how easily the centres blended into their local surroundings. In Brisbane, for example, Teegan recalled the difficulties she had experienced finding BITA on her first visit. The centre had a military air but didn't seem particularly out-of-place in the industrial landscape adjacent to Brisbane airport.

> 'It feels already quite military when you're getting there. And it's just a wire fence [...] just a driveway and a number 100 so we did drive past and we're not the first ones to drive past it and then realize, "no, that was it! Go back". When you arrive and there's a car park. There's only two or three visitor spots, but I think even the staff park on the grass. [...] It's not like they have any signpost of "receptions this way". It's really like we don't want people to come here.'

The comparative banality of these facades was – for some visitors – part of what made them confronting. Numerous visitors to urban facilities noted that, prior to their involvement in the asylum seeker support movement, they had not even realized that there was a detention centre in their area. Arriving at the centres, visitors began to comprehend that refugees and asylum seekers really were being imprisoned in their cities, sometimes just kilometres from their homes.

This disconcerting mix of high security architectural features and industrial banality continued within the facilities themselves. The initial entrance areas were often bland and unremarkable, but several visitors observed that their optics betrayed something of the broader institutional cultures within which they operated. Visitors to BITA in the early 2010s recognized the irony of a sign behind the reception desk that read 'WELCOME' in several languages. "We used to think that was funny; it's not very welcoming", Max (Brisbane) laughed. Yet these visitors also comprehended the symbolic significance when – with the introduction of the Coalition government's militarized border protection programme – the sign was removed and replaced with the words 'BORDER FORCE'. This small aesthetic change signalled a larger shift that would be felt by detainees and visitors for years to come.

Submitting to security screening

As noted above, entering detention was comparatively simple in the early years of the 2000s. Over time increasingly laborious visitor application processes were introduced; physical security screenings at the facilities were also progressively implemented during this period. By the time Operation Sovereign Borders was underway, visitors arriving at a detention facility were required to go through several layers of security before they could see the people they had booked to visit. First, they presented themselves to the reception desk with 100 points of identification, including one document that showed a colour photograph of themselves. Next, they received a fluorescent vest and wrist band to wear during their visit, and, in some cases, had a small mark made on their wrist in invisible ink. Visitors were then required to place all personal belongings – with the exception of any items they were taking to their visits – into a locker. The locker key was returned to the reception desk for safe keeping.

This removal of personal items was a source of concern for some visitors, including Brisbane retiree Alma who regularly took two asylum seeker children to visit their father at BITA.

'I just couldn't quite believe that this was a family visit, you know? [...] Their phone had to stay in the locker and I was a bit amazed at that. What if they had something they wanted to share with their dad? That wasn't going to happen.'

Other participants who left families at home when they visited detention were similarly concerned that their own loved ones would not be able to reach them easily if, for example, there was an emergency.

It was not unheard on for visitors to be turned away during this initial check-in stage, usually because they had insufficient identification. Yongah Hill IDC visitor Fiona (Perth) knew several visitors who had driven 90 minutes to the remote facility only to be denied entry because they had forgotten their passports. "They've just been told, 'sorry, you haven't got your ID'" (Fiona, Perth). Visitors could also be turned away on the basis that they were wearing inappropriate footwear. All visitors were required to wear closed-in shoes, purportedly due to Occupational Health and Safety concerns. This simple closed shoe rule could cause deep distress.

'This lady was before us [at reception] and she was refused entry to see her son – despite having come down from Sydney – because she had open-toed sandals. And no amount of explanation, pleading, complaining, speaking to the manager, was going to change it. "No, lady, if you want to come you better go to the shops and buy some enclosed shoes, but I suggest you do it fast because you've only got a half-hour window!" If you're not in the visitor centre within half-an-hour of your booking time you are also refused entry. And she didn't get to visit.' (Oliver, Mebourne)

The rule was a particular issue for visitors in Australia's hot northern states – so much so that Heather (Darwin) had taken to keeping four spare pairs of shoes in her car to share with other visitors. "[I]n Darwin no one ever wears closed shoes", she explained.

For visitors who made it through this initial check-in process, the next step was physical screening. The nature of these screenings escalated dramatically under Operation Sovereign Borders. Detention Services Manuals from as recently as 2013 indicate that visitors to (lower security) Immigration Transit Accommodation facilities could have their bags checked for alcohol or illegal items but were otherwise exempt from security screenings and searches (Immigration National Office, 2013). By 2018, visitors to all detention facilities were advised that submitting to intensive screening – including 'hand-held scanners, walk-through screening, x-ray and substance detection' (ABF, 2018b: 1) – was a condition of entry.

During my first interviews in 2015, the physical screening process involved walking through an airport-style metal detector and allowing any items that were being taken into the centres to be x-rayed. At this time, visitors described this process as intimidating but relatively unproblematic. By 2019, female interviewees in particular reported that the metal detection process had become considerably less comfortable, escalating beyond what might be encountered even at an international airport.

> 'Women have been turned away because the metal under their bras has shown up as metal. It depends on the guards – sometimes they let you through anyway. I haven't been turned away for that. But you have to prove what the metal is in some way so they have to use a wand if you go through the metal detector and it comes off as you're wearing some metal, then they'll use a wand and like do it over your body and you sort of have to justify, "well, it's my bra". And the majority of guards would be men and it can be really uncomfortable having to explain to them.' (Imogen, Melbourne)

Participants noted that some visitors had used these experiences as opportunities to vent their frustration. "I've had a friend literally take off her bra at reception and go 'there!'", Hannah (Melbourne) told me. The power discrepancy that characterized these occurrences, however, could be deeply unsettling. This was particularly the case for young women who felt their physical vulnerability beside the Serco officers.

Drug detection tests – where visitors' clothing was swabbed for the presence of illicit substances – also became the norm during this time and added to visitors' sense of intimidation. Complaints regarding the unreliability of these tests increased as my research progressed. In 2015, several Villawood IDC visitors reported being turned away from the centre because an illegal substance had been detected on their clothing. By 2019, stories of this kind were common. In Melbourne, Louise described a series of incidents in 2018 when she was repeatedly denied entry to MITA due to drug residue on her clothing.

> 'The first time I was just speechless because you are told to go home, which when you've come three hours is quite a way! [...] The second time I was told it was probably Fentanyl and I'd probably picked it up on public transport because I travel by train. So the last time I went when I got knocked back [...] I washed every article of clothing from the skin out. I did not go on the train. I drove my car. I washed the seat. I washed the steering wheel. I washed everything I came in contact with. I got in there and I'm positive [for traces of drugs]!'

Louise knew she had done nothing wrong but felt profoundly disempowered. There seemed to be little recourse available.

> 'I said I wanted to see the manager. What do you do? Anyway, a big bulky Serco guard came out and I was in the sort of no-man's-land. And I didn't realize at the time probably because I was so angry, but there

were two Serco guards either side of him, so I was standing against the wall and they had me like that. And when I reflected on it, I thought that was very intimidating. [...] I went down to Broadmeadows Police Station and asked them to test me. They said they couldn't because it was a federal matter, but that I could make a stat[utory] dec[laration].'

This experience fundamentally shifted Louise's experience of detention. "Every time I have the drug test, I just feel anxious now", she told me. "What can I do if they find it positive?" Yet it also contributed to a new and novel form of resistance. "I wear a coat or a big shirt in the summer over me on the train. I get off and I get to the reception area and I take the shirt off", Louise laughed. This ritual, while clearly pragmatic, entailed a performative element, communicating to the Serco officers the ridiculousness of the process.

Other participants shared similar stories of subtle resistance. In Perth, Bronte described her response when she received an "absurd" drug test result at Yongah Hill IDC.

'When it happened to us I said, "well, can I speak to the manager?" And they used the thing on his clothes and he had traces of cocaine on his clothes! So they let us in because it was obviously some problem with the machine. So I understand that you need to have some checks and balances around that but certainly there's a power dynamic between you and the people running the institution.'

Visitors who were not as "cranky and old and assertive" as she was, Bronte feared, may have turned around and driven the 90 minutes back to Perth.

Significantly, the Department appeared to be aware of these issues, as by 2019 some visitors were being offered no-contact visits when they failed a drug detection test. Yet as Maive (Brisbane) described with respect to her own experience at BITA, this apparent solution was far from perfect.

'I was testing positive to heroin. That was a bit weird because I'm pretty nerdy and straight and I don't drink, so that's definitely not something that's happening for me. So they did two tests and, apparently, they both came up as positive for heroin. [...] One time I even had to sit beside a screen to visit the young man that I was visiting. We weren't allowed to be in the same room! [...] It was so hard because there were aeroplanes going past and it was really hard to communicate and there's a guard on the doors outside.'

For Maive and many others, the drug detection process seemed like another hoop to jump through. "It just felt like another type of barrier, making it difficult to come in", she said.

The admission of gifts

As the previous chapter explored, research on psychological conditions in civilian prisons frequently observes that micro-level deprivations and frustrations are key in producing prisoner anguish. Among other pains, inmates are deprived access to desirable goods and services; while they typically have access to the basics required to sustain life, the luxuries that afford identity and pleasure are stripped away (Sykes, 2007 [1958]). Goffman's (1961) work on the mortification of self in total institutions offers a useful supplement to this idea. Upon entering a total institution, Goffman argued, a person undergoes a process of mortification where all markers of the old self, including material possessions that communicate personal or community identity beyond the institution, are removed.

One of the most striking aspects of Australia's detention centre visitation process concerns the enforcement of escalating rules to maintain Spartian conditions within the facilities. Detainees have often spoken about the small comforts they are denied in detention, expressing their longing for simple pleasures like "a big bed, a clean pillow, [a] comfortable blanket and a window that opens so that I can feel the wind and hear the rain at night" (Ali, 2021b: np). For many of the participants in this study, the most distressing aspect of the visitor entrance process under Operation Sovereign Borders concerned the challenges associated with admitting gifts. While a blanket or homemade meal would not end their friends' suffering, visitors recognized that such items could soften the abrasive edges of the institution and felt frustrated and upset when they were unable to deliver these items.

In the mid-2010s, visitors would often take boardgames or decks of cards to their visits. These activities provided a point of focus for the visits, allowing detainees and visitors from different CALD backgrounds to communicate with each other through a common language of laughter and play. As the years progressed, rules surrounding these items became less predictable. By 2019, MITA visitors were unable to take even simple card games into the centre.

'One of the things that they like doing even back home in Sri Lanka is they have a card game they call Rummy […] they love playing it but to play it you need three decks of cards. And we used to be able to take in things like that. No worries. And then they said, "no games". We said, "but this is a cultural activity". […] "Well we will provide any necessary entertainment". So they provided one deck of cards and that was always incomplete.' (Oliver, Melbourne)

The situation at Villawood IDC was similar. As Asha (Sydney) lamented, "[s]ometimes you're allowed to take cards, other times you're not".

These shifting rules caused particular concern when children were involved. In the early years of this study, when children were routinely detained, participants described thwarted efforts to take basic items to detained children to brighten their moods. In Darwin, Lauretta had taken playdough to her visits with a young family. This was initially permitted, but later banned.

> 'There was no explanation. [...] "Why am I not allowed to bring the playdough in?" "It's the new rule". [...] Even people who thought it was stupid on the [Serco] staff didn't do anything. I guess they couldn't.' (Lauretta, Darwin)

A separate property process existed where visitors could submit items to be screened, processed and (if approved) given to the detainees after their visits, but this did not resolve the problem. Visitors found the process to be highly capricious. Robyn (Brisbane), for instance, had taken doonas to BITA for detainees who told her they were cold.

> 'In the winter the families that I was visiting said that they were really cold – at night, you know. And I said, "well, put in a request for some blankets". They said, "we did but they're not coming". So I just brought a gift. I brought some doonas. I brought a couple more and then there was like a deluge – all the detainees – "can you bring me one? Can you bring me one?" So I started to get friends to donate them and I was bringing them in.'

Soon, she was reproached by centre staff.

> 'I got into trouble for that because "they get plenty, they're just stockpiling". I bought a new baby some clothes [too]. "They're just stockpiling, it's a fire hazard, you can't do it". I just commented, "well stockpiling clothes, that's what I call my wardrobe".'

As Robyn reflected, there was an institutional expectation that people in detention should have few personal possessions. Over time, fewer and fewer items were accepted.

As with other centre rules, the property process not only hardened over time but was implemented significantly differently from centre to centre and month to month. In Melbourne, Imogen explained that during 2019 MITA had displayed a typed list at reception, specifying what items were admissible via the property process.

'You say, "can I bring a sketchbook for someone?" Or "can I bring a toy for a child?" Or "can I bring a hair thing for a child?" Or "can I bring a scarf for a woman". And they're like, "no, if it doesn't fit that category it's not allowed in". You would question why those particular categories. There are other things that are incredibly important or particular things that people would really appreciate during religious festivities and they're not allowed, but they don't even care about giving an explanation. They just say, "that's the rules. Read the sign. That's the rules".'

These restrictions were strictly enforced at MITA for several months.

Visitors to other centres shared similar stories of necessities like toiletries and sanitary products being summarily rejected. Elizabeth (Sydney) described flying from Sydney to Melbourne to visit a detained friend in Maribyrnong IDC. She had brought him some basic items but was prevented from leaving most of them at the facility.

'When I went there I took two toothbrushes for him, toothpaste, a bag to put everything in, soap, soap dishes, deodorant, and a book that he wanted […] I was allowed to leave the bag to put things in, but I wasn't allowed to leave the toothpaste, the toothbrushes, the deodorant or the soap. Because "we provide all of those things". But I said […] "I'm told by the refugees they think the toothpaste is horrible and the toothbrushes are hard and you shouldn't have hard toothbrushes". [They said,] "No. It's against the rules".'

Being prevented from offering even modest provisions was a source of distress for many visitors. As Maive (Brisbane) emphasized, "when they're asking for very simple things [and you think,] 'that's something that I can provide', not being able to do that for them [is upsetting]".

The admission of food

This pattern of bureaucratically administered deprivation was also apparent in changing rules regarding the admission of food to visits. As Moina's story evidences, bringing food into detention had not always been a difficult process. Numerous visitors described their own previous practice of bringing fresh food into detention, such that the visit itself involved a shared meal and at times took on a quality of celebration. In Sydney, Elena would bring takeaway pizzas to her visits, while Roberta in Perth would make homemade casseroles and cakes. Many visitors asked their friends about their culinary preferences and tailored their offerings to the specific people they visited.

'I remember one time there were these two couples there from Sri Lanka and both of them had lost babies, and I knew a woman who had a Sri Lankan restaurant in town and I asked her if she wanted to give us some food to take out.' (Allie, Darwin)

Over time, providing these personalized food offerings became more difficult.

'The people who were Iranian – they liked flat bread, fetta cheese, olives, that kind of thing. One Iranian lady really liked peaches and I was really cross one day because I took in quite a few peaches and they said, "you can't bring in fruit". And I said, "well, you could have told me that. You haven't just made the rule this minute".' (Ronelle, Darwin)

The introduction of food restrictions occurred gradually and, at first, erratically. In 2015, study participants were already complaining about the difficulties associated with bringing fresh food into detention. As William (Sydney) told me at the time, "it varies from day to day depending on who's the officer who's there. Sometimes you're allowed to bring fruit, sometimes you're not; sometimes it's got to be in sealed packages, sometimes not." These restrictions gradually solidified and were ultimately formalized as official ABF policy.

In 2016, the ABF released a new information sheet, *Changes to the Food Policies in Immigration Detention Facilities*. From 11 September 2017, the sheet advised, visitors would only be permitted to bring food to their visits if: (a) the food was commercially packaged, labelled and factory sealed, had a visible and valid expiry date, and was identifiable; (b) the food's packaging was made of carton or soft plastic, rather than metal or glass; (c) the food was of quantity that could be consumed during the visiting hours; and (d) all left-over food was disposed of or removed from the facility at the end of the visit (detainees were no longer permitted to take food back to their compounds).[3] According to the ABF, these new rules were introduced to ensure the safety and security of detention spaces.

There are two guiding principles for regulating the types of food that can be brought in for detainees: (a) Health – Cooked and raw foods quickly become contaminated with bacteria and can cause illness if they are left out at room temperature. This is why perishable foods are not allowed in our detention facilities and why we will not allow food to be sent by postal or courier services or delivered as take-away meals. (b) Security – Food must be commercially packaged and sealed to reduce the risk of controlled and prohibited items entering the IDF. (ABF, 2016: 2)

As Chapter Four will elaborate, these restrictions had a significant negative impact on detainees' well-being. People in detention often requested fresh fruit and vegetables because they wished to supplement their institutional meals. The introduction of these rules meant visitors were largely limited to "bringing in what we'd classify as 'junk foods', and they don't necessarily want to be eating junk food" (Moina, Melbourne). At a socio-emotional level, the restrictions imposed even greater pain. Banning fresh and homemade meals fundamentally changed the atmosphere of visits. It dampened the tone of warmth and normality that detainees and their visitors worked to co-create, ensuring detainees had little respite from the sterile realities of institutional living. In her research on Russian prisons, Dominique Moran (2013: 346) has observed that the visiting room offers prisoners 'a form of escape from the everyday life of the prison'. Embodied activities like the sharing of food, as well as visitors' accessorizing of visitation spaces with items from 'outside' the institution, allow the therapeutic performance of 'a kind of "normal" life'. Without these items and the sensory reprieve they provide, the sanctuary provided by the visiting room is less complete.

With the introduction of these news rules, visitors who wished to bring fresh food into detention had to request advanced permission to do so using a designated form. Visitors mainly used this process to facilitate the admission of speciality items on occasions such as a detainee's birthday or a cultural or religious festival. Before food restrictions were introduced, visitors like Moina had at times baked *Australian Women's Weekly*-style birthday cakes ("where you made the doll into a cake and all those things") to help detained children celebrate their birthdays. The special 'controlled item' approval process theoretically allowed such practices to continue but was widely criticized for its unreliability. Serco officers at times rejected items on the basis that they were not permitted, despite pre-approval having been granted.

> 'A cake is not one of the items that are generally allowed, but in the online forms you're allowed to request prohibited items. So [some fellow visitors] had requested a cake and that had been approved. But they got there and, again, [were told] "cakes not allowed in". "It's for a two-year-old kid's birthday party!" "I'm sorry, you can't take a cake in. Not allowed".' (Oliver, Melbourne)

Such rejections were a source of deep frustration and disappointment for detainees and visitors alike. As Oliver (Melbourne) asked, "[w]hy would you set up a system that was just needlessly cruel and bureaucratic like this? Why not allow a two-year-old to […] at least have a birthday cake and people singing Happy Birthday?"

Questions of intentionality – in this case, *why* visitor entrance rules have become so restrictive that they cause harm – are difficult to answer from a purely empirical perspective. If Departmental statements are to be believed, the bureaucratic obstacles that surround detention centre visitations are in place to *mitigate* harm; the ABF's (2016) statement concerning the introduction of food restrictions insisted that these rules were made to ensure the 'health' of detainees and the 'security' of the facilities more broadly. As this chapter has begun to explore and the coming chapters will elaborate, however, visitation restrictions also serve another function – contributing to the isolation and deprivation of detention spaces.

Participants in this study were largely skeptical that the rules they encountered were in place to protect their friends. Their first-hand observations of these restrictions suggested that harm was being compounded rather than ameliorated. The main threat to people's health and welfare in detention was not food poisoning or contraband. Rather, it was the corrosive impacts of the institution itself.

Conclusion

In her research with visitors to a Californian prison, Megan Comfort (2003, 2008) observed that visiting a prison involves coming under the institution's gaze. At the entrance to a prison, visitors 'convert from legally free people into imprisoned bodies for the duration of their stay in the facility' (Comfort, 2008: 27). Participants in this study underwent a similar transformation. Entering detention involved struggling through a web of bureaucracy, before being subjected to a series of physical screenings that made visitors feel their comparative powerlessness and vulnerability.

For most of the participants in this study, this whole process was frustrating and unsettling. Yet this experience of subjectification also provided visitors with an embodied understanding that the centres they visited were akin to prisons. White participants from privileged, non-refugee backgrounds were often startled to be treated as they were. Where 'little violences' (Scheper-Hughes and Bourgois, 2004: 19) were often a routine occurrence in the lives of detainees' family members, many Australian visitors were accustomed to being treated with more respect. The entrance experience thus gave them a greater appreciation of detainees' day-to-day lives. As Lola (Melbourne) put it, "I'm getting a version of what they're experiencing, and in a way not having it sugar coated for me is a good reminder that I'm going into a prison".

What we see in visitors' stories is that the prison-like nature of Australia's detention facilities has increased dramatically over the last decade. Facilities that were once comparatively permeable have grown in their totality, and multiple rules and restrictions have been introduced to block the admission of items that might mitigate the deprivation detainees experience. Tightening visitation rules have thus functioned to increase detainee discomfort while maintaining the official fiction that these facilities are humane.

Chapter Four continues this theme. Following visitors into the centres, it reveals immigration detention as a Kafkaesque system of unpredictable deprivations where visitors both witness and are subject to shifting scheme of rules and indignities.

4

Witnessing the Pains
of Imprisonment

Kylie's story

*It's 2015 and I am at the modest premises of a Brisbane NGO. In an adjacent building,
a free meal is being served to disadvantaged members of the local community. I'm here to
interview Kylie – a vibrant young youth worker with blond hair and a contagious laugh.*

*Kylie first became aware of the challenges faced by asylum seekers in Australia
during a practicum for her youth work degree. The placement was at a high school
(working, she jokes, with "the naughty kids"), and brought her into contact with a
young woman who was fending for herself after arriving in Australia.*

> 'She's come here, she's trying to do year ten, and [having lost both her parents]
> basically has no supports – this beautiful young woman. [...] I just thought,
> as a person who has a lot of resources and knows the Australian culture, why
> not show young people and equip them to navigate the Australian system?'

*Just a few years later, Kylie is now a professional youth worker, supporting a culturally
diverse client base and visiting BITA in her spare time. She has become particularly
close to one detained family and feels a special obligation to support their children.
Despite the wealth of skills and enthusiasm she brings to the task, the realities of
Australia's asylum seeker policies present considerable challenges.*

*In her visits to detention – as well as in her broader work with asylum
seekers in the community – Kylie has seen the impacts of prolonged instability in the
lives of young people seeking asylum. Living without permanent protection is corrosive
to mental health.*

> 'It's really hard to work with asylum seekers because normally what you do
> with other young people is build hope and build dreams and build goals, and
> that brings their mental health up. It's really hard to do that if you're doing
> hypothetical goals and hypothetical dreams and hypothetical situations, so all

you can really do is really practical assistance in the here and now — that's the only way.'

In this context, providing meaningful support is hard. But Kylie focuses on what she can do.

'I'm going [to BITA] to entertain them because they're in this box and they're going to be bored. That was how I saw it. Everything else didn't matter. I'm not there to fix their problems because you can't fix them because of the political environment. I'm just there to have fun with them because they probably don't have fun in that environment.'

Yet even these modest goals have proven difficult for Kylie to achieve.

What is perhaps most difficult about detention, Kylie tells me, are the profound power imbalances that define institutional life. Indefinite detention makes it hard for asylum seekers to set long-term goals, but unpredictable and erratically enforced rules compound this harm — rendering even short-term plans unreliable. In her early visits to BITA, Kylie organized an activity for each visit — usually a soccer game — to distract the detained children. They clearly enjoyed seeing her and would wait in anticipation for these weekly visits.

'They'll run to the door and they'll wait for you to open the door — so you're quickly trying to sign in so you can hug them and they're all jumping on you. "Look I made you a necklace!" You felt like they wanted you there, and the girl would always make me a card, and she'd draw pictures of me and my boyfriend, who she'd never met.'

While Kylie has been careful to never miss a visit — "they really, really want a separate time that you're coming every week, so that they can look forward to it" — the activities she has planned have often been thwarted.

'Depending on what [Serco guard] is on [...] they have different sets of rules. For example, we would always play outside and the kids loved soccer. We would bring a soccer ball in and some guards won't care because they like the kids and some guards are like, "don't play soccer, you're annoying everyone". So sometimes we could play soccer, sometimes we weren't [allowed]. Then, when they realized we were doing it weekly, they started hanging up pictures on the post — like, a picture of a person playing soccer with a cross against it. So then we could no longer play soccer or have balls.'

Within this system, harm is inflicted through the small details of institutional life.

★★★

Immigration detention and harm

A large body of evidence now exists regarding the negative impacts of immigration detention on people who are detained. Psychological and psychiatric studies have consistently shown that people in detention experience high levels of anxiety, depression and post-traumatic stress disorder (PTSD) (von Werthern et al, 2018; Robjant et al, 2009; Ichikawa et al, 2006; Newman and Steel, 2008). Self-harm and suicidal ideation are widely reported (Hedrick et al, 2019; Mares and Jureidini, 2004; Procter et al, 2013) and detention has been shown to exacerbate pre-existing conditions such as postnatal depression, bipolar disorder and obsessive-compulsive disorder (Rivas and Bull, 2018). Longer periods of detention have been associated with worse mental health outcomes (Robjant et al, 2009; Silverman and Massa, 2012; Bull et al, 2012) and while some studies document a reduction in symptoms post–detention (Keller et al, 2003), there is evidence that people who are detained for long periods experience depleted mental health for years after their release (Steel et al, 2006; Coffey et al, 2010).

The effects of detention on minors are particularly acute. Detained children suffer serious physical and psychological illness as well as developmental delays (AHRC, 2014; Mares, 2021). While recent Australian governments have significantly reduced the number of children in secure detention facilities, minors are at times still incarcerated.

Responding to claims of a causal connection between immigration detention and physical and psychological deterioration, government representatives have often alleged that reports of ill-health among people in detention are overstated. On these occasions, claims of detainee illness have been dismissed as efforts to manipulate the Australian people into granting them freedom (Morrison, 2019). On other occasions, officials have accepted that some detainees *are* unwell, but have insisted that these ailments are not causally related to their incarceration. The 'real' problem has instead been represented as 'the pathologised state of merely being an asylum seeker' (Maglen, 2007: 62).

Physical and psychological disabilities *are* more common in people from refugee backgrounds than in the general public, and researchers have traditionally centred migration and pre-migration factors in explaining this disparity (Li et al, 2016). The forced migration experience, after all, is one of prolonged and cumulative traumatization (van der Veen, 1995; Hedrick et al, 2019). The majority of asylum seekers are fleeing persecution; some have witnessed or been subjected to violence or torture; and many have left or lost loved ones in their search for safety. In addition, forced migration often involves long and dangerous journeys which impose their own stresses and can result in further physical and psychological injury. To attribute the ill health that many people in detention experience exclusively to these occurrences, however, is to grossly understate the impacts of asylum seekers' *reception* experiences on their overall well-being.

When countries act to deter and detain refugees and asylum seekers, they do irreparable harm. Policies such as immigration detention both compound pre-existing health issues and impose additional injuries. A 2006 study by Zachary Steel and colleagues was among the first to demonstrate a causal relationship between deterrence policies and psychological suffering in the Australian context. Adjusting for the effects of age, gender and pre-migration trauma, the study found that past detention was a reliable and *independent* predictor of PTSD, depression and mental-health-related disability.

This identification of immigration detention facilities as places of trauma is perhaps unsurprising to those versed in the violence of Australia's offshore processing facilities in PNG and Nauru (AHRC, 2017a; Phillips and Spinks, 2013; Al Hussein, 2014; UN Committee against Torture, 2014; UN Human Rights Council, 2016; Stayner, 2020; Evershed et al, 2016; Boochani, 2018a; Gleeson, 2016). Yet health outcomes in Australia's *onshore* detention system are also extremely poor. Bringing together visitors' testimonies and public statements from people in detention, this chapter explores the specific carceral practices through which onshore detention facilities produce such devasting health outcomes.

Inside the visiting room
Everyday visits

Once visitors made it through the complex security apparatus described in Chapter Three, they entered a visiting area. In the initial years of my research, visits usually took place within the centres themselves. Kylie's visits to BITA, for example, occurred in the centre's large common area, where she played with children from several asylum seeker families under close Serco supervision. Within these communal spaces, it was easy for visitors to meet detainees they had not nominated on their official visitor application forms, and for detainees who did not have existing community support to make connections within the Australian community. These shared spaces also provided opportunities for individual visitors and detainees to spend time one-on-one – for example, by going on small walks together in an outside common area.

Most visits at this time were structured around a shared meal. Visitors brought fresh produce to their visits, including specialty items requested by their friends. Visitors and detainees ate together, sharing food and conversation.

> 'People used to bring cakes they baked. [My friend] was always making biscuits and things. People would bring home made food. There'd be a smell of food everywhere. Toys for the children. I took

my grandchildren there to visit other little children and we used to take Lego and dolls and the whole lot. Everything you can think of. [...] You'd have kids running around with the toys.' (Deb, Melbourne)

Visitors across Australia emphasized the power of these meals in creating an atmosphere of trust. Sharing food, after all, is an intimate act. As Tan Chee-Beng (2015: 17) observes, the most basic form of commensality is the family meal – a social event characterized 'by the expectation of care and sharing'. To eat together is to both express and foster closeness (Fischler, 2011). Through the sharing of food, visitors and detainees engaged in an affective practice of relationship building. Feelings of closeness often grew, and meaningful friendships developed.

Over time, however, the structure of visits became more regimented. Pockets of normality became harder to create as the atmosphere of the visiting room became austere and institutional. Purpose-built visiting rooms were erected at many centres, and new rules were imposed surrounding the use of these spaces. By 2019, visitors and detainees were assigned specific tables within the visiting room and expected to remain in their allocated seats for the duration of their visits. Restrictions on the admission of food and belongings were also introduced (see Chapter Three), which altered the tone of visits.

'We used to be able to all sit at the same table – the whole visit room – and people would just come and bring all that they'd cooked – foods, cakes, everything – and eat together. Now, we have to sit at a table across from the person you're visiting. [...] You can visit one-on-one and you sit across like in a prison and you can't move now from that position.' (Hannah, Melbourne)

If a visitor or detainee left their seat to speak with someone at another table, they risked reprimand.

'It's demeaning. It's horrible. It's unnecessary. I mean, there's a few people scattered around this big visiting area often, and because their person hasn't arrived to see them or whatever they move over to see you. [...] And the guard will come up and say, "excuse me, you're not at your right table. Go back to your right table". It is just awful. It's treating them as though they're children. But also, if you know what's good for you, you'll obey absolutely to the last letter of the law.' (Claire, Melbourne)

Rules of this kind felt petty and pedantic.

Visitors noted that encroaching rules had a marked impact on centre relationships. In Brisbane, Alma visited BITA as the guardian of two young children whose father was in detention. The visiting room, Alma noted, afforded minimal privacy. Being required to sit at a designated table in a pre-decided configuration prevented natural interaction and made it harder for the children to sustain extended visits.

> 'Because you're stuck in a little place like this for an-hour-and-a-half, you're quite constrained. It would be much nicer as a family if you could say, "let's go into the garden and the girls can play football", or all that sort of thing. By the end of an-hour-and-a-half the little one starts to get a bit restless.'

While the impacts of these constraints were most evident to Alma in the relationships her young charges shared with their father, she saw that they would place pressure on any relationship.

> 'I just see that as another barrier [to] having a normal relationship with the person you're visiting. And even if it was me visiting another adult who had been in detention a while, the thought of, "let's go outside and sit under the tree and have a cup of tea" would be much nicer than sitting in this horrible little space where everyone can hear your conversation. There's not a lot of privacy. I've only seen one lady I thought was visiting her husband and that looked very, very awkward. So those sort of things would be much nicer if you had a bit of space, a bit of privacy, a bit of room for children to play.'

The deprivations of detention thus extending beyond detainees to impact and harm visitors, including young children.

These pains came on top of the more fundamental anguish friends and family members felt being separated from each other. In Brisbane, Laleh described a detained child's distress when her father – who had arrived in Australia before his family and was now living in the community – had to leave the centre at the end of a visit.

> 'He used to come and meet them every night, but they couldn't be released into the community detention with him. [...] That evening when it was time for us to leave the little girl couldn't stop crying "cause she just wanted to leave with her daddy". And she would huddle under his jacket and just didn't let go. The Serco guard had to take her by force and remove her. [...] All that little girl wanted was her daddy.'

Lola in Melbourne had a partner in detention and knew better than most how hard it was to be divided in this way. Her partner's incarceration in a crowded institution meant she was never able to spend time with him alone. Even their phone calls were not truly private.

'It's a terrible path to go to be involved with someone like this, because you see detention from the inside – the violence of it. [...] The lack of privacy. What it means to have someone sharing [a room] with you. We'll be on the phone for an hour and people are constantly in and out. [...] You hear people fighting. You hear guards bullying people. You feel quite immersed in it. That side of it I really hate.' (Lola, Melbourne)

Hardening visitation rules were salt in an already painful wound.

Communal celebrations

While individual and small group visits were the norm throughout the study period, long-term visitors noted it had once been possible to hold larger group festivities within the facilities. As recently as the mid-2010s, visitors had been involved in communal celebrations to mark Eid, Nowruz (Persian New Year), Christmas, Mother's Day and other holidays. Deb (Melbourne), for example, described a Nowruz event she had helped to organize at MITA. In hindsight, she observed, the scale of the celebration was remarkable.

'I remember one year we asked if we could have permission to have a Nowruz celebration and we were given it. The whole centre for the whole evening – like, night time! Imagine it now days? Night time! We had a Nowruz table with the seven things, the whole bit, we had music, everything. And all the detainees were there. The music blasting, dancing, singing. A pile of visitors. It was astonishing, really, but it was permitted. [...] It was absolutely nothing like things are now.' (Deb, Melbourne)

Hannah (Melbourne) had been part of the same events.

'We would organize Christmas, Eid parties, circus performances, bands. There was a kind of community liaison person. I used to manage an annual Christmas shoebox appeal [...] I'd get kids in our community to decorate shoeboxes and then adults would buy gifts and we would fill them all and then go in there with the Sisters of Brigidine who would do the food for lunch, and then we would give out all the Christmas parcels and stuff like that. And we would have to work pretty hard with management around that kind of stuff and provided the entertainment. [...] After several years they started to cut back all of that back.' (Hannah, Melbourne)

Like Deb, Hannah stressed that the situation at MITA was now markedly different. Community liaison officers were no longer employed. Communal gatherings were rarely allowed. Even bringing everyday foods and gifts into the centres had become challenging.

Yet effective prohibitions against communal celebrations had not been introduced overnight. The system had hardened slowly and somewhat erratically through the early and mid-2010s. In Darwin, Heather recalled one Christmas during this time when she had worked with detention centre staff and local supporters to organize gifts for children in detention. Local children in the Darwin area had planned to visit the centre on Christmas Day to deliver the gifts in person.

'We arranged that we were going to bring all these people Christmas presents for the kids, and someone made Christmas crackers and stuff. And it had all been arranged with the person who was the head of the centre who wasn't [working] on Christmas Day. And these kids said they'd do this on Christmas Day – they came on their Christmas Day – and we got there and they said, "oh, no you can't. You've got to open all of those presents before you give them to the kids". And "you can't give them crayons because they might draw on the walls". It was so bad!'

As Heather reflected, this was a painful day both for the people in detention and for the Australian children who had worked so hard to prepare their presents. It was also a politicizing experience for the local Darwin community, as participating children and their families began to ask, " 'what is this place?!'" (Heather, Darwin).

Death by a thousand cuts

Inadequate recreation

Everyday life in detention is a grind of boredom, distress and discomfort. As detainee Moz Azimitabar put it in 2021, "[s]ometimes we don't realize how important these simple things are like walking into the street, hugging a friend, visiting family. I haven't had these things in eight years" (in Gillespie 2021: np).

After months or years visiting detention, many of the participants in this study had developed a good understanding of their friends' daily lives. There had been a time when detainees had been permitted to leave their places of detention for small excursions, but as the system hardened these outings became rare.

> 'They were doing day trips, so they were taking him to swim at one of the local pools. He did three or four visits and they told him that it would be a regular thing. That was his one opportunity to be out in the community and he was talking to the local people and he had that chance to think that he was part of something. That he wasn't just a detainee. So there were about four trips and then they suddenly stopped it. Knowing how much joy it brought him, and they just suddenly stopped it.' (Lewis, Sydney)

Each day was now much like the others. Detainees lived their lives almost exclusively within the facility walls. On the rare occasions that they left their places of detention to attend medical appointments, they were accompanied by guards and required to wear handcuffs (AHRC, 2020).[1]

It was common for interviewees to describe exchanges where detainees asked them for updates concerning their lives but had no news of their own to share. Samantha (Perth) had one friend who asked her during every visit, "'oh, have you eaten? How is your mum? How are your family?'" Answering was difficult. "You can respond to that," she explained, "but if you say, 'what have you done today?' it's the same thing every day". Nathaniel (Melbourne) described a similar dynamic.

> 'There's this constant sense of crushing boredom. You do that thing when you go in and say, "how are you?" and they say, "still the same". And some of them roll their eyes, you know. "Absolutely nothing has changed since last week!" Boring and boring and nothing's changed.'

The contrast between visitors' lives and those of the people they visited was stark.

> '[Y]ou go back the following week perhaps, and you realize that in that week you've gone out for dinner, you've gone to the movies, you've gone visited friends, you've gone shopping – moving about. These people that you visited last week, they have not moved. They've gone to their room to the community area to maybe the sporting oval to the community area back to their room to the internet area, but they haven't moved outside a space of 100 square metres or whatever it is.' (Max, Brisbane)

To be detained was to live a life in which each day was largely indistinguishable from the next.

Limited access to recreational facilities at the centres was an important part of this picture. All centres had designated recreational spaces, but their size, quality and accessibility varied considerably (AHRC, 2020). Early in my research, when dozens of minors were in institutional detention, Jess (Brisbane) told me how excruciating BITA was during school holidays. There were limited facilities for children there, and those facilities that were provided could be removed at any moment.

> 'There was one of the boys and I could really tell he was struggling. [...] He was 11. He was going through that, like, "becoming a man" thing and all there was was painting and colouring and a slippery dip. There's nothing else beyond that! And then they stopped letting them use soccer balls.'

At one point, Jess told me, people at BITA had been able to play pool, but this did not last.

> 'We had a pool table, we used to play pool every time, and I think that was really good for him 'cause he got to do it with the older men. He was, like, going through puberty or whatever. And then they took the balls away. [...] Apparently – this is what the kids said – people were taking them and to try and kill themselves. [...] And then they just took all the balls away. But the table's still sitting there so it's still really frustrating for them.' (Jess, Brisbane)

As Jess reflected, this abandoned pool table served as a vivid reminder of the children's hopelessness. It was "like the epitome of their lives – just disappointing", she said.

For detainees held in APODs, such as commercial hotels, even fewer recreational facilities were available. Where the main detention centres provided some equipment and outdoor space, APOD hotels typically did not. Alma (Brisbane) recollected one detainee's appraisal of the Kangeroo Point Hotel where he was being held in Brisbane.

> 'I said, "is this better than being out at the other detention centre?" He said, "no, it's not". I said, "why not?" He said, "well, there's no gym, there's no football, there's not a library. There's nothing". They're bored out of their skulls. So he was sitting there thinking, "what is my future? Why am I being held in here for six years or however long?" I think it would just antagonize.'

The "nice sheets" (Teegan, Brisbane) and striking views that some of these APODs offered disguised their more fundamental deprivations.

'They're imprisoned in a hotel room. You know, the hotel room has no air. They can't go outside. They cannot move. [...] Yeah, they're still feeling safer than being on Manus or Nauru, but they plummet back down to that [feeling of] "I'm caged. I'm back in a cage 24/7, heavily guarded". And so that's hard.' (Hannah, Melbourne)

In the ways that counted for detainee's well-being, these makeshift detention facilities were far from luxurious. These were – to again quote detainee Moz Azimitabar – "luxury torture cells" (in Doherty, 2020). Within them, detained refugee Farhad Bandesh explained, detainees had to "fight for basic human rights like fresh air and sunshine" (in MC, 2021: np).

In addition to offering basic recreational facilities, the main detention facilities ran a small number of organized activities. Most centres held weekly activities such as art, English, yoga and music lessons. People in detention were incentivized to participate in these activities through a rewards system, where those who participated were given 'points' to spend at the detention centre shop.

The idea that rewards can be used as an instrument of power is well established in the prison literature. Sykes (2007 [1958]) himself observed that prison guards often have limited capacity to control inmates using physical force. Prisoners dramatically outnumber correctional staff, meaning 'the ability of officials to physically coerce their captives into the paths of compliance is something of an illusion' (2007 [1958]: 49). In this context, Sykes (2007 [1958]: 49) argued that prisons use rewards system to ensure inmates' cooperation.

'It may be that when men are chronically deprived of liberty, material goods and services, recreational opportunities and so on, the few pleasures that are granted take on a new importance and the threat of their withdrawal is a more powerful motive for conformity than those of us in the free community can realise.'

This carrot and stick approach continues to be employed in many carceral institutions. Rewards for desirable behaviour may be formalized, but they can also take informal form, as when guards enforce rules more leniently to incentivize cooperation (Ibsen, 2013).

Visitors had mixed feeling about the points systems utilized in detention, and about their friends' participation in the activities offered. During the initial years of my research – before visits were moved to purpose-built visiting rooms – visitors regularly witnessed and joined in with these activities. Their reflections on what they saw were sometimes scathing. In Brisbane, Robyn recalled her confusion when – on her first visit to BITA – she had found the Muslim adult detainees colouring in pictures of Easter bunnies.

'It was near Easter and they were colouring in things I would say were pre-school sort of Easter bunnies and Easter eggs, and all these Muslim adults doing this. And I couldn't understand. "Why are they doing it? Why are they cooperating?" I just said to [one woman], "do you like colouring in?" you know. And she said, "no". And I said, "oh, why are you doing it then?" And then she explained that it was for the points that they get. [...] So they do an activity for half-an-hour they get two points. So with three or six points they can buy some shampoo or nicer soap or whatever, chocolate. So that's why they do it, to get the points. I just thought, "this is really demeaning. This is really demeaning".'

Moina (Melbourne) had a similar view of the activities offered.

'They get a lolly if they win bingo. This is an adult. They know that's hopeless and they hate it. So I've got to turn it into a joke. "Did you share?" You know what I mean? You've got to make it funny because it's actually an awful experience but it's something to do, and they know it's degrading to get a lolly for winning bingo when you're an Afghani man and you're the head of the family and you've had all your family die and here you are fighting for a lolly.'

In Darwin, retired psychologist Josephine observed that even activities like yoga, which had some clinical merit, could seem demeaning to people who were experiencing ongoing suffering.

'They didn't want [yoga classes]. Because the official psychologist did that and they found that insulting because of what they had experienced to be told just to relax. And I can well understand it. [...] Many of them had been tortured and had terrible experiences of the journey; what they suffered in Indonesia; what they suffered on the boats; and then they were on Christmas Island. So by the time they got to Darwin they'd often already had years of intense suffering. So to think they could lie down and close their eyes and slow their breathing and do meditation. I can understand why it was insulting.'

For visitors like Josephine, pressuring detainees to participate in these sessions without addressing the underlying causes of their pain was offensive.

In the course of my research, I spoke to several people who had been personally involved in running recreational activities in detention. In most cases, they, like other visitors, had begun this work in an attempt to help people in detention. Yet over time some had come to share other visitors' reservations regarding aspects of the programmes. Ambrose (Melbourne) had been pivotal in starting a music programme at MITA. With other volunteer musicians, he took musical instruments to the centre each week to play with the detainees. Ambrose believed in the value of the sessions: he conceived them as "a little island" where people in detention could find joy and reprieve within a harsh institutional setting. His hope was that "it was some space away from whatever else was happening in the centres for them". The reality that these sessions existed within the coercive structures of the institution was thus a source of discomfort.

> 'The points system that they have there, where you do an activity and you get a point and then you can use that in the commissary. On the one hand, it's like, "yeah, okay. That's a system and perhaps I'm not the person running the organization. So perhaps it's got merit". [But] just give them some chocolate! […] I always felt quite conflicted about that whole system.'

Furthermore, Ambrose was deeply uncomfortable with the way detainees' participation in the sessions was policed by guards.

> 'The staff started making decisions about who was "participating" in the music sessions, and there was this one person who would sit up the back, cross their legs and close their eyes, and just listen to the session. That *is* participating in a music session because you listen to the music. Just because you're not banging a drum or singing along doesn't mean that you're not participating. That's very active listening! […] And that's where this points system gets a little bit frustrating for me because they get to dole out the points as they see fit.'

While Ambrose understood that the guards were doing their job, this encroachment of institutional power into the sessions risked compromising their therapeutic value. It also complicated Ambrose's own position as he sought to mitigate the centre's deleterious impacts, but ultimately had to operate within and conform to the system's demands.

Reduced agency

In July 2021, Jalah Mahamede – a refugee and artist who had been incarcerated by Australia for over eight years – tweeted his frustration from BITA.

We live by the laws of a God. [...] But our God is security guards, immigration agents and security cameras. We have to live by their rules. They tell us what to eat and when to eat. They tell us how to behave. They tell us what is good and what is bad. They reward us if they think we are being good. We are not criminals. We need our freedom (Mahamede, 2021a: np)

This perception of the institution as cruelly omnipotent was a recurring theme in the study. Micro-level rules asserted a debilitating asymmetry of power within detention, making detainees acutely aware of their structural vulnerability. Mother and school teacher Esme (Brisbane) had witnessing the disempowerment detainees experienced in detention in her visits with young families.

'I found it very confronting and difficult that those mums couldn't look after their children properly. That they had children going to school in the mornings [but] they couldn't see their school, nor could they see their teachers. They couldn't go to [P]arents and [C]itizens night, athletics carnival or any of the normal school events where parents engage in the school community. There was an enormous disconnect between home and school, which we know to be really limiting for children's education. To watch mums not be able to parent their children – and dads – but as a mum myself, to see that. I just found it incredibly distressing [crying].'

As Esme's examples illuminated, the deprivation of autonomy in detention went well beyond the forced nature of her friends' imprisonment.

'The logistics of someone being detained and your idea of it is probably a bit different. Practical things that you take for granted when you've got freedom are not there for those parents. Their everyday life is dictated. Choosing what their children can take to school for lunch. They sound like really insignificant things perhaps but they're the things that you can control as a parent and those mums and dads can't do that. They cannot give their children money to buy food from the tuckshop or take on excursions. They don't even have a choice when it comes to choosing clothes for their children. Relying on someone else to get them clothes or food is incredibly disempowering for a parent. All of those things that contribute to your sense of identity. All that being removed from you.'

The institution assumed control over parents' smallest decisions, diminishing their influence over their own lives and those of their children. These controls infantilized detainees, stripping them of their adult responsibilities and reducing them to the 'dependent status of childhood' (Sykes, 2007 [1958]: 75).

Security practices within the centres further corroded detainees' autonomy. Detainees' rooms, for example, were liable to be searched at any moment. Such interruptions prevented detainees from relaxing and at times interrupted their sleep. The denial of control over their immediate environments – for example, not being able to set the temperature of the air conditioning in their bedrooms, not having easy access to additional blankets, and sharing all spaces with other people – added to their stress. These intrusions kept detainees "on tenterhooks" (Terry, Brisbane) and were particularly stressful for individuals who were managing symptoms of trauma.

Chapter Three observed that detention centre admission rules have escalated considerably in recent years and have not always been applied consistently. Interviewees described a similar trajectory inside the centres, noting that internal rules were regularly changed and tightened, and that different guards applied rules in different ways. In Darwin, Allie spoke about a detained couple who had been allowed to plant a small herb garden, only for this permission to be revoked. "They had these herbs growing", she told me, "and then one day, one of the guards came and ripped them all out". In Brisbane, Robyn similarly noted that the colouring in activities she had found so demeaning on her first visit to BITA had been abruptly stopped one day. Friends who had been actively encouraged to colour in through the centre's points system were now informed that the activity would cease. As the woman Jodie (Brisbane) visited in detention told her, " '[e]very week they've got new rules'".

In the absence of explanation, rule changes of this kind came to feel arbitrary and punitive. Some detainees told their visitors that they believed the institution was playing with them. It was even difficult to ascertain which decisions had been made by site personnel and which originated with higher levels of management, making recourse difficult (Neil and Peterie, 2018). Complaint processes seemed largely futile, and a wall of bureaucratic evasion and silence met all who sought answers. "You can ask any questions or as many questions as you like and there is never an answer", Elena in Sydney told me.

The pain associated with the deprivation of autonomy is well documented even beyond prison studies. Psychological research supports the view that agency is vital for human flourishing; indeed, there is evidence that perceived autonomy – feeling 'a sense of choice about one's behaviour' (Ntoumanis et al, 2020: 2) – is a vital pre-condition for psychological health (Deci and Ryan, 2014). The pain associated with reduced agency in detention runs even deeper. As Louise Newman and colleagues (2008: 121, emphasis added) argue, in some cases the detention environment 'reinforces a sense of loss of control over daily life [...] *re-enacting the environment of persecution* from which the individual has fled' (see also Canning, 2019). The embodied experience of disempowerment in detention thus both adds to and compounds pre-migration and migration traumas.

Lack of certainty

The disempowerment that people in detention experience at the micro-level of institutional life also reflects and reinforces a more fundamental powerlessness. That is, small assaults and indignities underline the reality that potentially life-and-death decisions concerning detainees' futures are beyond their control (Neil and Peterie, 2018). One of the main deprivations experienced by people in detention is the deprivation of certainty (Crewe, 2011; Kox et al, 2020; Warr, 2016; Ugelvik and Damsa, 2018). Detainees do not know how long they will be detained. Indeed, they have no guarantee that they will be released at all. Those fleeing violence or persecution live in the knowledge that they might ultimately be deported to danger.

As of August 2021, the average duration of detention for people in Australia's onshore immigration detention system is 696 days (Department of Home Affairs, 2021a). Some people have been in detention for over ten years (Commonwealth Ombudsman, 2020a). Extended periods of detention with no clear timeline or guarantee of release are the norm in Australia's detention system. As detainee Jalal Mahamede (2021b: np) wrote as he began his ninth year of incarceration, "[w]e asked for help but all we got is torture. [...] Every year we tell ourselves, 'this year we will be free'. But nothing has happened".

Visitors saw the impacts of this prolonged uncertainty in the lives of their friends. Many shared stories of people who had been in detention for years – often during the formative period of early adulthood.

> 'I get teary to even think about it, just thinking about this poor person. [...] It just makes me sad. It's mostly young people in their 20s. They've been living there eight years or coming on nine years for some of them. It's just such a waste of their young life.' (Maive, Brisbane)

In Sydney, Lewis reflected on his own experiences as a young man to underline what this loss of time meant for the young man he visited.

> 'I couldn't even imagine what it would be like to go six years without ever being outside. Ever being able to start your life. 'Cause he's the same age as I am. So to know that he's 26 and knowing how much I've grown from being 20 to 26. He hasn't had that chance to experience

all the things that I've experienced in six years. Things that people take for granted, often. The little things like getting your licence, travelling around. All those kinds of little things. Even just making friends, being in relationships, all those types of things. He's missed out on a lot.'

Other visitors described their friends' grief at being unable to start families, pursue tertiary education, secure paid work or progress careers. Even being unable to 'contribute' to society through volunteer work could be a source of distress for people in detention, including one man – a trained firefighter – who watched news stories of bushfires ravaging Australia and told Rachel (Darwin) about his growing sense of powerlessness and purposelessness. "[H]e said, 'I'm a firefighter. Just let me out for two weeks. I'll go and help fight the fires and then I'll come back'".

Detainees who had left families overseas to seek safety in Australia were particularly impacted by this sense of passing time. For these individuals, the lack of certainty concerning their futures had collateral impacts for which they felt responsible. Prolonged detention meant prolonged inability to provide for loved ones and dependents. As Jocelyn (Melbourne) explained,

'Everyone comes here for their families, they're not just coming here for themselves. The whole time they're detained they're frightened for what's happening to their families back home because they've come here to try and give their family the opportunity for a safe future and time is just ticking away. Ticking away.'

In some cases, detainees had chosen not to tell overseas family members that they were in detention as they did not want to burden them with additional worry. These individuals bore a weight of guilt as they languished in detention, unable to send money or resources to support their families' survival. Moina (Melbourne) described arriving at a visit to find a detained man "terribly upset". "They actually just got a message [from] the mother saying she's hungry. Hungry! And he has to sit there doing nothing!" she recalled.

Maintaining hope when life is on hold and the future is uncertain is far from easy. Visitors explained that the people they visited often seemed upbeat and positive in the initial weeks or months of their incarceration. They were eager to talk about Australia and looked forward to beginning new lives in safety. But as time passed, their demeanours changed.

'Even in the space of six months or a year – in that time they become a totally different person. You see communications drop off. They're less engaged. Initially you might be able to joke around with them and have more prolonged conversations and then it becomes two-word responses, kind of thing, and you can see the decline. Which is quite difficult to watch.' (Samantha, Perth)

Some people in detention withdrew from company and became lethargic. Hopes and dreams that had once been energizing now seemed distant and futile. In Sydney, Luke watched a friend who had studied law in Afghanistan deteriorate to the point that he could no longer read a book.

> 'I'd asked him if we can try to get access to some books so you can brush up on Australian law and perhaps [...] get [your qualifications] recognized here. And he was saying, "I just start to read a book and it just feels like, what's the point".'

Where it might have been possible to endure the pains of imprisonment for a finite period, the indefinite nature of this suffering made prolonged resistance difficult.

Harm and hope(lessness)

Detainee pain

Speaking from his Melbourne APOD in 2020, Moz Azimitabar told *The Guardian* that his body was becoming weak. "Every day weaker", he said. "They are killing my time, killing my potential. Slowly they are killing me" (in Doherty, 2020: np). The following year, adopting the language of the Black Lives Matter movement, fellow refugee and detainee Mohammed spoke through tears. "I can't breathe in this situation", he cried. "We can't breathe" (in Foster, 2021).

The participants in this study saw these devastating impacts of detention first-hand. At times, engaging in banter and laughter was the most important part of a visit, and people in detention would take a leading role in creating an atmosphere of fun.

> 'There is the humour. [...] They have their own personalities and we'll play cards with them or something and we really enjoy that – that sort of light-hearted nonsense. [...] They spring off each other and they're fun. They're just fun.' (Louise, Melbourne)

On other occasions, visits were more sombre. In Sydney, Luke told me about a detained friend who felt so defeated by the system that he was unable to maintain conversation. "[A] lot of the time it was just sitting with him and being in his company", Luke explained.

'We had this guy tell us at one stage, "I don't want to hear anything from anyone unless it's get your stuff, we're leaving now. That's the only thing I want to hear anyone talk about". But even then, he still stayed around with us for the next few hours and he's there waiting when we turn up to visit. He's eager to see us. And he'll follow us to the gate to say goodbye.' (Luke, Sydney)

Jude (Sydney) concurred. "I suppose the main thing about it is just sitting beside [them]. Saying, 'we're with you. For whatever it means, we see your pain'".

The mental health impacts of detention were such that detainees were sometimes too unwell to receive visitors at all. In Darwin, Emily recalled receiving a small note from an adolescent detainee who was too depressed to attend a visit.

'I was visiting a father and his daughter – his 16-year-old daughter who I never met but [who] other advocates were really concerned about. […] I still have this piece of paper that she wrote me a note on saying that she basically would really love to talk to me but she wasn't well enough today. And something about that piece of paper. […] It's sort of really poignant. I guess because it's so, so painful that this young girl is sitting in a room with a pencil. You know, a young girl who's, like, sixteen – what an incredible time of life – is just sitting in this room.'

Other visitors described friends cancelling or skipping visits because they were unable to "even muster enough energy to get out of bed in the morning" (Roberta, Perth). Over time, visitors gained a clearer understanding of this psychological pain and saw how institutional practices contributed to their friends' suffering.

The participants in this study were acutely aware of the prevalence of self-harm within the centres. One interviewee had been present at a facility during a detainee's suicide attempt. The alarm had been sounded, she remembered, when the man had climbed onto the centre roof. At first, she had assumed he was on the roof to retrieve a ball – in her world, she told me, that's what it meant when someone was on the roof. But as the detained children began running to their parents and burying their faces in their clothes, she understood that something very different was taking place.

Other visitors spoke of close friends who had made suicide attempts. In Sydney, Lewis told me that a man he visited had tried to take his own life after being separated from his partner and newborn child. Initially, other detainees at Villawood IDC had given Lewis the news, but he had later seen the man in person and seen the wounds on his body. That period, Lewis told me, had been harrowing for everyone. "[H]e's this happy, sweet person and to know that his circumstances had driven him to a point where he just didn't want to be around anymore. That was definitely one of the lowest, saddest points about visiting the guys". It affected everyone within the centres – as well as the detainees' community-based friends and loved ones – when a detainee attempted suicide.

Kyli Hedrick (2017) has undertaken statistical analysis of self-harm incident reports from Australian immigration detention facilities to identify the factors that precipitate these events. The majority of self-harm incidents (39.1 per cent) are triggered by 'detention conditions', including specific stressors like 'being transferred within existing detention facilities or to another detention facility, noise levels, rooming arrangements and delays in accessing medical treatment and/or medication' (Hedrick, 2017: 92). Other common triggers include processing arrangements, negative decisions on refugee claims, and family separations. As Moina (Melbourne) noted, however, individual triggering events exist in a broader context of deprivation and frustration, where detainees are permitted few sources of hope.

> 'If you look at all the things that people say give you good strong mental health, you'd almost say that everything [is taken away]. Thinking of the future, having work that has some value to it, having loved ones, contributing in a community. All of those things are what keep us sane. And the fact is they have none of them. And a level of control over your life. […] All that's taken away.'

Put differently, people in detention are subject to serious psychological stressors even as key protective factors – which usually afford meaning and guard against self-harm and suicide – are stripped away.

Prolonged social isolation has physiological impacts as well. It would be difficult to overstate the importance of social connections for human thriving. A 2021 review of research on the relationship between social connection and health found that social isolation is associated with a staggeringly high number of health problems. Indeed, the review concluded that social isolation is implicated in 'chronic physical symptoms, frailty, coronary heart disease, malnutrition, hospital readmission, reduced vaccine uptake, early mortality, depression, social anxiety, psychosis, cognitive impairment in later life and suicidal ideation' (Morina et al, 2021: 1; see also Masi et al, 2011). When immigration detention facilities repelled visitors and systematically corroded detainees' access to support, they thus did profound harm.

Institutional responses

In his foundational work on the pains of imprisonment, Sykes (2007 [1958]) suggested that prisoners have their basic physical needs met while they are in prison. It is, he said, the Spartan existence that is imposed on prisoners rather than any straightforward denial of life necessities that causes prisoners pain. This idea of prisoners being denied access to the goods and services that make life bearable clearly resonates with visitor stories of Australia's detention system. Yet to suggest that asylum seekers in this system retain access to everything they need to survive would perhaps be misleading.

Contemporary scholars make a similar point with respect to civilian prisons. In recent decades, prison scholars have highlighted the inadequate health care that some prisoners receive while incarcerated. Deaths in custody are a significant issue and have often been linked to systemic failures, including failure to provide (or heed inmates' requests to access) appropriate medical attention (Stoller, 2003). Research has also shown that physical 'intimidation and unprovoked aggression [are] used to punish prisoners and ensure compliance' (Crewe, 2011: 511). Put differently, contemporary prison studies suggest that Sykes may have been overly optimistic when he said that inmates' basic needs are met in prisons.

Participants in this study were often alarmed by the inadequacy of detainees' access to healthcare to address their physical and psychological injuries. Several visitors had been shocked when suicidal friends were placed in solitary confinement or under constant surveillance to ensure they did not take their own lives. Serco's *Supportive Monitoring and Engagement* protocols meant detainees who were deemed to be at high risk of self-harm or suicide were commonly subject to 'significant restrictions on freedom of movement and privacy, as a person may be subject to 24-hour-a-day direct personal supervision by a Serco officer, including when they are in their rooms or going to the bathroom' (AHRC, 2020: 55).

In Brisbane, Robyn described her phone conversations with a suicidal woman at a local APOD who was being monitored under this protocol. During the calls, Robyn heard Serco officers interacting with her friend.

'I'm on the phone. There's four [guards] – three women and one man – in the hotel room with her and they were making her leave the door open while she peed. And she's screeching that she wants to pee in private. And it was just shocking. [...] The next morning she rang me from the airport. They transferred her to [Melbourne's] MITA. I was her support Brisbane.'

"Their response to someone suicidal", Robyn emphasized, "doesn't seem to be to give them immediate mental health treatment, but to give them four guards to make sure they don't do it". As a response to acute distress, actions of this kind seemed counterproductive at best. "It seems to me that it's all about punishment", Robyn reflected.

Inspection reports from the AHRC, which draw on first-hand interviews with detained asylum seekers, paint a mixed picture of these practices. During their 2019 inspections, several detainees told the Commission that they appreciated not been left alone when distressed. Others, however, reported that constant monitoring increased their suffering. One detainee told the Commission that the way this system responded to suicidal ideation discouraged detainees from asking for help.

> I wanted to hurt myself and the security guards started to guard me so I'm scared to talk to the doctors and nurses. When I say something to the nurse, they tell Serco and then they start guarding us, that places bad character on us. (AHRC, 2020: 55)

The Commission concluded that 'the role of non-clinical staff in constant one-on-one monitoring and engagement may not be suitable to establish a safe environment for all people at risk of self-harm or suicide in immigration detention' (AHRC, 2020: 55) and called for an independent review into the practice.

Responses to physical illnesses and injuries were equally troubling and underlined the broader inadequacy of the health care provided. In Brisbane, Terry described a conversation with a detained friend whose son had been taken ill.

> 'The boy had […] convulsions in the middle of the night so he went to that guards and they said, "sorry, the medical office doesn't open till 8 o'clock in the morning". This is true. He said, "well, let's get an ambulance". "Sorry, we can't do that". He tells me this the next night. He's a very strong man. I've only seen him cry twice. He was sobbing on my shoulder. He said, "I thought my son was going to die!" He said, "why do they treat us like animals?"'

In Sydney, William had lost a friend because – as he understood it – his friends' calls for medical attention had not been heeded.

> 'Several people have died in detention with medical conditions, I'm sure. The first one I was really aware of was our lovely friend. He was the most beautiful man. He gave me his papers as I was leaving visiting him at 5 o'clock. I was going to work on them. And at 11 o'clock that night I got a phone call that [he] had died of a heart attack. And it was partly because the response to his cries for help with chest pains were greeted with mirth. "Come on, pull the other leg, you're just trying to get attention". He died in the ambulance on the way to hospital.'

Available evidence confirms that access to medical care in detention is far from dependable. This has been most striking offshore, where several deaths have been directly linked to incorrect, inadequate or delayed medical treatment (see Chapter One). Yet even within the onshore system, detainees regularly wait months, if not years, for medical attention (Public Interest Advocacy Centre, 2021). In numerous cases treatment has only been granted after legal intervention (Holt, 2019). Even then, therapeutic interventions are of limited value while incarceration continues. To quote long-term detainee Mehdi Ali, "[o]nly freedom can save me" (2021c: np).

Conclusion

It is broadly accepted that a causal relationship exists between immigration detention and psychological pain. Precisely what it is about being detained that produces this outcome, however, has received comparatively little scholarly attention. As Coffey and colleagues (2010: 2070–1) note,

> Existing studies have examined the consequences of immigration detention of varying duration largely in terms of diagnosable disorder and mental health symptoms. Less research has been done to expose the psychological experience of detention and how the nature of that experience relates to future psychological well-being.

This chapter has shown that – like inmates in civilian prisons – detained asylum seekers are subject to a range of deprivations and frustrations that diminish health.

Individually, many of the controls described in this chapter could be dismissed as institutional oversights or bureaucratic blunders. Alternatively, they could be interpreted as warranted measures to ensure the safety and security of detention spaces. What this chapter has revealed, however, is that these interlocking technologies of deprivation and frustration do not make detention safer, but gradually destroy detainees' spirits. Additionally, this chapter has shown that – like their prison counterparts – detention centre visitors are not only witnesses to the pains of imprisonment, but are at times subject to them.

Against this backdrop of institutionally manufactured pain, the next chapter turns to consider the relationships that develop within these spaces, and their social and political role in combatting deterrence.

5

Care and Resistance

Paul's story

It's a Saturday morning in 2016 and I'm meeting Paul at the University of Sydney Library. Paul is twenty-something and casually dressed, but his easy confidence and measured speech give him an air of professionalism.

Paul has been visiting Sydney's Villawood IDC for two-and-a-half years. In that same period, he has established a small charity that runs community education campaigns and delivers tutoring and resources to asylum seeker children. Paul's corporate connections (he works in HR) have been an asset in this work, allowing him to access more reliable funding by becoming a preferred charity for his large corporation.

Just a few short years ago, Paul knew little about the experiences of refugees and asylum seekers in Australia. The turning point came when he sat next to an Iranian man at a wedding. The man – a refugee – showed Paul his torture scars and shared his story.

> *'He was telling me his story and I thought it was pretty emotional. I didn't really think of the issue before. [...] If you don't know about it you may not necessarily have strong opinions about it, but you can probably be swayed when you hear a personal account.'*

This experience was so powerful that Paul embarked on a research journey and ultimately decided he needed to act. Several months later, he made his first visit to Villawood IDC.

On that first day visiting detention, Paul tells me, he was "a nervous wreck". The entrance procedures were strict and intimidating, and he was unsure what awaited him within the centre. When he met Kamal, however, Paul's anxiety vanished. Kamal was young, friendly and upbeat. Paul liked him immediately.

In the years since that meeting, Paul has visited Kamal every week or fortnight, and most of his close friends and family members have been to Villawood IDC too. Paul has also formed connections with Kamal's friends in detention and often visits them as a group. While the detention environment is not the most conventional backdrop for a friendship, Paul emphasizes that these are genuine relationships. He is not visiting detention as an act of charity, but because he sincerely likes the people detained there. Most of the detainees are just regular young men, craving 'normal' friendships with people their age.

To spend your twenties in detention, Paul tells me, is to lose important, formative years. Kamal can't leave detention to enjoy the freedom and frivolity of youth, but Paul can bring a taste of that to him within the centre walls.

> 'They're in my life basically. I tell them everything – girlfriends, friends, what's happening outside. It's as if they're outside like one of my mates. They get the exact same thing of what my mates would outside, except for a smaller period of time, I guess. I just go in and see them for that time. It's as if I'm going to go and have a coffee with a friend who just happens to be in a detention centre. [...] I'm not tiptoeing around them. I'll try to beat them at cards. There'll be banter. It's a proper friendship.'

Paul's friendship with Kamal is now so strong that he views Kamal as a 'brother'. In fact, Paul uses this language in two ways. Paul's tight group of friends is like a 'brotherhood', he tells me, and Kamal is an integral member. But as someone with no relatives in Australia, Kamal has also found a family with Paul's own biological relatives.

> 'All his stuff's in my parents' attic. My Mum calls him every week. [...] I have a very close relationship with him and I've had quite emotional moments with him where he's told me after bad days that the only reason he's still going is because of us and our friendship and the fact that all the guys I bring in to see him, we'll just treat him like another guy. Because he's 26 or 27 – he's just another young guy.'

When they speak on the phone, Kamal never fails to ask after Paul's family. And at the end of each call, "he'll say that he loves us". "He's just a young guy who wanted a family", Paul stresses. "We've treated him like that".

★★★

Theorizing resistance

At its most recognisable, political resistance involves open acts of defiance and dissent. In the context of immigration detention, this might involve supporters participating in public demonstrations, or detained asylum seekers openly protesting or defying centre authorities. Yet resistance can also take subtler forms (Scott 1986, 1989, 1990; Hynes, 2013; Baaz et al, 2017; Vinthagen and Johansson, 2013). Lucy Fiske (2016) has written at length about the multiple resistances enacted by immigration detainees in

Australia. Friske (2016: 80) highlights diverse practices including 'refusal and riot, hunger strike and lip sewing, letter writing and cultivating contacts with journalists'. Not all of these activities, she notes, are readily recognisable as resistance, but all function 'to subvert, disrupt or manipulate the state's power' (Fiske, 2016: 53).

This acknowledgement that diverse practices *count* as resistance is important for this book, particularly given the propensity of social scientists to view care-based responses to injustice with some suspicion. Interventions that respond directly to the needs of individuals have often been charged with ignoring and obscuring the structural causes of suffering (see, for example, Gosden, 2007; Rackley, 2002; Hutchinson, 2014; Korf, 2007). Equally, scholars have cautioned that altruistic interventions frequently involve paternalistic modes of relating that can disempower care recipients, compounding and perpetuating their marginalization (Berlant, 2004; Erickson, 2012; Darling, 2011; Lange et al, 2007).

It is easy to see how people from non-refugee backgrounds visiting detention could be vulnerable to charges of this kind. Indeed, numerous study participants actively raised and grappled with these very issues within their interviews.

> 'The more I visited the more I became aware of the political dimensions of why people were suffering and the range of abuses that they suffer, and it was like, well, if I'm coming I'm going to do some good with that! [...] I don't want to be that person who just watches you suffer and holds your hand while you suffer. For me if felt a little bit perverse.' (Lola, Melbourne)

Lola's point is undoubtedly a powerful one. The darker potentialities of 'compassion' weighed heavily on many visitors, who wrestled with the problem of how to offer support in a way that was meaningful, practical and, ultimately, ethical. Like Lola, many visitors concluded that more was required of them than mere 'hand holding'. Yet to dismiss detention centre visits as such would not only mischaracterize the work that most visitors performed; it would also somewhat misunderstand the way that power operates in detention, and, by extension, what constitutes subversion within this environment.

As the previous chapter demonstrated, Australia's onshore immigration detention facilities use an interlocking system of deprivations and frustrations to inflict psychological pain on people in detention. These pains are not accidental. They serve and reflect a broader government policy of asylum seeker deterrence, discouraging prospective asylum seekers from coming to Australia and encouraging those already in detention to return home. In the context of these institutional efforts to break detainees' spirits, detention visitation takes on heightened significance. If deterrence is enacted through the creation of isolated and demoralized detainees, any efforts to disrupt the socio-emotional conditions of detention have political potential. This chapter thus interrogates the intimate relationship between care and resistance within detention spaces, highlighting the (sometimes subtle) roles visitors play in supporting detainees' resistance.

Disrupting despair
Recognizing personhood

In Australia, people seeking asylum have been regularly vilified as 'illegal immigrants' (van Kooy et al, 2021; Pickering, 2001; Klocker and Dunn, 2003), maligned as selfish 'queue-jumpers' (Martin, 2020; Gelber, 2003), dismissed as manipulative non-genuine refugees and 'economic migrants' (Rowe and O'Brien 20, 2016; Every and Augoustinos, 2008; McKay et al, 2010), and portrayed as a danger to Australia and the Australian way of life (Every and Augoustinos, 2007; Clyne, 2005; Dunn et al, 2007; Poynting et al, 2004). When governments have expressed qualified support for people seeking asylum, they have tended to do so by portraying them as two-dimensional victims of evil people smugglers (Peterie, 2017).

Within the detention system as well, detainees have had their personhood systematically erased. One of the hardest aspects of incarceration is the sense of social rejection that prisoners feel. Imprisonment means losing one's claim to 'the status of a full-fledged, trusted member of society' (Sykes (2007 [1958]). For people in immigration detention, who have committed no crime, the perceived injustice of this ostracization adds to their pain. As Thomas Ugelvik and Dorina Damsa (2018: 1029) observe, detainees typically experience detention centres as 'racist institution[s] built on a logic of discrimination' (see also Bosworth, 2014; Mountz et al, 2012; Lietaert et al, 2015).

In a series of letters published during his detention in PNG, Behrouz Boochani underlined the importance of caring relationships for detainees' resistance in dehumanizing carceral settings. In one letter – an open manifesto – Boochani thanked Australians for *caring* about detainees. 'We decided to resist on our own', he stressed, 'but your support gave us faith that there are still people who care, and who are willing to stand up for justice' (2017: np). In a subsequent letter Boochani (2018b: 529) expanded on this theme, explaining that the detention system diminished those within it, and that it was politically important to see people in detention as individuals.

One must not reduce refugees to a general category as the Australian media has so often done. Indeed, they must not be reduced to a vague notion such as 'refugee'. Their existence as unique persons must not be fragmented or eroded. [...] [W]e are unique human beings in opposition to a system and culture that has instrumentalized us, and our sense of selfhood, for political ends. The manifesto stands against a system that identifies refugees as numbers, that atomizes each situation as a calculable equation and that tries to change people into machines. A system that diminishes human beings.

As Boochani stressed, asserting personhood – and, indeed, recognizing and affirming another's personhood – can be important political work.

People incarcerated in Australian detention facilities are acutely aware of their portrayal in mainstream political and media discourse. Kylie (Brisbane) saw this during one of her early visits to BITA, at a time when visits took place within the centre's communal living areas. Kylie had been at the centre when the Australian documentary series *Go Back to Where You Came From* came onto the television. During the show – which highlighted the plight of asylum seekers by taking six Australians on perilous (reverse refugee) journeys from Australia to crowded refugee camps or war-torn countries – the detainees gathered around the television.

'Everyone in the whole centre went to watch it. And so I went, obviously, to watch it as well. And the episode was on the refugee camp in Bangladesh which is where the family that I visit are from, and they stayed there for 12 years. And so they were, like, "oh my gosh!" They were showing us and [saying], "see, this is why, this is why!"'

As Kylie explained, the people she visited had wanted her to know that they had had no choice but to flee to Australia. "'See! This is why we had to come here! This is why we had to come by boat'", they kept telling her. Her friends were clearly concerned, Kylie reflected, that the Australian community – and perhaps even Kylie herself – viewed them as 'illegals' and 'criminals', and not as people in genuine need of protection. "They felt like they had to justify that they're good people", she said.

One of the key roles that visitors played in this respect was to demonstrate to their friends that they were seen and believed. As William (Sydney) put it,

'the system basically says, "we don't trust you guys. We think you're criminals". [...] It's a very debilitating situation to be in where you've got no one around you that trusts you. Believes you. Believes your story and believes you're worthy. So they're treated very inhumanely because they're rejected and they've got no support. And what we can do is to be there offering unconditional friendship and taking people as they are and trusting them.'

People in detention had been maligned and rejected by Australian society. Through their presence and actions, visitors tried to communicate that some people still cared.

The personal nature of visitor-detainee relationships was important here, and served as a striking counterpoint to the homogenizing force of the institution. Visitors not only demonstrated that some Australians saw and supported people in detention in general; the *specificity* of their relationships meant that individual detainees had opportunities to be seen and known as unique people. They were not universalized into 'an abstraction' (Held, 2004: 151).

The friendships that developed between people in detention and their visitors were often grounded in points of commonality. As is the case in society more broadly (McPherson et al, 2001), people with shared interests, comparable sociodemographic characteristics or similar personalities often felt friendships spark naturally. Progressive Christian Nathaniel (Melbourne), for example, connected with a Muslim man at MITA over a shared love of theology.

'He and I found out that we had a lot in common when it came to our understanding of our faith and our religion. So we would go off and have these bizarre long-winded conversations about theology which would bore everyone else at the table completely to tears, but we would end up laughing about bizarre theological things that we had both learnt.'

Other visitors connected with detainees who were their own age, or who shared their passion for music, gardening, art or politics, among other pursuits. In all instances, the process of building a friendship involved a mutual process of seeing and affirming specific dimensions of their friends' identities.

Visitors frequently used the language of friendship or even family to underline the intimacy of some of the relationships that resulted (see Tilbury, 2007; Lange et al, 2007). In Sydney, Lewis considered the young men he visited at Villawood IDC to be among his closest friends.

'You've built this relationship with someone you could almost classify as being a best friend, and the fact that it's solely been visiting four hours each weekend in a detention centre – it doesn't even feel as though that's how I've gotten to know these guys.'

Rebekah in Brisbane felt the same about a young woman she visited at BITA: "we talk about each other as sisters," she told me. "She is my best friend". In several instances, more literal family ties had also formed through

83

romantic attachments or guardianship arrangements for community-based children.

Familial titles were generally bestowed by people in detention initially, but many visitors embraced them as both welcome endearments and accurate representations of the relationships they shared. The lexis of brothers and sisters, aunts and uncles, parents and grandparents spoke to the closeness and commitment of many friendships. Visitors also used this language of family to communicate welcome and belonging. Many asylum seekers had no family in Australia; some had no living family at all. Adopting familial titles was therefore a way for visitors to reassure their friends that they were not without support. As Moina (Melbourne) reflected, "I always give them my name and address to have with them. […] As 'Grandma', you can always come to me once you're out [of detention]".

As connections grew, the visiting room could become a space of sanctuary. Visitors and detainees worked together to co-create small pockets of comparative normality – including through the curation of a sensory experience of home. As discussed earlier, the sharing of food was an important part of visits in the early years of this study. Visitors and detainees used food in a practice of place-making, whereby the hostile environment of the detention centre was rendered (comparatively) friendly and familiar though the introduction of comforting tastes and smells. Food is important for our sense of home, and familiar foods can provide an embodied sensation of safety. As Robin Vandervoordt (2017: 616) explains,

> Home is not so much a place, but a situation where people, objects, scents and tastes feel familiar, safe and warm. Reviving those sensory experiences is crucial to create a home even, or perhaps especially, in a hostile environment. Eating and drinking serve as an anchor for a socio-structural situation in which all 'ontological securities' seem to have turned into quicksand.

The participants in this study seemed innately aware of this potential and worked to provide the people they visited with the foods they required to create such an escape.

Visits could also be a space where detainees embodied social identities beyond those imposed by the institution. In Sydney, Regina described the joyous scene that unfolded when a young couple visited Villawood IDC with their ten-month-old daughter. The baby's presence, Regina recalled, had allowing the detained men to communicate identities as fathers and caregivers, and to experience a glimpse of their past lives.

> '[T]hat baby attracted everyone like a magnet. These were men who were away from their families. Away from their wives and children

that they hadn't seen. And it was just heartbreaking in a way, but gosh it was beautiful. That little baby put her little hands out to everybody and smiled and laughed. [...] She was passed around like a parcel. It was beautiful. [...] That really stands out to me as a wonderful afternoon. To see some of these people smile who I've never seen smile before. They got out musical instruments, and I didn't even know they had any. And they started singing silly songs and everybody was cracking up laughing, and it was wonderful to watch them laughing. All from a little baby. All from just the normality of having a normal life.'

While scenes of this kind became significantly less common as visiting rules hardened, visitors' presence in the centres nonetheless continued to offer a semblance of normality, and to provide opportunities for detainees to express and assert identities beyond the institution.

Affirming agency

Social scientists frequently caution that asylum seeker support work – and equivalent work in interracial spaces – can reflect and reproduce colonial patterns of violence and domination. Colonization often involved (and/or involves) overt violence and brutality, but 'care' can also be a tool of colonial oppression. Early colonizers at times offered 'paternalistic and disingenuous sentiments of compassion and care' (Sirriyeh, 2018: 39) to Indigenous peoples, instead of engaging with them as sovereign rights holders. This logic continues into the present not only through policies of 'tough love' (see Chapter One), but also through some forms of paternalistic advocacy and activism. When white benefactors assume positions of power in their efforts to 'support' people of colour, for example, they risk reproducing the very social hierarchies they purport to contest.

Jonathan Darling demonstrated the applicability of this critique to asylum seeker support work in his 2011 study of an asylum seeker drop-in centre in the UK. Darling showed that while volunteers at the centre welcomed asylum seekers, they retained ownership and control of the centre's spaces. In this way, programme volunteers adopted privileged and emotionally rewarding identities as morally virtuous benefactors, while asylum seekers were positioned as 'vulnerable, dependent and rightless' (Darling, 2011: 414). The coding of the privileged and empowered citizen as generous patron, Darling argued, functioned to naturalize and depoliticize the vast inequalities that distinguished these parties. While Darling (2011: 414) was careful not to 'dismiss those gifts which were offered here, as for many [asylum seekers] they were central to finding a way to "go on" with their lives', he nonetheless argued that the programme reproduced the 'exclusions and inequalities' that the asylum seekers experienced in society more broadly.

Jennifer Erickson (2012) observed a similar phenomenon in her study of a volunteer programme that helped newly arrived refugees to resettle in North Dakota. Volunteer participants in her study had 'more access to power and knowledge' within the programmes than the participating refugees, and some volunteers displayed 'the "white man's burden", a need to "teach" refugees rather than collaborate with or learn from them' (Erickson, 2012: 174). Such volunteers, Erickson (2012: 167) argued, served 'as foot soldiers for hegemonic forms of citizenship that privilege Whiteness, Christianity, a Protestant work ethic, and gendered practices of care'. In the Australian context, Cheryl Lange and colleagues (2007: 39) have similarly observed that volunteer English tutors who support Hazara refugees in Albany, Western Australia, at times interact with refugee participants in ways that reinforce the power these tutors already hold by virtue of 'their English language ability, formal citizenship status and sense of belonging'.

The reality of inequality is a constant backdrop to detention centre visitation work, and many of the participants in this study regularly grappled with the implications of their comparative privilege and the moral questions this raised. The stark differences between their own life circumstances and those of the people they visited were difficult to ignore. The juxtaposition was perhaps most starkly apparent at the end of each visit: while visitors were free to leave the facilities, their friends were frisked by guards and returned to their secure compounds.

> '[Y]ou're saying goodbye to everyone and you're like, "OK, I'm going to go home to my family, to everything else now. They're going to go [...] back to the same room that they've been stuck in for the last three or five years of whatever it is. Back to the same routine". [...] I always find the goodbyes quite difficult.' (Samantha, Perth)

Once outside the centres, small pleasures such as an air-conditioned car reminded visitors of their friends' ongoing deprivation.

> 'You know that you're going to walk out the gates and get into your car and drive home and resume your normal sort of life. And these people are going to go back to their compounds, eat the same crappy food at the canteen, have the same very limited range of things that they can do, be depressed, worry about what's going to happen, take their pills to make them sleep. So that's very difficult.' (Oliver, Melbourne)

Many visitors consequently struggled with the larger question of why *they* were able to enjoy freedom and resources while the people they visited in detention were not.

The unsettling answer that many visitors from non-refugee backgrounds reached was that their white skin and/or Australian citizenship/permanent residency afforded privileges they had not earned. Visitors like Imogen further recognized that the luxuries they enjoyed as Australians were theirs because of a global system that concentrated resources with the privileged few.

'[I]t's always in the back of your mind. You have to be really wary of the way that you talk about your country and the types of opportunities that I've had here that so many people are denied. [...] It just feels so obvious that the very place we're sitting in is a result of me being entitled to some of those opportunities – that I'm benefiting from a system that is also doing this to you. So it's difficult to navigate that.'

Imogen did not support mandatory detention or the governments that perpetuated it, yet she experienced the striking disparity between her own life and those of her friends as a moral indictment.

In this context, many visitors engaged in the reflexive, iterative work of noticing asymmetries in their relationships and trying to become more ethical allies. At the most basic level, this involved visitors confirming with their friends that they did, in fact, want them to visit. In Sydney, John had asked one man in detention, "is there any point in me coming?" The man's answer had been definitive: "he said, 'keep coming'". Nathaniel (Melbourne) had sought similar feedback from his friends at MITA. One of the people in detention, he noted, had chosen not to continue seeing him as he did not enjoy group visits. This was "completely legitimate", Nathaniel told me, and he had been careful to affirm and respect the man's decision.

Many visitors also deferred to their friends regarding how their visits should run. Several visitors started taking their children or grandchildren to the centres because detained children – who had few peers their own age to play with – had asked them to do so. Other visitors consulted with their friends regarding who to nominate on their group visit request forms, recognizing that their friends (like all people) had preferences, and may not get along with all of the other detainees. Visitors also tailored their food offerings (insofar as they were permitted to bring food into the centres) to their friends' preferences, and within their commensal meals they worked to ensure that their friends' agency was respected.

The sharing of food was a common strategy through which visitors and people in detention worked to build more equal relationships. Food has long been recognized as a valuable tool in the production of belonging (Bailey,

2017; Hughes, 2019; Schermuly and Forbes-Mewett, 2016) and this potential has often been leveraged in refugee and asylum seeker support programmes (Khorana, 2018). As Robin Vandervoordt (2017) observes, the shared table can be a space where new arrivals assert equality by positioning themselves as hosts, not guests (Vandervoort, 2017). Vandervoordt experienced this directly in his own research interviews with refugees in Belgium, who subverted dominant constructions of refugees as dependent by offering him – a privileged Belgian researcher – food and beverages.

> [I]n that particular situation, they were giving food and drinks, rather than receiving them; they were hosting me, a Belgian guest, thereby subjecting me to their eating and drinking routines. In this sense, they were engaging in the power struggle springing forth from any such 'gift', by trying to shift and change their position vis-à-vis the giver. (Vandevoordt, 2017: 609)

Visitors and detainees in Australian detention facilities engaged in similar scenes of subtle negotiation. While visitors were responsible for bringing food to their visits, their detained friends routinely claimed agentic roles as the hosts of these meals. Detainees prepared hot drinks in the centre kitchens and took it upon themselves to serve and distribute the food their visitors provided. As Regina in Sydney told me, "[t]hey're very hospitable. We take in a bit of food and you go to [...] make a cuppa and [they say], 'no, no, no'. You've come to them to visit and their tradition is they'll look after you". Samantha in Perth agreed. "The guys will make us tea and offer us things. Kind of like we're their guests in this horrible immigration prison". Where the volunteers in Darling's (2011) study had retained control over the centre spaces, asylum seekers in Australian detention facilities asserted their moral equality and agency by assuming the role of hosts.

These expressions of agency and hospitality could be jarring to visitors who often imagined, in their early visits, that *they* were the ones offering care and making asylum seekers welcome. In Brisbane, for example, Jess recalled that she had not wanted to accept anything from the people she visited at first, as doing so felt unfair when she had so much and they had so little.

> 'I thought, "I'm not in detention, I'm not an asylum seeker, I can give you things. I've got things I can give you! You can't give me anything". But that changed because they give me things too!'

Over time, the detainees' hospitality – and, indeed, their gentle resistance to Jess' paternalistic care – helped Jess to reimagine her visits not as acts of charity, but as two-way relationships. As her relationships grew, Jess came to recognize the people she visited as friends and equals. "Friendship is the right word", she told me. "I wouldn't want to call myself a volunteer". Through simple acts like accepting cups of tea, visitors did the deeper self-work of unlearning identities as privileged benefactors and learning to honour their friends' agency. As Moina (Melbourne) told me, "if they offer you a cup of tea you always take it, because that's something they can do for you".

A similar trend surrounded language acquisition in detention. Australian visitors often assisted their friends as they studied or perfected English, but many also tried to learn their friends' languages. For some visitors, these efforts were a way of combatting any stigma their friends might be feeling: stumbling over Farsi or Tamil words, for example, was a way of affirming that learning a new language was difficult. But these language exchanges could also become spaces where visitors learnt to recognize their friends "as valuable sources of knowledge, especially with regards to their first language" (Rebekah, Brisbane). As Rebekah explained, "[w]e were all students and teachers within our relationships, which I think helps to demonstrate respect – for their culture and language, and for them as people. [It] can have something of an equalizing effect". This reflexive commitment to language *exchange* differs significantly from the paternalism Erickson (2012) and Lange and colleagues (2007) observed in their respective studies.

Actions of this kind were clearly insufficient to counteract the marked differences between detainees' and visitors' situations. As Hazel (Brisbane) stressed, "[m]e going in there for two hours and then walking off and getting in my car. What can be equal [about that] if the other person's locked up and bored and frightened?" These strategies, however, were an important way that visitors tried – however imperfectly – to affirm the humanity and moral equality of the people they visited. By extension, they were also an important way that visitors endeavoured to counteract the corrosive impacts of the detention machine.

In subverting the logic of detention and the social hierarchies it entrenched, the participants in this study were doing subtle political work. As they engaged in reflexive solidarity building, many also found ways to extend their resistance into more recognizable forms of political advocacy and activism.

Agitating for change

Advocating for detainees

Beyond helping the people they supported to endure detention, visitors to detention engaged in a range of activities to expedite their friends' release. Educated, English-speaking visitors used their privilege to "stand between" (Lola, Melbourne) detainees and the ABF, ensuring their friends had access to the information, documentation and support they needed. Detainees were given minimal state assistance accessing justice and were often confused about their rights and legal options within Australia. Seasoned visitors thus played an important role in connecting the people they met in detention with migration agents and lawyers.

Less experienced visitors also helped their friends to access justice, most notably by assisting with legal paperwork. In Perth, Greta explained that she had "just gradually started doing paperwork for people". This typically involved helping detainees to read and fill out forms, but sometimes extended to lodging Freedom of Information requests and data breach complaints on a detainee's behalf. At times, visitors worked closely with their friends' legal teams and became the conveyors of legal information and documentation between these parties. In one notable example, Josephine had worked with a team of lawyers to prevent the deportation of eight people from Darwin.

'I went in every afternoon to [the centre] and got the information every lawyer needed and [...] we saved the whole lot. [...] The lawyers couldn't have all come to Darwin – they had all their clients in Sydney or Melbourne or Brisbane or wherever – but they would do this pro bono work and we'd give them the information.'

Other visitors supported their friends' legal cases by helping them to record the experiences that underpinned their refugee claims. It was common for visitors to accompany their friends to subsequent legal hearings, and in a minority of cases visitors were also called to give testimony.

In addition to supporting their friends in their protection claims, visitors were at times involved in advocating regarding conditions in the centres. Work of this kind was less widespread but was frequently taken up by visitors with a strong background in advocacy or activism. In Perth, long-term activist Siobhan described her efforts to help a man who had become suicidal at Yongah Hill IDC. The man, Siobhan explained, used a wheelchair but had been forcibly separated from his wife and primary caregiver. Unable to maintain hygiene or access regular meals, his condition had deteriorated dramatically.

'So he's in a room on his own. No one's helping him toilet. No one's helping him shower. There's no rails in the shower. He's got severe blisters on his hands because he's got no gloves and he's having to try to get himself up to the mess hall [in the wheelchair].'

Siobhan's response had been swift and decisive.

'Part of my role was contacting the disability association – getting somebody from Disability WA to go out and see him and assess him. I did a statutory declaration as part of an official complaint to the Human Rights Commission, Department of Immigration, Serco etc.

And explaining to him and his wife, together and separately, that when they meet with their case manager the point that they need to make is not, "I feel really bad because I'm separated from my husband", but "if my husband has a fall while he's showering by himself and injures himself, that's a lawsuit and you will be liable".'

Under this pressure the authorities relented and the couple were reunited.

While advocacy of this kind could improve the situation of individual detainees, many visitors explained that their actions also entailed a universalist intent. Visitors advocated for their close friends and loved ones, but many also sought out opportunities to share their skills with other people detained at the centres. Insofar as their efforts assisted detainees to push back and access their rights, visitors hoped this work might disrupt the operation of the detention system more broadly. It was harder for authorities to deport detainees or push them into despair when advocates and legal teams were working to protect their rights. As Samantha (Perth) told me, these efforts could also place resource pressure on the detention system, as authorities were forced to respond to each legal challenge and information request. Bureaucracy was frequently used in detention to harm detainees and their supporters, but it could also be leveraged to serve detainees' interests.

Bearing witness

The regular presence of visitors in detention is highly disruptive to the secrecy and totality of these institutions. On the one hand, visitors' presence ensures that conditions in detention do not go unnoticed. On the other hand, it conceivably prevents some abuses from occurring by providing accountability. Visitors like Samantha (Perth) understood the importance of their role in this respect and saw their presence within detention as a grain of sand in the cogs of the detention machine (Ugelvik, 2011).

'I think going there is in itself a bit of a political act because it says to the government "there are people watching [...] even if you put a detention centre an hour-and-a-half drive away from Perth in a more remote area, people will still go out to that centre. You can't hide it". And entering into that space. That's the Department's space. It's their territory where they can do whatever they want, essentially. Going into that space is an act of resistance.' (Samantha, Perth)

This potential for detention centre visitors to hold the government and its contractors to account has been explored in detail by Caroline Fleay and Linda Briskman (2013). Given the secure and inaccessible nature of many of

Australia's detention facilities, Fleay and Briskman argue, community-based visitors serve an important oversight role within these centres. Yet the efficacy of this oversight mechanism depends on visitors' willingness to not only see and recognize what is happening in detention, but to also *communicate* their experiences with others. Bearing witness, Fleay and Briskman (2013: 114) explain, involves 'communicating what has been seen and heard in ways that encourage the receivers of the message to take action in response'.

Participants in this study took the obligation to share their experiences seriously, and their witnessing efforts took a number of forms. Some visitors, including many who did not identify as activists, described their efforts to bear witness by humanizing asylum seekers and sharing their testimonies in private conversations. As Louise (Melbourne) understood the situation, hardline asylum seeker policies were only politically viable because ordinary Australians accepted the government's vilifying narratives.

'[Y]ou've got to ask yourself, "why is it so secret? Why is it so secret?" And it's so secret because the political implication is "we're saving you from all these terrible people so you better vote for us". That's what it's about, unfortunately, in my view. It's about politics.' (Louise, Melbourne)

Louise and others like her thus used the relationships they developed in detention to challenge prejudice in their social circles. They gave personal testimony that asylum seekers were not enemies and Others, but potential friends. And they strengthened these statements through the ongoing embodied testimony of their detention centre visits.

In Brisbane, Kylie intentionally worked to humanize asylum seekers in her workplace by speaking casually about her BITA visits. When colleagues asked what she had done on the weekend, she would tell them about the people she visited in detention, framing them as her friends. "It creates conversation", Kylie explained. "Normal conversation". These natural interactions seemed to cut through layers of defensiveness, fear and prejudice in ways that rehearsed arguments could not.

This perception that personal stories have more persuasive power than facts alone is born out in the literature. Research from a range of disciplines indicates that stories are one of the most efficient forms of communication, and that the human brain may be uniquely equipped to process information presented in story form (Morris et al, 2019). As Brandi Morris and colleagues (2019) explain, the presentation of information alone may actually *increase* polarization, rather than providing opportunities for people to reconsider false beliefs. Individuals presented with cold scientific facts tend to become more galvanized in their pre-existing opinions. In contrast, those presented with stories 'experience higher empathy and are more likely to exhibit story-consistent beliefs and pro-social behavior in real life, even when controlling for individual dispositions toward empathy and transportability' (Morris et al, 2019: 22). This effect may be particularly pronounced when the stories presented are personal testimonies, as visitors vouch for their detained friends, lending them their social capital.

It was not only through these personal testimonies that visitors bore witness to what was happening in detention. Many also pursued more public forms of witnessing – most notably by participating in political protests. While some participants had been attending public demonstrations long before they commenced visiting, others explained that visiting detention had 'politicized' them.

> 'At the start I think as a person of faith – as a Christian person – you think, "okay, I will go and offer compassion or offer empathy and bring some light into a dark place". So I think that's what I thought to begin with. […] It has shifted because of the experience of visiting and because of the steps that ABF and Serco have taken to make it just more difficult and more horrible. It's kind of pushed many of the visitors much more towards activism.' (Oliver, Melbourne)

As visitors like Oliver came to recognize the political causes of their friends' suffering, overt political action felt increasingly essential.

In addition to attending public protests, some visitors played a key role in organizing these events or speaking to those who attended. Many of these visitors emphasized the importance of centring and amplifying detainees' voices during such activities. In Perth, for example, Samantha told me that she always tried to use detainees' words when she spoke at public rallies: she would tell her detained friends about any upcoming speaking opportunities, and they would give her messages to share. Consulting in this way, Samantha told me, lent authority to the claims she made and the stories she told. Members of the Australian public were often deeply affected hearing the words of the people their country detained. Yet this approach transcended pragmatic considerations. It was also about recognizing detainees' agency and ensuring her activities as an activist did not compound inequalities.

Siobhan (Perth) regularly did media work, helping detainees to get "their images, their names, out in public space as part of their own agency and human rights work". Ethical allyship, she explained, meant honouring the leadership of those in detention.

> 'We're there to be a voice and a conduit, in order to be able to create a channel of communication that filters and protects them from repercussions as often as possible. […] I always try to remember that

many of the people that we're connected with and engaged with were human rights activists, political activists, in their own countries. They're not children.'

In Melbourne, Hannah agreed. Her activism involved working with detainees on creative projects that helped people in detention to tell their own stories on their own terms.

'I think it's generally important that we amplify voices. People call asylum seekers voiceless and this and that and there's a lot of issues in this space with the white saviour kind of complex, or that benevolent kind of attitude and we start being the voice for people who have big strong beautiful voices. And for me it's important that we provide a space for those voices, so it's not about us or what you know, it's about these people and their stories and how they want to say it.'

Visitors could thus become an important resource for people in detention who wished to share their stories in the public sphere. As Samantha (Perth) put it, visitor activism was "kind of like a partnership, for lack of a better word, against this horrible machine".

Conclusion

In her book *The Politics of Compassion*, Ala Sirriyeh (2018) distinguishes between solidaric and paternalistic forms of compassion as structuring logics of justice struggles (see also Hoggett, 2006). She argues for a model of compassion grounded in proximity and solidarity, rather than the hierarchical power relations typically associated with compassionate relationships. Many of the participants in this study actively embraced a comparable ethic of care. They recognized that true solidarity was premised on a basic recognition of the Other's equality. At both the micro-level of their personal relationships and in their broader efforts to enact policy change, these visitors strived to pursue an equalizing redistribution of social power, honouring their detained friends' agency and, in many cases, their leadership (Anderson, 2002; RISE, 2020).

In underlining the social and political functions of detention centre visits, this chapter facilitates a new appreciation of why detention centres make it so difficult for prospective visitors to gain access (see Chapter Three), and why visiting room rules continue to harden (see Chapter Four). Visits have the potential to subvert and disrupt the logic of the detention system and provide pathways to more recognisable forms of resistance. It is thus unsurprising that authorities work to keep visitors out. As refugee Farhad Bandesh told *The Guardian* upon his release from detention in late 2020, "we have some people in the community who are beside us. They walk beside us in this battle and the nightmare will be over, and we will be free and we deserve to be free. [...] My message is resistance brings life, resistance brings freedom" (in Zhou, 2020: np).

Forced Relocations

Carole's story

Carole – a smartly dressed woman with short grey hair – sits opposite me at the Brisbane Square Library. It's 2015 and Carole has been visiting BITA for a little over two years. She has been concerned about Australia's asylum seeker policies for significantly longer. For years, Carole tells me, she was "appalled" by the government's treatment of asylum seekers. "I thought that was an area where I wanted to make some contribution once I had time". When she retired from medicine in 2011, Carole seized the opportunity to act on these convictions – first tutoring a refugee student in her local community, and later commencing visits to BITA.

There is tenderness in Carole's voice as she talks about the main family she has visited during her time at BITA. The family arrived in Australia by boat several years ago and was initially sent to Nauru for offshore processing. When they were later transferred to Brisbane to access medical care, a fellow visitor introduced Carole to the family. Learning that Carole was a retired doctor, the mother asked whether Carole might visit her teenage daughter, Farah, in the nearby hospital. Carole gladly agreed.

In the weeks that followed, a quiet friendship developed. Farah was warm and intelligent, and despite the bleakness of her situation, she clung to the prospect of a happier future. Farah wanted to be an astronomer, Carole recalls, and that dream infused even her most painful memories.

> 'She told me that they came [to Australia] by boat. [...] The boat trip from the very little she told me sounded terrifying, but she said the only good bit was the skies were just incredible when they were out on the sea. That stuck with me.'

One of the greatest sorrows of Farah's life was the loss of her education.

> 'She was very down all the time and would rally and have these bits of comparative lightness, but she was really, really concerned that because she hadn't been to school for three years she wouldn't be able to learn and she'd

forgotten it all. Because she was clearly quite a clever girl and quite ambitious and that was a recurring theme that she was scared about it.'

Like so many young asylum seekers, Farah recognized that detention was robbing her of valuable years. Where other people spent their adolescence securing an education, embarking on careers, and meeting likeminded friends and future partners, Farah was watching her hopes gradually dim.

When Farah was released from hospital and sent back to BITA, Carole continued her visits. Sometimes – when Farah's mental health allowed – they played Scrabble together.

'She was a big reader, but I think that her depression was such that she couldn't really concentrate a lot. I thought that [bringing her a Scrabble set] might be a good idea, and we played Scrabble together. She was hilarious. She was delightful. She cheated – openly – and I would say, "that's not the rules, I told you!" And she would say, "it doesn't matter, I'm going to win!" When she wasn't desperate, she was full of fun.'

When Farah began attending a local high school, Carole felt hopeful. With the prospect of an education, there was a new spark in her young friend's eyes. This joy, however, was to be short lived.

Intellectually, Carole had known that the family's situation in Brisbane was far from stable. She had heard of other detainees being relocated between detention centres, or – in the case of medical transferees – occasionally being sent back offshore after receiving treatment. Yet when she received a call from BITA to cancel a pre-booked visit, Carole was not prepared. Farah and her family, Carole was told, were no longer at BITA. When pressed for details, the Serco officer advised that they had been relocated to a facility in Darwin.

Sitting in front of me two months later, Carole blinks back tears. In the time since her friends' relocation, she has been unable to contact them. She has considered travelling to Darwin to see the family, but with little information that feels like a risky proposition. Instead, Carole has gleaned what she can from other visitors. Gathering information is difficult, but not knowing what to do is even harder.

'I was completely floored by [their relocation], which is stupid because I knew their situation. But there was this sort of vicarious trauma and feeling "I've got to do something", but there wasn't anything. [...] I just knew how absolutely devastating this would be for them.'

The overall experience of visiting immigration detention, Carole tells me, is one of powerlessness. But these feelings are particularly acute when relocations occur. Her own emotional well-being, Carole insists, is comparatively unimportant. Yet she believes that 'traumatised' is the right word to describe her emotional state. And if she feels this way as a privileged Australian, she can only imagine what Farah's family is experiencing.

★★★

Carceral mobility

When we think of immigration detention centres, we often envisage places of confinement (Peters and Turner, 2017). As the previous chapters have explored, detainees in Australia's detention system are routinely held for years on end (Department of Home Affairs, 2021a). Facilities are prison-like in their architecture and security features, and the 'totality' (Goffman 1961) of these institutions has increased as entrance procedures have become more complex. Yet in focusing on the use of confinement within detention systems, it is easy to overlook the use of forced *movement* as an instrument of carceral power.

Between July 2017 and May 2019, there were 8,000 involuntary movements of detainees in Australia's immigration detention system (O'Malley, 2019). Some of these movements were deportations, but others were forced transfers between different detention facilities. In just one year – July 2018 to August 2019 – the Immigration Department spent AU$6.1 million on flights moving immigration detainees around the onshore system (Department of Home Affairs, 2019a). This included AU$5.7 million for charter flights and AU$400,000 for commercial flights. It did not include the cost of keeping planes on standby and transporting the staff who accompany detainees; neither did it include the cost of transporting detainees by road.

Within the existing academic literature on immigration detention, involuntary movement has received considerably less attention than involuntary confinement. In the last decade, however, a body of research has emerged regarding forced movements in prison settings, contesting orthodox analyses of carceral spaces as 'environments of fixity and stability' (Disney, 2017: 1907) and positing that 'mobility is part and parcel of carcerality' (Peters and Turner, 2017: 3; see also Moran, 2016; Turner and Peters, 2017). Scholars have described inmates being transferred between different prison facilities in places including the UK, Sweden, Russia and Latin America (Follis, 2015; Svensson and Svensson, 2006; Moran, Piacentini and Pallot, 2012; Gutierrez Rivera, 2017). With respect to immigration detention specifically, studies have shown that forced movement is also used in some UK, US and European detention facilities (Gill, 2009; Hiemstra, 2013; Michalon, 2013; Conlon and Hiemstra, 2017b), highlighting another sense in which immigration detention centres increasingly resemble prisons. A consistent finding from this research is that involuntary movement is being employed a tool to punish, control and discipline prisoners (Michalon, 2013; Mountz, 2013). The use of forced movement as an instrument of carceral power, however, has been largely overlooked in studies of Australia's detention network.

Internationally, we also know comparatively little about how forced relocations impact those left behind. Research concerning the human costs of these transfers has, quite understandably, tended to focus on the people who are moved. Nonetheless, within these studies there has been a general recognition that forced relocations can have a detrimental impact on civilian prisoners' relationships as family members and friends struggle to visit loved ones in geographically distant locations (Christian, 2005; Roguski and Chauvel, 2009). These impacts can in turn damage criminal prisoners' prospects of rehabilitation; as Dominigue Moran (2013: 178) notes, the reality that 'prison inmates who are visited during imprisonment "do better" on release' has been accepted by criminologists for decades. With respect to immigration detention specifically, it has similarly been observed that forced relocations can reduce detainees' access to advocacy and support services, with potential implications not only for their health and well-being, but also for the success of their legal claims (Martin, 2019; García Hernández, 2011; Moran, Piacentini and Pallot, 2012; Heimstra, 2013).

In a rare study of immigration detention centre visitors' experiences of forced relocations, Nick Gill (2009: 192) found that frequent transfers within the UK detention estate made it difficult for advocacy groups to maintain motivation. Relocations impacted not only what advocates could and could not achieve, but also what they wanted and did not want to achieve. In keeping detention populations transient, Gill argued, authorities prevent the formation of close personal relationships between detainees and supporters, which in turn reduces advocacy efforts. Findings of this kind are concerning, not least because they imply a concerted effort to increase the considerable isolation that immigration detainees already face (Gill, 2013; Briskman, 2013; Fleay and Briskman, 2013). Yet Gill's findings – and the picture they paint of an increasingly disengaged supporter base – do not sit comfortably with the testimonies this book has presented so far, or with Carole's story of intimacy and trauma. The question of how and why forced relocations impact detainee-supporter relationships therefore warrants further exploration.

This chapter explores forced relocations in Australia's onshore detention facilities, as witnessed and experienced by centre visitors. It describes the relocation process and documents the impact of relocations on detainees and their supporter, adding to our emerging picture of the human costs – both direct and collateral – that Australia's detention regime imposes.

The relocation process

'Disappearances'

Detention centre visitors are rarely present during forced relocation operations, but they see and feel the impacts of these transfers in profound and sometimes debilitating ways. For most of the visitors interviewed for this book, the story of their friend's relocation was initially the story of their disappearance. Dozens of interviewees described arriving at a detention facility for a pre-booked visit, only to learn that their friends were no longer there. Other interviewees, like Carole, had received a call from a facility to cancel a booking. While some visitors were given basic information regarding what had occurred, centre personnel were often unwilling and unable to tell visitors where their friends or loved ones had been taken. As Angela recalled regarding her friend's disappearance,

'They said, "she's been moved", and I said, "oh, where to?" and they said, "oh, we don't know where she's been moved to. Or when it happened. Or nothing. We just know she's been moved". So I thought, she could have been deported. She could be in another city in Australia. She could be in another detention centre, onshore or offshore. I have absolutely no idea.' (Angela, Brisbane)

This lack of information was distressing for visitors. They were desperate for reassurance that their friends were at least safe, and understood that the institution – rather than their friends – had made the decision to withhold details of their new location.

The problem, visitors explained, was that it was not always possible to contact a detainee directly after a relocation to find out what had happened. This was particularly true for less experienced visitors, who may not have thought to exchange contact details with their friends early in their relationships. In Darwin, for instance, I heard the story of a community member who – after her first visit to Wickham Point IDC – sewed a dress for a child she had met there. When the dress was complete, she returned to the centre to deliver her gift, only to learn that the family had been relocated. This woman wanted the child to receive the dress she had made her, but the centre staff refused to disclose the family's location or to even forward the package on the woman's behalf.

On other occasions, visitors had the necessary details to contact their friends, but limited access to phones and computers within the detention facilities made communicating difficult (Briskman, 2013). Staying in contact was particularly challenging when detainees did not have access to personal mobile phones – for example, during a period when detainees were expressly banned from having mobile devices in detention. As Amnesty International Australia has observed regarding the necessity of mobile technology in detention, 'Amnesty's experience has been that land lines and internet access have consistently proven to be inadequate in meeting the needs of people in detention, especially for people seeking asylum' (2017: 4). Nonetheless, access to mobile phones in detention has not always been reliable, and the Department has attempted to legislate to ban mobile devices in detention on two separate occasions.[1]

Interviewees stressed that the shock of the transfer process compounded these logistical challenges, leaving some detainees with little capacity to respond to or initiate communication.

'In moments of crisis it's so hard for someone to share what they're going through with everyone that's important to them – a little bit easier now because they have access to mobile phones, but that's only been [recent]. [...] Before that it was so hard for people to update us on what was going on in their life and therefore for us to be able to provide any support to them because as a friend, a visitor, we're not really entitled to anything.' (Imogen, Melbourne)

In this context, visitors frequently turned to one other – using the "bush telegraph" (Charlotte, Brisbane) of Australia's asylum seeker support network to contact local and interstate advocates and ask if anyone had news. They also reached out to other detainees within their network to see if they had heard or seen anything within the facilities.

For the small number of interviewees who heard from their friends as their relocations were occurring, the experience could be equally tough. Long-term MITA visitor Claire, for example, recalled the terror in one friend's voice when he called her from the airport. He was already psychologically unwell, and the stress of a transfer threatened to destabilize him further.

'He rang me from the airport at six o'clock in the morning and said, [...] "they're taking me somewhere and taking me to another detention centre, but I don't know where". [...] The next I heard was that he was in Perth and then that he was on his way to Yongah Hill.' (Claire, Melbourne)

Powerless to stop these relocations, visitors like Claire spent hours waiting for further news. When news came – typically when their friends arrived at the new facility – the stories they shared were harrowing.

Being transferred

While Carole's experience of a forced relocation culminated in the abrupt severing of her friendship with Farah's family, many of the people interviewed for this book had at least some contact with their friends after they were moved. In describing the forced relocation process, these interviewees shared not only their own first-person accounts of their friends' disappearances, but also their friends' stories – as they had been recounted to them when contact resumed.

In sharing these accounts, interviewees overwhelmingly stressed the secrecy and trauma of the transfer process. Interviewees described friends being woken in pre-dawn or early morning bedroom 'raids' and given just minutes to prepare for departure. Explanations were rarely provided, and, in many instances, detainees were not even told where they were being taken. As Yongah Hill IDC visitor Ava explained,

'Whenever they got comfortable somewhere they were taken somewhere else. It was always early in the morning – "you've got 10mins to pack your bags". […] They were always in such a hurry.'

Stories of this kind recurred across the network and aligned with detainees' own testimonies. Speaking publicly in 2020, refugee and detainee Farhad Rahmati – who had been relocated twice in the preceding five months – underlined the domination involved in the transfer process. The first involuntary transfer he had endured had been from a Brisbane hotel APOD to BITA.

'At 8 o'clock about five or six officers rushed into my room and handcuffed me. There was one on my right, one at the left and one at the back. That's the way I was moved out of Kangaroo Point [APOD] in June.'

Just months later he was transferred again, this time from BITA to Villawood IDC.

'This time, I was doing my daily exercise early morning and they called me for a meeting with the ABF. I went to the interview room. I was told I was going to be transferred without any explanation. They confiscated my phone right away. And I had no way of knowing what was going on. They put me in a van, drove me to Brisbane airport, handcuffed me at the airport and put me on a charter flight.'

"Why are there such security measures for someone who has never committed a crime?" Rahmati asked (in Gregoire, 2020: np).

Reflecting on their friends' experiences, visitors emphasized that the violence of the relocation process continued during transit. The use of handcuffs was standard practice in transfer operations (Commonwealth Ombudsman, 2020b), and these physical restraints compounded detainees' feelings of powerlessness and intimidation. As Maive's detained friend had explained it to her,

'They're handcuffed – so they're handcuffed on the plane for the whole ride, and there's a Border Force person sitting either side of them as well, so it's a pretty full on and scary experience.' (Maive, Brisbane)

For visitors like Maive, this use of force seemed both disproportionate and inhumane. Indeed, visitors often used emotive and emphatic language – 'man-handled', 'dragged', 'abducted' – to describe what they saw as the physical and psychological violence of the relocation process.

One consequence of these abrupt removals was that detainees often lost precious belongings. On the surface, such losses might appear insignificant compared to the broader suffering that detention imposes. As MITA visitor Moina told me, however, the loss of physical possessions could be a source of significant grief. The forced migration experience had left many asylum seekers with few material possessions; many therefore felt strong attachments to any belongings that had survived their journeys, as they connected them to their pasts and to the families they had left behind.

'With every move their belongings are lost and lost. By the time you see them they've got nothing of what [they had]. […] When they left home often the family had put together money to help them. Often there'd be little things bought for them. Their mother would often buy them some warm clothing or something and these become important, but these get lost by the time they've moved a few times.' (Moina, Melbourne)

Because detainees had little control over their day-to-day lives, material belongings could also afford a sense of comfort and individuality, helping them to feel safe and to maintain a sense of personal identity and belonging. As Leora Auslander and Tara Zahra (2018: 3) write in their book *Objects of War*, '[p]eople in desperate circumstances rely on familiar things in their efforts to retain memories and maintain a sense of self'. In stripping away these personal belongings, the forced relocation process thus inflicted a painful deprivation, attacking detainees 'at the deepest layers of personality' (Sykes, 2007 [1958]: 69).

While involuntary relocations were (as will be shown) distressing for detainees completely apart from this transfer procedure, several interviewees suggested that the anguish of their friends' relocations could have been reduced if advanced notice had been provided. The difference such warning could make was highlighted by Lewis – a Villawood IDC visitor who explained that his detained friend had been advised of his pending transfer the day before it occurred. Lewis described his friend phoning him in tears: "he was scared, and he said, 'they're moving me to Melbourne'. He goes, 'they're moving me tomorrow morning at 9 o'clock in the morning'". Given the tight restrictions surrounding visitor applications and processing times (see Chapter Three), a face-to-face farewell seemed impossible.

> 'There was no way we could send in our forms to go and visit on the Saturday morning. And visiting hours don't even start until 10 o'clock. [...] Just this overwhelming sense of despair, like there was no way – I thought there was no way we were going to be able to say goodbye and that was really hard.' (Lewis, Sydney)

Ultimately, one of the Serco managers intervened to allow Lewis and some other close visitors to see and farewell their friend.

> 'For people to be able to visit outside of visiting hours you need to get permission from the Immigration Department which as you can imagine isn't something easy. We wouldn't be able to put in that request, especially in less than 24 hours. And so that manager – the Serco manager – made a call to someone that he knew in the Immigration Department and actually pulled some strings and allowed us to come in at 9 o'clock that Saturday morning.' (Lewis, Sydney)

In this farewell visit, member of the detainee's 'Australian family' were able to hug him, offer encouragement and say their goodbyes.

Sharing this story, Lewis reflected that the care and empathy shown by the Serco manager was deeply appreciated ("he was a really good guy"), but that his actions underlined the inhumanity of the system itself. These goodbyes were only possible because an individual Serco manager had advocated for an exception to the usual procedure. In a system where involuntary transfers typically occurred within minutes of their announcement, goodbyes of this kind were exceedingly rare. Indeed, the Australia's Immigration Department has confirmed that abrupt removals, with little time for goodbyes or the collection of belongings, are standard practice in the detention system. 'Where a detainee is not aware of a prospective transfer (i.e., "involuntary" transfers), transfer operations are usually conducted at short notice to the detainee(s)' (Department of Home Affairs, 2019b: 3). It is thus unsurprising that across the five years of this study, I only heard of this one instance when visitors were permitted to properly farewell a friend.

The human costs
Disruption and disorientation

As visitors heard their friends' transfer stories and tried, in the weeks and months that followed, to provide support, they came to understand just how disruptive forced relocations could be. Chapter Four explored how pain and instability are produced through the shifting details of detention centre life. Forced relocations added to this volatility and, in doing so, further corroded detainees' well-being.

Visitors explained that as much as life in detention was characterized by capricious rules and restrictions, detainees who remained in one facility for an extended period were often able to create a semblance of normality. While much of detention centre life was unpredictable, detainees developed rhythms around their daily activities and institutional relationships. They learnt their roommates' sleep patterns and idiosyncrasies, and how to maximize their own rest and privacy. They met other detainees, including speakers of their own first language, and formed friendships. They developed a basic understanding of how their facility worked and how different guards operated – knowledge that helped them to stay out of trouble and to maintain their equilibrium in a harsh and capricious environment.

In this context, the stress relocations caused continued long after the transfers had taken place. The impacts of relocations on detainees' 'inside' relationships were acute. People in detention relied on fellow detainees within the centres for social connection and emotional sustenance, and that relocation to a new facility left them with depleted support.

'The detainees have a network of people inside who sustain them […], who contribute to their mental health, who look after them, who if there's conflict or impacts of drug use they're buffered by that – they have their little kind of posse inside. And then they're picked up and put somewhere else away from those people who have been their everyday support network.' (Lola, Melbourne)

Transferees therefore had to negotiate the everyday stresses of detention centre life without the buffer of trusted friends.

Relocated detainees also embarked on a steep learning curve regarding how their new facilities operated and how they might survive within them. Visitors explained that, before this knowledge was accumulated, their friends often lived in a state of vigilance.

'There's no consistency between centres. That's the thing that really strikes me for detainees when they move. There's no consistency of rules. There's no consistency of visiting experiences. People are in detention for years and years and they're shuffled around at the convenience of Serco to be in these different centres. As a visitor it's remarkably different but as a detainee they say it's retraumatizing because you've got to start again every time.' (Lola, Melbourne)

The patterns and habits that structured detainees' lives at one facility were not necessarily available to anchor and support them in the next.

'You had to know the system and work within the system for each, and the poor asylum seekers who had no idea where they went to – I don't think they were usually told "it's different here", they had to find out the hard way. What they were trained was the right way to do things in one place and then they were told they were doing it wrong in the next one.' (Josephine, Darwin)

Beginning again in a new and potentially threatening environment could be stressful at the best of times. For people who were already under significant psychological strain, the instability that relocations produced could be dangerous – pushing them beyond the limits of their ability to cope.

Being thrust into a new and unfamiliar environment imposed serious psychological costs for some detainees. Several interviewees described friends self-harming immediately before or after a relocation. Robyn's (Brisbane) story exemplifies this trend.

'[One friend] was on suicide watch in Brisbane for a while, and she […] sort of got past that because they were in Brisbane for quite a few months and she went off to school and she was really changing. I could see how much better she was – her whole demeanour. And she was enjoying going to school. And then they were taken to Darwin and back on suicide watch.'

Accounts like Robyn's accord with quantitative research conducted by Kyli Hedrick and colleagues (Hedrick et al, 2019; Hedrick, 2017) which has identified forced relocations as one of a number of triggers for self-harm in Australia's immigration detention system. The strain these relocations inflicted was clearly considerable.

Interviewees observed that the frequency with which transfers occurred also contributed to general anxiety levels within the detention facilities, which could exacerbate mental health concerns even for detainees who had not previously been moved. Visitors explained that the transfers created an atmosphere of threat as detainees recognized that they were also vulnerable to potential relocation.

'There's constantly distressing scenes as one family or another is being dragged away to be put on a plane with very little notice. And it's so upsetting for all the other refugees [...] they're seeing people get hauled off and people are crying and begging and it's all enacted in the middle of BITA in front of everyone else, and this happens day after day. [...] That was the thing that I learnt that I didn't know about. How dreadfully stressful it is for everybody there when other people are suddenly dragged away. Because they've gotten to know people. [...] And you never know if it's going to be you tomorrow morning." (Jodie, Brisbane)

As Lisa in Sydney confirmed, "there's always a nervousness about 'are we going to be deported?' 'Are we going to be moved?' [...] This whole thing of there not being any sort of control [is] very difficult for people". Involuntary transfers – and the abrupt and forceful way in which they were performed – made detainees *feel* their vulnerability. Just as a centre's pool balls might be confiscated or their soccer games banned (see Chapter Four), so too might a detainee be woken in the early hours of the morning and flown hundreds of kilometres across Australia. What was perhaps most distressing about this practice, BITA visitor Jodie told me, was "the sheer random cruelty of it". "Absolute power", she explained, "might be enacted randomly at any time without warning", and this created an amorphous mood of fear.

Interviewees explained that their friends did their best to manage these difficult psychological conditions, and frequently displayed more fortitude than they, as visitors, were able to. One detainee used humour to help both himself and his visitors cope, joking to Bronte, "I've seen Australia! I've been to Darwin and Curtin and Brisbane and Adelaide and Perth [detention centres]" (Bronte, Perth). Another tried to be prepared, packing his bag before bed each night "just in case he was moved on to somewhere else" (Fiona, Perth). Many detainees also took it upon themselves to care for new arrivals and offer whatever assistance they could. In small acts of care and concern, they made room in their friendship groups for new detainees, used their community connections to find them visitors, and quietly monitored those who were not coping. "Despite everything they've been through", Yongah Hill IDC visitor Siobhan (Perth) stressed, many of the detainees retained "more humanity, more human decency, than a great deal of our politicians".

Isolation and radiating harms

Critics of Australia's immigration detention system have frequently observed that detainees are hidden from the public by high walls, remote locations and restrictions on access (McLoughlin and Warin, 2008). Secrecy and inaccessibility have been recognized as core features of Australia's detention regime (McMaster, 2002b; Fleay, 2015). Studies have similarly found that political and media discourses contribute both to detainees' sense of ostracism and to the popularity of draconian detention policies by fostering false beliefs and negative community attitudes (Pedersen et al, 2006; see also Augoustinos and Quinn, 2003; McHugh-Dillon, 2015; Peterie and Neil, 2020). What has received less attention is the way that forced relocations compound detainee isolation and, in doing so, breed anguish and despair.

Participants in this study emphasized that forced relocations not only impacted their friends' relationships with other detainees in the centres. They also damaged detainees' connections with services, supporters and loved ones within the community. This frequently included legal and medical professionals, as well as detainees' community-based friends and family members.

At an instrumental level, forced relocations jeopardized detainees' connections with legal and medical professionals, with potentially serious consequences. A pro-bono migration agent who participated in the study described the damage relocations could cause to asylum seekers' legal cases.

'I was representing [a detainee as a migration agent] and just before her [Administrative Appeals Tribunal (AAT)] case – about a month before her AAT case – they sent her to Perth! Here am I in Melbourne; [my client] was in Perth!' (Deb, Melbourne)

While people in detention could converse with their legal representatives via phone or internet when this technology was available, ensuring the privacy and confidentiality of communications was difficult in shared detention spaces. As Amnesty International Australia (2017) has noted, detainees are sometimes reluctant to discuss their legal cases in spaces where they might be overheard. Time zone differences create additional challenges, as do the difficulties presented by language barriers. When detainees are held in one location for extended periods, they are often able to recruit Australian visitors to help them with communication and language issues. Forced relocations disrupt these support systems. Available evidence suggests that asylum seekers with legal representation are more likely to succeed in their cases than those who represent themselves (Ghezelbash, 2020; Kenny et al, 2016). When access to legal support is disrupted by forced transfers, the implications can therefore be serious.

Interviewees similarly explained that detainees who needed medical care – including medical evacuees from Australia's offshore processing facilities in PNG and Nauru – were often on waiting lists to see local doctors or specialists. When they were relocated within the onshore network their treatment was delayed.

'I've seen people who they're here [from PNG or Nauru] for treatment and then they get moved before they get their treatment. And that means going back to another doctor and starting again.' (Moina, Melbourne)

As has been discussed, detention environments often produce or inflame physical and psychological ailments (Essex, 2019; St Guillaume and Finlay, 2018; Briskman et al, 2008; Coffey et al, 2010). In this context, the disruption of medical care through forced transfers could seem particularly cruel.

In addition to compromizing access to essential professional services, relocations disrupted detainees' access to intimate relationships and informal sources of emotional and social support. When I began interviews for this book in 2015, asylum seeker women and children were regularly held in institutional detention (Department of Immigration and Border Protection, 2015b). Since that time, most have been released into community detention or granted short-term visas (AHRC, 2017a), such that by January 2021 there were fewer than five children in closed detention and over 96 per cent of detainees were men (Department of Home Affairs, 2021b). These releases, while welcome, have seen numerous families separated as husbands and fathers have been refused release. Psychologists warn that – even in situations where families remain geographically close, so that visits are possible – separating families in this way can increase the risk of self-harm or suicide (HREOC, 2004). For families divided by longer distances through forced relocations, the risks are even greater.

In Perth, Roberta shared the story of one such family. The wife, living in community detention in Perth, had struggled to visit her husband during his detention at Yongah Hill IDC. When he was transferred to BITA, the situation became even more dire.

'From Perth it's a one-and-a-half hour drive out of the city to get to Yongah Hill, so for any day that we visit we spend three hours commuting, so it is a commitment for anyone to try to do that. And for this family to try to do that – they have no vehicle, they have no means of getting there, they are completely reliant on volunteers to make that commute with them. And that was difficult enough, but then they moved the father to Brisbane. And so of course there was no way that they could visit. [...] It's incredibly cruel.' (Roberta, Perth)

Another interviewee, John, shared a comparable story about the man he visited in Villawood IDC. The detainee had a wife in Australia but was relocated to Perth without notice or explanation. While the man's wife was employed and had social and financial resources in Australia, making regular trips to Perth was not a realistic option given her work commitments. In these cases, as in many others, the practice of relocating detainees prevented already fractured families from even seeing each other. This was distressing for all involved.

As has been explored, community visitors – including friends, volunteers, advocates and activists – are highly valued by many people in detention and can become a family, of sorts, to those without relatives in Australia (RCOA, 2017; Coffey et al, 2010). Even when relationships are more superficial, visits can help break the monotony of detention centre life, providing distraction and a connection to the outside world. When detainees are relocated, these connections with supporters are frequently lost or weakened.

> 'That's one of the really horrible things about [detention]. People – particularly the ones who have been in for a long time – some of them do make these connections and form these relationships with people in the community. And they can be severed at any moment. […] And they have no control over that. They have no say in that. And then suddenly they're in this new place. They don't have visitors. They don't have the same support that they had before.' (Samantha, Perth)

Following their friends' removal, some visitors did whatever they could to maintain these relationships.

> 'You start making a connection with people and get into a supportive rhythm with them and then they're gone, so you have to decide do I just sort of forget them or do I actually make the effort to see them again, which means you have to go to wherever they are.' (Lola, Melbourne)

In many cases, however, visitors found that they were unable to provide the same level of support to their friends post-relocation. They wanted to help, but regular interstate travel was not financially or logistically feasible for many.

Maintaining communications online or via phone offered a partial solution in these circumstances but was far from ideal. One Villawood IDC visitor, Elizabeth, recalled that when one detained friend was transferred interstate, he stopped communicating completely. Months later he contacted her to apologize, explaining that following his relocation he had gone into a deep depression and been placed on suicide watch. "'I couldn't write to you from Darwin'", he had told her. "'I didn't go out of my room in Darwin. I was so depressed and I lost seven kilos'". Another interviewee provided ongoing support to a suicidal friend who – since his interstate transfer – had no one else to turn to. "He regularly tells me, 'you saved my life today'" (Frannie, Sydney), she explained, but it was much harder to provide support at a distance.

In some cases, the distress that relocations caused was so pronounced that it contributed to detainees' decisions to abandon their refugee claims. William (Sydney) spoke of one friend who, after years of detention, elected to return to his country of origin after a particularly stressful transfer operation. "They sent him to Christmas Island, and he just said, 'I'll go back and die. A quick death. It's better than this slow death'", William said. "This can happen. It does happen".

It was common for interviewees to cry when talking about their friends' relocations and the harms that resulted. In explaining their tears, most underlined their feelings of impotence in the face of profound and preventable suffering. Even before relocations occurred many visitors felt frustrated and helpless in the face of institutional rules. This sense of powerlessness was even stronger after transfer operations, as visitors witnessed their friends' heightened distress but had even less capacity to render assistance. As Jodie in Brisbane told me, standing idly by while people you cared about were being irreparably harmed was almost too much to bear.

Conclusion

Previous chapters have shown how detainees and their supporters create small pockets of normality to make life in detention more tolerable. They have also shown that committed friendships frequently develop in these spaces. This chapter has added to this picture – demonstrating that forced relocations can wipe away these havens at any moment, producing a world in which there is no safe ground on which to stand.

The participants in this study testified to the corrosive impacts of forced relocations on their friends' emotional well-being and networks of support. Immigration detention emerged from their stories as a tool to disrupt and disorient detainees – making them feel their powerlessness and vulnerability by placing them in new and unpredictable settings. Visitors stressed the role of increased social isolation in achieving this anguish. Physically separating detainees from their friends, family members and supporters, interviewees explained, left detainees with depleted social and emotion resources. It also reduced their access to vital legal, medical and instrumental support and thus, visitors feared, increased their vulnerability to repatriation.

This perception of forced relocations as a tool to punish and coerce is consistent with the burgeoning international literature on carceral mobility. As Gill (2013: 28) explains, a key take-away from this scholarship is that 'mobility is used by authorities to increase the discomfort, invisibility and insecurity of carceral spaces'. To use the language of earlier chapters, involuntary movement is being utilized as a tool to accentuate the pains of imprisonment for immigration detainees (see Moran, 2017).

Yet the stories offered in this chapter contribute something new to understandings of involuntary transfers and the production of pain in carceral settings. Where Chapters Three and Four showed that visitors experience a form of the deprivations and frustrations of imprisonment when they enter detention spaces, this chapter has shown that forced relocations compound these experiences of 'secondary prisonization' (Comfort, 2003; 2008), amplifying visitors' pain and perceived powerlessness.

In his 2009 study of detainee relocations in the UK detention estate, Gill argued that regular detainee movements blocked the formation of personal relationships between detainees and advocates, which reduced advocates' motivation to offer committed help and support. This chapter has documented something slightly different – not the *prevention* of relationship formation, but abrupt and painful attacks on those connections that already exist. It has thus not only highlighted the trauma of relocations for immigration detainees, but also the stress that this practice causes to detainees' supporters and loved ones. The next chapter will explore this theme further, delving deeper into the impacts of immigration detention on visitors' socio-emotional well-being and, ultimately, on their capacity to continue visiting.

7

Reverberating Harms

Robyn's story

It's 2019 and over four years since I last saw Robyn. But entering the State Library of Queensland I recognize her immediately. Robyn was among the first people I interviewed when I commenced interviews for this project in 2015. At that time, I was struck by her unassuming manner and by the disarming candour with which she described her experiences visiting detention.

In that first interview, Robyn painted a vivid picture of the small frustrations and larger disruptions that characterize detention centre life. She talked about her friendships with many people in detention, but one family had seemed to hold a special place in her affections. This family, Robyn told me, included a "bubbly little girl" of five-years-old; keeping her entertained was at once a highlight and lowlight of Robyn's visits.

Robyn's story of the family's forced relocation from BITA to Darwin was among the first I heard concerning the transfer process. On one level, her story had a happy ending. The family were returned to BITA and later released into the community. On another level, Robyn's story underlined the staggering human costs of practices like these.

'They came back to Brisbane because the mum had to go back to hospital. So I wanted to [see the daughter at BITA]. [...] Her dad came out. He said, "she's not coming out much, she's not coming out much". Anyway, he came out into the common room with her, and she would normally have run up to me and cuddled me and all that sort of stuff. And I said "hi", you know. And the little girl just looked at me really blankly. And the other Iranians that I was with at the time said something to her in Persian, which would have been "say hello". And she just waved. I was very close to tears that day. And I didn't want them to have to comfort me. But that image of this blank little girl – completely changed to how I knew her. That really affected me. And I don't think I've ever quite got that out of my head.'

113

Adults and children alike were being damaged by detention, Robyn told me. And witnessing this "needless, needless" suffering took a toll on visitors too.

Back in 2015, Robyn had been somewhat hesitant to discuss her own distress. The pain experienced by those in detention, she emphasized, was far greater and more important than her own discomfort. "I try to tell myself I've got no right [...] to feel sorry for myself", Robyn explained. "I don't want to become a martyr and all that bullshit".

Four years and many dozens of visits later, Robyn is now less dismissive. She cannot ignore the reverberating impacts of the detention system. The anguish of visiting detention, she tells me, has not diminished. Rather, "it's got worse".

> *'I go to see a psychologist now. I'm showing symptoms of PTSD. [...] There are many, many stories that you hear or things you've witnessed that stay with you that keep you awake at night. [...] And the feeling of helplessness and hopelessness.'*

Robyn continues to visit BITA, but in a reduced capacity.

> *'When you're face-to-face with people and you've known people for a number of years, you can't just say, "I can't do it anymore". You can't turn away. Because they're people. [...] I started limiting my visits because if someone said, "oh, there's someone who needs visiting, will you go?" I'd always go. Whereas now I'll try and find someone to go so that I don't increase my visits too much. Because it did become just too many people, too much.'*

As Robyn recognizes, her story is not unique. "A lot of advocates can't sustain it".

Despite her clinical diagnosis, Robyn continues to grapple with the moral legitimacy of her pain.

> *'You still feel like, "do I have the right to feel like this?" This trauma isn't happening to me. It's so much worse for them and [...] you feel guilty for feeling bad. You feel guilty when you're not feeling bad because you're forgetting or you're living your life. And that's the thing I struggle with most. [...] But I am more aware now that if you're going to keep going — and this has been going for some time now — you do need some sort of sustenance and support.'*

Robyn is undoubtedly correct that visitors occupy a privileged place within the detention system. Being an Australian affords visitors like Robyn rights that detainees are not granted. Yet, as the wider narrative of this book has revealed, visitors are also targeted by Australia's detention regime. This is a system that harms detainees, but it is also a system that harms supporters. The well-being of both groups is bound up together.

★★★

The benefits of volunteering

There is broad consensus in the interdisciplinary literature on volunteering that volunteer work affords a sense of meaning and purpose, which in turn improves volunteers' physical and mental health (Grimm et al, 2007). This finding is particularly strong in studies of older people and those not engaged in paid work (Herzog et al,, 1998; Greenfield and Marks, 2004; Harlow and Cantor, 1996), whose identities are often more tightly aligned with their volunteer roles (Greenfield and Marks, 2004). In this respect, volunteering can become an important expression and affirmation of a person's social value (Erickson, 2012).

Previous studies of refugee and asylum seeker support work accord with this research, showing that programme volunteers often derive significant meaning from their programme participation, including the gratifying perception that they have 'made a difference' in the lives of those they support (Erickson, 2012; RCOA, 2017). Volunteers also value the friendships they develop within these programmes and may gain new life perspective as they witness their friends' fortitude. As numerous studies attest, witnessing other people's strength can inspire vicarious forms of growth and resilience (Cohen and Collens, 2013).

Many of the participants in this study had developed close and committed relationships through their visits to detention, and they held these friendships dear. Some also reported emotional benefits similar to those described above. In Melbourne, for example, Lola explained that her teenaged children – who regularly accompanied her on her visits to MITA – were extremely grounded as a consequence of their relationships with people in detention.

> 'For them, a lot of the young [detained] men have become role models of sorts, because they are so resilient and positive in the face of all these difficulties. I've grown up with teenagers who don't complain about their lives. But I think it's because they've got this enormous perspective. They understand their privilege. They understand how fortunate they are.'

Orthodox portrayals of volunteer work as a rewarding and rejuvenating activity, however, speak to only one aspect of the detention visitation experience. This characterization does not sit comfortably with stories of anguish and trauma like those Robyn shared. Visitors find their activities meaningful, but many also suffer significant distress as a result of their experiences.

Visiting detention can inspire complex and at times contradictory emotions. As Hannah (Melbourne) explained,

'It's kind of conflicting really because you learn so much about how privileged you are, how lucky you are, actually how *non* resilient. I don't know if I could sustain what these people have been through. I struggle with visiting and being exposed to everything that's gone on in these spaces. I'm so affected by it that I cannot imagine living it. So there's all these conflicting things of privilege, so conscious of your own human rights and things like that. At the same time you're traumatized by what's happening to these people. You suffer from depression, anxiety, powerlessness, frustration. It's huge.'

Visitors enjoyed their friends' company and were grateful for elements of their experience. But these rewards did not negate the deleterious impacts of detention on their health and well-being. Neither did they alter the fact that the system appeared to be designed to harm detainees, and frequently targeted them, as visitors, to achieve this end.

As Robyn alluded, of course, focusing on visitors' pain is not unproblematic. Detained refugees and asylum seekers undoubtedly suffer exponentially more than their supporters, yet white voices and white stories are frequently prioritized in public debate. To fully understand the human and societal costs of immigration detention, however, stories like Robyn's cannot be ignored. As this chapter will show, they reveal something important not only about the reverberating impacts of immigration detention, but also about how detainee isolation and despair is produced and reproduced through micro-level institutional practices – including through those that target and repel visitors. This chapter thus explores the emotional contours of visitors' experiences in Australian detention centres, exposing the reverberating impacts this system imposes and what these harms means for detainees' access to support.

The collateral impacts of immigration detention

To date, comparatively little research has been conducted regarding the 'collateral impacts' of immigration detention. Work has understandably focused on the impacts of detention on those who are incarcerated. An embryonic body of work is starting to emerge, however, regarding the adverse impacts of working in detention spaces. Previous studies have gestured towards the toll that detention centre work can take on researchers, detention centre employees, and the care professionals who enter detention facilities to provide support (Bosworth, 2014; Puthoopparambil et al, 2015). In her book *Inside Immigration Detention*, Mary Bosworth (2014: 59) noted that all the researchers who conducted fieldwork for the book in the UK detention system "reported depression, anxiety, uncertainty, sadness, anger, and guilt". Evidence of psychological distress is also emerging among those employed within these spaces. Indeed, numerous compensation claims have been lodged concerning psychological injuries obtained by staff in Australian immigration detention facilities in just the last few years (Hashman, 2016).

While the ways that immigration detention impacts professionals are thus beginning to garner recognition, the effects of detention on detainees' personal visitors have gone largely unstudied. One notable exception is a 2008 study by Nadya Surawski, Anne Pedersen and Linda Briskman, which explored stress and coping among asylum seeker advocates in Australia. Their survey research found that advocates experience high levels of stress and vicarious trauma in the course of their work. Indeed, asylum seeker support work was found to be more stressful than equivalent forms of work with other disadvantaged groups. While the study documented the extent to which asylum seeker advocates suffer from stress and vicarious trauma, however, it did not distinguish between different forms of advocacy work, and it provided little qualitative detail surrounding these emotional experiences.

The idea that working with traumatized people can have emotional and psychological costs is not new. The multiple terms that have been coined to describe these effects ('secondary trauma', 'vicarious trauma' and 'compassion fatigue', among others (Figley, 2012)) point to the issue's growing prominence within academic discussions of both trauma and care work. What these terms have in common is the premise that individuals can be significantly harmed by 'indirect' exposure to trauma. The concepts are generally illustrated with examples of care professionals hearing about traumatic events in the context of (for example) counselling sessions with people who have themselves been exposed to significant danger (Dass–Brailsford and Thomley, 2012). In these examples, the affected care professionals are generally separated – both physically and temporally – from the traumatic incidents, only hearing about them through the people they are helping. For detention centre visitors, the encounter with trauma is somewhat different. Visitors in these spaces are direct witnesses to suffering. They spend time within, contribute to, and are affected by the very environments that have been shown to be traumatic for detainees. Furthermore, most share strong emotional bonds with the people they visit. As such, ideas regarding emotional contagion and secondary exposure to traumatic incidents may provide only a partial explanation of visitors' distress.

The sociology of trauma

While many visitors acknowledged the satisfaction they derived from their detention centre relationships, emotional anguish was a constant theme in the study. Visitors regularly expressed distress concerning their friends' suffering and described the particular pain of being frustrated in their efforts to provide help. While many visitors emphasized that their pain was trivial compared to that of their friends, their accounts resonated with psychological descriptions of traumatic experiences.

In their book *Coping with Trauma*, Rolf Kleber and colleagues (1992) explain that traumatic situations involve extreme discomfort, as well as feelings of powerlessness and disruption. While the language of powerlessness requires little explanation (in a traumatic situation, the individual 'barely has any influence upon the occurrence and development of the event'(Kleber et al, 1992: 4)), the notion of disruption needs some elaboration. According to Kleber and colleagues, a traumatic event disrupts the individual's perception of the world such that everything suddenly looks different. Life no longer makes sense or feels secure as it once did, and the individual's sense of themselves and their environment 'no longer adequately fit the new situation' (Kleber et al, 1992: 6). Put differently, '[t]he existing certainties of life' disappear and core assumptions shatter (Figley and Kleber, 1995: 78).

The encounter with a traumatic situation may be direct, as where an individual is personally present during an extreme event. Individuals may also experience traumatic environments indirectly, through the stories of others. As Charles Figley and Rolf Kleber (1995: 78) explain, intimate knowledge of traumatizing events can evoke feelings of powerlessness and disruption, just as living through these events directly can.

> For people who are in some way close to a victim, the exposure to this knowledge may also be a confrontation with powerlessness and disruption. Secondary traumatic stress refers to the behaviors and emotions resulting from this knowledge. It is the stress resulting from hearing about the event and/or from helping or attempting to help a traumatized or suffering person. This conceptualization of primary and secondary traumatic stress describes the distinction between those 'in harm's way' and those who care for them and become impaired in the process.

Trauma can thus be transmitted from person to person, just as individuals might experience vicarious growth as they observe another's strength and thriving.

This understanding of trauma as a response to (direct or indirect) exposure to a traumatic situation is significant for the emphasis it places on the traumatic environment. Experiences of powerlessness and disruption are, of course, at least somewhat subjective. A situation that causes disruption for one individual may not evoke the same response in another whose past and ontological perspective imbue an event with different meaning (Berger, 2015). Understandings of trauma that centre the traumatic situation are critical, however, as they de-pathologize the trauma sufferer (Snyder, 2009) and facilitate a more nuanced discussion of the social and political factors that can contribute to traumatization. Such a model invites a more sociological engagement with the idea of trauma, where social environments and institutions – rather than individuals – can be analysed and 'diagnosed' (Peterie, 2018b).

The participants in this study frequently used the language of trauma to describe their experiences visiting detention, and almost all underlined the powerlessness and disruption they experienced in their visits. Visitors were exposed to traumatic situations both indirectly and directly. On the one hand, their friends told them about their harrowing experiences in detention. On the other, participants experienced first-hand the carceral environments that traumatized their friends.

Perceived powerlessness

Everyday disempowerment

Most of the participants in this study began visiting detention because they wanted to help the people Australia imprisoned. They also wanted to demonstrate their opposition to the government's asylum seeker policies, and to escape morally compromising identities as complicit bystanders (see Chapter One). The way that power operates in detention, however, made it difficult for participants to realize these aims. Visitors' efforts to render assistance were frequently frustrated by institutional rules and micro-level controls, and many visitors described a debilitating sense of powerlessness surrounding their visits.

From the frustrations of completing onerous application documents to the intimidation of the entrance process itself, visitors were made to understand that visitors were not in control (see Chapter 3). As Yvette (Sydney) explained with respect to her Villawood IDC visits, "[g]oing into Villawood you were going into an institution in which you were utterly powerless. [...] You sign yourself in, you leave your licence, you go through scanners".

This subjectification continued within the centres themselves, as visitors were subject to a diluted form of the pains of imprisonment and thwarted in their efforts to provide distraction and relief (see chapter 4). As restrictions escalated under Operation Sovereign Borders, even simple acts of care like providing a homemade meal or engaging a detained child in a game of soccer became difficult to perform. These frustrations reflected and communicated a more fundamental powerlessness: an inability to secure their friends' release.

'It does take a toll on you. I mean, when people say to you, "how much longer will I be here?" Or you say, "can I bring you anything?" [and they say,] "no, just give me my freedom". That's really hard.' (Yvette, Sydney)

Visitors' lack of power extended beyond – but was painfully reflected through – their inability to provide food and recreation.

This reality placed visitors in a difficult position vis-à-vis the people they visited. Many visitors were privileged Australians and the people they visited sometimes assumed they should be able to do more than they could. One detained man, for example, had told John (Sydney), " 'you need to tell them to get me out'". But visitors were themselves positioned as quasi-prisoners within the detention system, and had little recourse to enact change. As Angela (Brisbane) explained,

> 'You have no more power than they do in affecting the way that their lives are driven. So that's a hard thing. Being someone who in their eyes is in a much more empowered position – which we are obviously – but we still can't help in any legal way that will affect the policies or anything else around their case.'

Visiting detention thus meant witnessing preventable suffering but being largely unable to make it stop.

In this context, visitors expended considerable energy managing feelings of powerlessness so that these emotions would not prevent them from providing support. As they made their way through security at the start of each visit, visitors suppressed feelings of intimidation and frustration. To show that they were afraid would be to concede that the institution was succeeding in making them feel powerless and visitors were loath to grant the institution this small victory. Yet expressing frustration might give centre staff an excuse to deny them entry.

> 'You're very conscious that you are managing yourself and containing your own emotional responses [...] When you're going through that system you've got to just abide by the rules, do what they say.' (Emily, Darwin)

Within the visiting room, participants again worked hard to contain their feelings, although their focus now turned to being strong for their friends. To this end, many visitors worked to hide their distress and project reassuring positivity.

> 'I think it's sort of a bravery thing [...] that you've got to kind of suck it up as the one who in this situation is the privileged and powerful person who has complete autonomy in your own life. You need to be able to manage this! [...] You know, these guys are dealing with it everyday. [...] We probably have an expectation that you put on your strong suit and can deal with it.' (Emily, Darwin)

As numerous visitors told me, it would not be fair to ask their friends to offer them comfort.

To keep their feelings in check, visitors gave themselves firm pep talks and reminded themselves why they were there. Ambrose (Melbourne), for example, described "always trying to remind myself [to be strong], because it would be so easy for me to just burst into tears". As part of this process, visitors worked to transfer their attention from their own emotions to those of their friends. Frannie (Sydney) explained, "[I'm] not someone who usually compartmentalizes emotions, but you have to in detention. Have to realize that it's not about you. [...] This is their whole life and what you face is trivial in comparison".

While visitors were often successful in temporarily suppressing feelings of powerlessness and associated despair, the realities of detention were never far from mind. Suppressed emotions typically resurfaced shortly after a visit, meaning the journey home could be challenging.

'When I was there and you were talking to them it was always a really nice energy. It felt very positive. There were moments where things were hinted at that were negative – never explicitly spoken about – and when you'd leave and you'd start driving home all of those things would sink in and take meaning. Which couldn't at the time probably because you didn't want to ruin the nice moment you were having with these people. So it was mostly confronting afterwards.' (Angela, Brisbane)

Visitors like Angela often spent hours or days recovering from their visits and working through the emotions they had not permitted themselves to feel.

'I had a lot of difficult nights after leaving those groups where I just would take hours to process what we'd talked about, what it really meant, and how powerless we were to do anything about it.' (Angela, Brisbane)

As Elizabeth (Sydney) told me, "[s]ometimes it's desperate. Sometimes I go to bed and I think, 'what can I do, what can I do?'"

Moments of crisis

Beyond the protracted disempowerment of a 'normal' detention centre visit, almost all study participants described at least one crisis moment that had shaken them and triggered crippling feelings of powerlessness. Some of these instances involved detainees' self-harm or suicide attempts. Several interviewees described moments of panic and fear when they received calls or messages from detained friends who had reached the limits of their ability to cope. These occurrences – which could occur anywhere in the onshore or offshore detention network – had lasting impacts.

> 'He rang me in Nauru saying he had petrol and was going to set himself alight. He never did. I got his sister to go and watch him so that didn't happen. But his voice that night stayed with me. […] Earlier this year he came here [to Australia], and I flew down to Melbourne to meet him and I went into the MITA detention centre and I met him and his sister. We couldn't stop hugging each other. I don't know who was comforting who.' (Robyn, Brisbane)

Part of the problem, several interviewees told me, was that visitors were often left in a state of fearful uncertainty – not knowing if their friends were even alive and having little recourse to help. The contradictions inherent to the visitor role compounded this sense of helplessness. When Imogen's (Brisbane) detained friend became suicidal, for example, his overseas family had contacted her for updates. Yet as a visitor she was entitled to very little information. "I couldn't answer his family's questions and I felt really guilty about that", Imogen recalled.

Forced relocations were another common trigger of debilitating feelings of powerlessness. As Chapter Six explained, visitors described the relocation process as they had experienced it: receiving an urgent phone call from a distraught friend during their transfer, or arriving at a centre for a pre-booked visit, only to learn that their friend had been moved. While the details of these stories varied, visitors described similar experiences of shock and powerlessness which seemed to echo the emotions of their transferred friends. As Jodie (Brisbane) told me,

> 'To be powerless to help as people you like and admire are persecuted in such horrible ways – that's what's upsetting for me personally. And there's a billion reasons why Australia's treatment of refugees is wrong and horrible and upsetting and dreadful and disgusting. But in concrete practical terms what's upsetting about the situation with people you know is just that randomness. That absolute power that might be enacted randomly at any time without warning. Because people do. They get abducted pretty much.'

Visitors who had lost friends to deportation shared similar feelings. The anguish was particularly strong for visitors who believed their friends would face torture or death if returned to their country of origin. In Melbourne, Moina described one agonizing farewell where a friend facing deportation gave her his photograph and asked her to remember him. "He said, 'I

122

know I will be killed and you're the only person who'll care. Please keep my photo'", Moina recalled. "He promised me he'd get in touch with me if he was OK, but I never heard from him again".

In these moments of crisis, visitors did their best to offer whatever help they could. Sometimes, when all legal avenues of appeal had been exhausted, this simply meant being with someone until the end. At other times, visitors found more active ways to resist. In Perth, for example, Greta described her involvement in a last-minute action to support a friend facing deportation.

'We did the anti-deportation action at the airport. We thought we had the correct flight. We thought we'd been really successful. We talked to just about every passenger on that flight. We flyer-ed them. We gave them general information about the situation for minorities in Afghanistan and we gave them specific information about our young man who some of his family had been killed by the Taliban, including his two little brothers, while he was in detention here. [...] We were just asking them to either stand and refuse to take their seats, or to refuse to do their seatbelts up and ask to see the Captain. And say they were concerned about this person.'

Despite the group's efforts and initial signs of success (several of the passengers had indicated that they would take the requested action), Greta later learnt that "they'd taken him on an earlier flight, an extremely long circuitous way". While Greta emphasized that she had learnt strategic lessons from this disappointment (next time, she told me, she would arrive at the airport early and stay all day) the sense of failure was difficult to carry. It was important to continue this work, Greta reflected, but feelings of grief, hopelessness and futility were never far away.

Hannah (Melbourne), who had been involved in numerous such actions, agreed. Sometimes a detainee would learn of their imminent deportation and there would be a "mass mad panic inside and outside [the detention facility] trying to organize legal representation, a protest or a vigil or blockade trying to stop their deportation", she explained. "We've delayed them by protesting and blockading the centre, but generally they win".

In the context of these difficult experiences, visitors reported a range of physical symptoms that betrayed high levels of distress, even when they were not fully aware of how traumatic their experiences had become. Sleep problems were extremely common and ranged from difficulties falling or staying asleep in the immediate aftermath of a visit to recurring nightmares and insomnia. It was also common for visitors to experience heightened emotionality, including periods when – in the privacy of their own homes – they were unable to stop crying. At times visitors struggled to concentrate at work or to meet family and social responsibilities because they felt so depleted from and defeated by their experiences in detention. Several visitors had received clinical diagnoses of depression, anxiety and/or PTSD which they attributed to their experiences in detention.

Ontological disruption

In addition to this sense of powerlessness, the detention visitation experience left many visitors experiencing what Kleber and colleagues (1992) describe as 'disruption'. That is, visitors felt disoriented and unsafe in their social worlds. Life no longer seemed secure in the ways it once had. This psychological concept of disruption bears striking resemblance to the more sociological notion of ontological insecurity. While the term ontological security – and its counterpoint ontological insecurity – was coined by a psychologist (Laing, 1990 [1960]), it was later taken up by Anthony Giddens (1991) and has inspired a diverse literature in the social and political sciences (Gustafsson and Krickel-Choi, 2020). Within this scholarship, ontological security usually refers to 'security not of the body but of the self, the subjective sense of who one is, which enables and motivates action and choice' (Mitzens, 2006: 344).

It was partly at this ontological level that immigration detention impacted visitors. As previously dependable principles like 'justice' broke down before them, visitors became aware of their own vulnerability, and of the instability of that which they had once taken for granted. As Snyder (2009: 110) puts it in his sociological study of trauma, visitors began to notice the 'cracks in the world through which violence can come rushing at you'.

Harmful institutions

While the specific injustices they had witnessed in detention weighted heavily on visitors' minds, the fact that these abuses had been able to take place at all was also a cause of stress. As they met people in detention and saw what detention really involved, Australian visitors became increasingly aware that their government was responsible for inexplicable human suffering. They also perceived that the government was getting away with its actions as institutions like the law and the media – not to mention the broader Australian community – failed to hold the government to account. As such, visitors began to wonder whether Australia was really as safe as they had once imagined.

Time and again, visitors described experiences of moral shock as they connected and reconnected with the reality that *their* country was perpetrating human rights abuses (McAdam and Chong, 2014). While most of the participants in this study had commenced visiting detention with a solid understanding of the asylum seeker issue, visitors nonetheless experienced moments of cognitive dissonance as abstract facts took physical form before them. In Melbourne, Louise recalled her shock the first time she saw a deportation notice – printed on "quality paper" and emblazed with the national emblem. "I couldn't believe that", she explained. "I think it was because it was so official. And this was Australia, *my* country. I had nightmares for a week after that".

The system's apparent lack of interest in the abuses it was perpetrating was also jarring for many. Numerous participants were incredulous, for instance, that people with serious mental illnesses were not only kept in detention, but were sometimes subject to even harsher conditions, such as solitary confinement. Visitors also described the sometimes horrific consequences of inadequate access to physical health care.

'A family that I'm supporting at the moment, where [the] dad's arm was broken on Christmas Island: it wasn't x-rayed, it was never reset. He was a professional sportsman back in Iran and his arm is now in need of fairly significant orthopaedic reconstruction. And I know we've got a waiting list for Queensland Health but he doesn't seem to be given the same or afforded the same level of care and concern that I would be as a citizen. And I just find that – those examples of injustice – really traumatic.' (Esme, Brisbane)

This apparent disregard for human life and well-being shocked many visitors, but also revealed a deeper and more distressing reality: this was a "scary" (Alma, Brisbane) system in which harm was the norm.

In Sydney, William illustrated this point with the story of a friend who was granted refugee status and told he would be released from detention shortly, only to be held in detention for an additional eight months.

'They just kept him there, kept them there, kept him there. […] They wouldn't let him out. And looking back now, part of it at least was they were waiting for the Governor General to sign the legislation that denied permanent protection. And as soon as that was signed they let him out. And he could then apply for a Temporary Protection Visa not a Permanent Protection Visa. Now if he'd been allowed to apply for his protection visa straight away he would have got permanent protection, now he's only got temporary protection. And we found out that was what was happening to a whole lot of people.'

The pain that his friend experienced, William insisted, was not an accidental oversight but a deliberate government attempt to skirt its obligations.

This experience of disruption was reinforced by visitors' own positioning as quasi-prisoners within detention. In Melbourne, Louise underlined the powerlessness she felt when she was declined entry to MITA and given no avenues of appeal.

'There was this whole system just against me and I had nowhere to go. They just said, "go home". "What? I'm an Australian citizen. I obey the law. I don't have criminal record and you're just saying I can't do this and I've got no options?" On reflection it was that disempowerment – taking away everything I had or thought I had. And that's I'd say similar to what they feel, but they feel it over a long period of time.'

Experiences like these allowed visitors to better understand their friends' circumstances, but they also contributed to a burgeoning ontological insecurity.

'I think when you're probably a bit of an idealist and you do think that we do live in a very fortunate country, and that we're a country of fairness, welcome and inclusivity and the rule of law applies, that there are processes to obtain justice, it can be shocking when it is clearly not the case. [...] [T]hat sense of justice has gone. That maybe avenues of appeal that feel – maybe they're not – but feel like they're open to me as a citizen. That people that are relying on us for support and who we are responsible for, and they're not afforded those same avenues of justice. I find that appalling and brutally confronting.' (Esme, Brisbane)

As Esme's aside – "maybe they're not" – suggests, the fact that Australia could withhold justice from people in its care caused some visitors to question whether they could trust the system to uphold their own rights either. If abuses like this were possible, their social world was not as secure as they had thought.

For many of the participants in the study, this growing sense of ontological danger was highly debilitating. Visitors felt anxious and unsafe, and struggled to contain fight-or-flight responses. They came to understand – in a newly embodied way – that the government's treatment of refugees and asylum seekers set a dangerous precedent. "When we allow our government to undermine [asylum seekers'] human rights," Siobhan (Perth) stressed, "governments then get used to that power and authority and control, and it then begins to bleed into other areas." The same systems that were used to harm asylum seekers could be (and, to some extent, already had been) used to harm them.

Complacent citizens

As described in Chapter One, the issue of 'the boats' has a long and contentious history in Australian politics. Asylum seekers have routinely been maligned as 'queue jumpers', 'economic migrants', criminals and potential terrorists, and numerous governments have achieved electoral success on the back of 'tough' policies to deter this foreign threat. Part of the disruption that visitors felt surrounding their experiences in detention concerned the public's general acceptance of the government's actions. Visitors observed that many Australians – including members of their own social circles – were complacent about the harm being inflicted in their name. Moreover, some of their acquaintances supported the government's hardline policies and saw detainees' suffering as an appropriate punishment for the perceived crime of entering Australian waters 'illegally'.

For visitors who had believed that Australia was a country of justice and human rights, the realization that their fellow Australians were unconcerned by what was happening in detention could be a source of anguish. Moina (Melbourne) explained that in her past work advocating for people with disabilities, exposing an injustice had typically been enough to change it. This was not the case where asylum seekers were concerned. Australians were unwilling or unable to see what was happening in detention, even when it was brought to their attention.

'You can see things that are wrong but that's the end of it. [...] To try to tell people how bad it is. It's almost impossible. Or else you sound like you're being fanatical. [Crying] [...] I always thought that if I saw something inhumane happen, if I could tell people that would be enough to change it. So that continually shocks me.' (Moina, Melbourne)

This complacency was a source of moral shock for many visitors, who felt increasingly alienated from their communities. Just as visitors lost faith in Australia's social institutions, so too did they begin to doubt the moral fortitude of their fellow Australians. Nathaniel (Melbourne) charged the Australian public with willful ignorance. "[I]t seems to me very much that people will pay a lot of money to not have to think about the 'problem' of refugees and asylum seekers", he noted. "They're quite happy for a government to throw vast amounts of money at putting people offshore or in detention centres".

Against this backdrop, visitors' attempts to raise awareness regarding the plight of asylum seekers were not always well received. In Sydney, Tanya explained that she lived in a conservative area, and that she had been derided and laughed at when she expressed solidarity with detainees. Robyn (Brisbane) had faced similar experiences. The secrecy that shrouded detention, she explained, made it harder to convince friends that conditions in the facilities were really *that bad*. When she told friends and acquaintances that the government was actively harming asylum seekers, many did not believe her.

'I'm not a conspiracy theorist. I'm not someone who thinks like that all the time. [...] Other people who I have things to do with don't believe it. Because this is Australia. Things like that don't happen in

Australia. And I think the complacency of other people really gets to me more than anything else.'

This mistrust, Robyn reflected, was hurtful.

'[If] you're an ambo or a firefighter, you're a hero. You're lorded by the community. You're doing wonderful work. How selfless and wonderful. If you're a refugee advocate, you're regarded with suspicion. [...] You're not just working in traumatic situations, but you're having to deal with that kind of vilification all the time.'

Many visitors thus found themselves feeling alone and misunderstood when they most needed support. As Lola (Melbourne) put it, "you end up feeling socially very disconnected".

In seeing the complacency and complicity of some Australians, visitors experienced a growing sense of isolation. Many Australian visitors also felt shame concerning their own status as citizens. Being a 'privileged Australian', innumerable interviewees told me, carried weight and guilt that they wished set down. Australian visitors understood that their dominant position in a system of oppression delivered unearned privileges, but they also felt the costs of these privileges for their own humanity and that of their society. Systems of oppression harm everyone, including their apparent beneficiaries (see Edwards, 2020; Edwards, 2006; Brod 1987). Visitors grieved for their country.

Visitor attrition

Against the backdrop of these emotional experiences, numerous interviewees recounted stories of fellow supporters who had stopped visiting detention because the personal toll was too great. Agnes (Sydney), who began visiting Villawood IDC around the turn of the century, had seen a lot of people "fall out along the way". "There were a lot [of visitors] after the *Tampa* crisis that just dropped away and stopped visiting", she recalled. "They just said, 'we can't cope, we can't cope'". Max (Brisbane) coordinated a visitation programme in Brisbane and had observed a similar trend.

'You are looking at people who are just about to give up hope. Have lost hope totally. People go along [to visit detention] and they hear these stories and they [...] say "what can I say to this person?" It can be very difficult and I think some people can do that for a while but after a while it gets to them and they have a break and come back, and then others feel like they'd rather just be working more on the campaign. Not having to face that sort of trauma.'

Ultimately, Max explained, a lot of people stopped visiting detention because "they found it too distressing".

In addition to describing this phenomenon with respect to fellow visitors, several participants reflected on their own difficult decisions to cease visiting detention. In Brisbane, Jodie explained that she had stepped back from visiting BITA because she "was just waking up crying at 3 o'clock in the morning". That didn't feel like a productive use of her energies. A friend of hers had stopped visiting for the "same exact reason". Tanya (Sydney) visited Villawood IDC for around eighteen months before she decided to stop.

> 'I was just too unhappy. And it's no good arriving and wanting to burst into tears. [...] I just felt like I was completely ineffective so there was no point my going. I was just too upset. [...] It was constantly in your mind. I don't think there's any other way is there. You could hardly come away and shut it off and get on with your life.'

Tanya had visited Villawood IDC until the emotional toll became too great. "I kept going as long as I could", she explained. Yet, like Robyn, Tanya felt significant shame regarding her decision to pull back. "I feel a failure. Truly. That I wasn't able to keep going", she confided. "And I sort of feel everyone who does keep going probably thinks of me as, 'oh, she probably just went along to see what it was like'".

This fear of judgement was a real concern for some individuals, who worried that any decision to prioritize their health might be read as a moral failure. Visitors were acutely aware that people incarcerated in detention facilities did not have the option of pulling back to prioritize their health.

> '[Y]ou only have to deal with it for a few hours, whereas your friends have to deal with it for years. And so while you're really uncomfortable with it or angry or frustrated [...] you also feel really guilty about complaining because in comparison to what other people put up with it's very little or it's in a very short period of time so you feel very conflicted.' (Imogen, Melbourne)

As Lisa (Sydney) explained, "they can't walk away. They've got to keep on keeping on so there's a bit of a psychological emotional pressure for you to keep on as well".

Yet long-term visitors were generally sympathetic towards those who pulled back. Escalating application and entrance processes, systematic disempowerment within detention spaces, and prolonged exposure to a traumatizing environment, they understood, had influenced these decisions. Just as the detention system sought to 'deter' current and prospective asylum seekers, so too did it work to deter the visitors who endeavoured to support them.

In Melbourne, Oliver spoke for many study participants when he explained that breaking visitors was part of a larger project of asylum seeker deterrence.

> 'They want to make life so unbearable for detainees that eventually they will crack and break and say, "well things back home in my home country are awful, I may be persecuted, I may face all sorts of horrible things. But being here is even worse. Being locked up indefinitely with no rights and no anything is even worse. So I'll go back". And I think for visitors it's the same. They want to make it harder and harder and tougher and tougher so that less and less people will visit. So that detainees will get less human contact, will get less support, will therefore have an even worse existence than they do to make it more likely that they will sign and say, you know, "I'm prepared to go back".'

Imogen (Melbourne) agreed.

> 'I think it's really intentional about making the experience of detention as unpleasant as possible. And if they can [...] decrease the amount of visitors, that's certainly making it more unpleasant for a lot of people in detention. The visitors' room is the only time that they can forget some of their concerns or have a little bit of fun or have some support from someone who genuinely cares about them as a person. And it's a really important part of their day or their week or however often they get visited. So I think it's targeted by authorities.'

As Frannie in Sydney reflected, "official documents all say that they want visitors to come and that it's good for the detainees, but [...] the way the system works tells a very different story". This was a designed system, and it was functioning to separate detainees from their sources of support.

Freedom of Information requests lodged as part of this study failed to deliver statistics regarding visitor numbers in Australian detention facilities. By all accounts, however, they have fallen dramatically under Operation Sovereign Borders. As Hannah (Melbourne) explained and innumerable interviewees corroborated, "[t]he amount of visitors has just dropped off".

Visitor endurance

Despite these concerted efforts to break visitors and end their resistance, a remarkable number of visitors managed to endure – continuing their detention centre visits, at least for a time. When asked how they were able to survive in these challenging conditions, visitors typically identified three main factors.

First and foremost, visitors stressed their commitment to and affection for specific people detained within the network. While they may not straightforwardly *want* to visit detention, participants told me, they would not abandon their friends and loved ones. By focusing on these relationships and allowing them to sustain them, many visitors were able to maintain their visits until the people they visited were released from detention, transferred interstate, or (in some cases) deported. At this junction, many took the opportunity to re-evaluate their activities and often transitioned into other forms of advocacy, such as supporting refugees and asylum seekers in the local community or participating in political protests.

Beyond the sustaining impact of personal relationships, some visitors found motivation in the fact that the system was actively working to repel them. As Oliver (Melbourne) told me, efforts to deter visitors could "cut both ways" – breaking some visitors but galvanizing others in continued action. If authorities did not want them to visit, these visitors deduced, their visits must *matter*.

In this context, visitors like Nathaniel (Melbourne) leant into feelings of anger, using them to combat despair and sustain ongoing resistance.

'I've seen many people who I started visiting with who just had to give up because they really can't cope with it. I use a judicious amount of anger because I say, "no, fuck you!" Because if the government puts in processes like this damned if they're going to stop me visiting somebody, because that's exactly what they would like. For less people to be in there. They would like them to be forgotten.'

Claire (Melbourne) observed that stubbornness could be a valuable asset in the fight against oppression. "A bit of it is probably sheer doggedness that they're not going to stop people like me going in. Sheer pigheadedness", she laughed. "I'll just keep doing it in spite of them". Understood in this way, activities like "jumping through [bureaucratic] hoops" (Imogen, Melbourne) took on new meaning. Where these activities had once been demoralizing, they were now reconceived as acts of resistance in a larger battle of wills.

Finally, visitors identified a third factor that helped them to sustain their visits: an unshakeable conviction that resisting immigration detention was the right thing to do. In Darwin, there was a time when Heather had worked more than 80 hours per week advocating for detained asylum seekers, on top of her regular employment and family commitment. This was a period, Heather explained, when people in detention were in particular need of visitors who could do the 'grunt work' of getting information and documentation to their legal teams; additionally, several detainees at the local centre were experiencing suicidal ideation and had turned to Heather for emotional support. It was "a complete mind fuck", Heather told me, but she "would do it again". When lives were at risk there was little alternative.

Heather was certainly not alone in this conviction. Lola (Melbourne) stressed that it was sometimes necessary to do hard things, simply because they were right.

> 'I think that my life is harder and sadder than it's been in a long time, but I also know that when my 80-year-old self looks at this time I'll be absolutely clear that I'm glad I did what I did.'

For visitors like these, the personal costs of visiting detention were considerable but giving up would be costlier still. To turn away would be a betrayal of themselves, their friends, and their principles. They could not blame others who pulled back, but resolved to continue, themselves, for as long as they were able to.

Conclusion

Australia's onshore immigration detention system harms the people detained within it. As this chapter has revealed, it also harms their loved ones and supporters. Within Australian detention centres, visitors encounter profound and preventable human suffering. They are frequently witness to large and small injustices, and they experience emotional anguish concerning their friends' circumstances. Additionally, the way that visitors are treated within these spaces adds to their distress. Experiences of perceived powerlessness and ontological disruption were almost ubiquitous in my interviews. Put differently, visitors routinely experienced detention facilities as traumatizing environments.

To say that visitors are harmed by detention, of course, it not to negate the reality that it is detainees themselves who are most acutely impacted by this system. Neither is it to suggest that visitors from the Global North are not also beneficiaries of the broader global political-economic system in which detention exists. What it is to say is that detention isn't *only* bad for the health of people in detention. It is also bad for detainees' friends, supporters and loved ones. And it is ultimately bad for the health of society at large.

To say that visitors are harmed by detention is also to foreground another mechanism though which people in detention are made to suffer. Visitor attrition was a recurring theme withing this study. Given the basic human need for social connection, as well as the roles visitors play in supporting detainees' resistance, institutional efforts to repel and deter visitors can compound the pain detainees already experience.

Conclusion: Tacit Intentionality and the Weaponization of Despair

Rebekah's story

It is 2019 and a beautiful day in Brisbane. I have come to the University of Queensland's leafy St Lucia campus to meet undergraduate student Rebekah. We sight each other through a crowd of students, then find a quiet picnic table to sit and talk. Rebekah is slightly built and softly spoken. Her face lights up when she talks about her best friend, Sahar.

The story of Rebekah's involvement with Australia's asylum seeker support movement is somewhat unique. She visited BITA once in 2013, she tells me, but logistical and health challenges made her involvement short-lived. Two years later, the issue found her again.

Rebekah was an inpatient in a local Brisbane hospital when she learnt that a young asylum seeker woman was receiving care in the same ward. The woman – Sahar – had been brought to Australia from Nauru for emergency treatment in the aftermath of a violent sexual assault. "She couldn't walk when she got here", Rebekah recalls. "She was in a wheelchair for a while. It was a locked ward, but she had guards".

In the weeks that followed, Rebekah made a concerted effort to befriend Sahar. When the Serco officers guarding Sahar forbade her from using the internet, Rebekah surreptitiously shared her mobile data. The two young women listened to music together and talked about their lives. "When we met, we were both in really awful situations", Rebekah tells me. "It really made such a difference having her. I just found that I connected with her like I hadn't really connected with other people before". When Sahar was discharged from hospital and taken to BITA, Rebekah promised to visit regularly.

Rebekah still remembers her first trip to visit Sahar at BITA. It was nothing short of devastating.

'I did everything wrong. I wasn't even wearing closed-in shoes and so [they said], "we can't let you in without closed-in shoes". But the lady [Serco officer] had a spare pair of flats. [...] And I brought all this food in in metal containers. "You can't take this in! What's this?" I brought in CDs and "no, you can't take these in. Haven't you been here before? Don't you know all this?" I was just in tears by the time I got in. [...] And then one of the guards said, "it's not going to be *like it was in hospital. [...] You're not going to be able to do the sorts of things that you did".'*

In the weeks and months that followed, Rebekah did her best to navigate BITA's rules. On her birthday, she brought her parents and siblings to the facility to meet Sahar and the family members who had accompanied her to Australia. Rebekah had to fight to convince the Serco guards that this group visit "fit with all [their] stupid rules", but she, her parents and her siblings were eventually allowed in.

> *'It was really good to be able to get everyone to meet. [...] That was before all the [fresh food] restrictions, so we brought in pizza, we brought in a cake. That was pretty good. You can't bring in metals, through, so I had a plastic cake slicer that I broke trying to cut the cake!'*

Rebekah laughs telling this story. It is a fond memory, but one that underlines the dissonance of the detention environment.

Today, Rebekah tells me, Sahar and her family are living in the community. While it's a relief to know that they are no longer imprisoned, Rebekah notes that Sahar's new life has not been without challenges. Sahar's brother was kept in detention for several months after she and her female relatives were released, and the strain this placed on the family was considerable. "[They] struggled to visit", Rebekah explains. "They found visiting the centre traumatic after their experiences, and I think it was also difficult for him to have them see him like that."

The family was also moved to another city upon their release, where they had no pre-existing support networks.

> *'Perhaps Immigration sent them [there] because that was where they had housing available – or for some other practical reason – but it felt like they were deliberately trying to cut [Sahar] and her family off from their support network, to sever the ties they had made with the Brisbane community.'*

Living in the community without permanent protection, income support, access to education or proximate friends is difficult, Rebekah stresses. Immigration detention is brutal, but the logic of deterrence extends far beyond detention centre walls. Both during and after detention, this is a system that breeds despair.

★★★

The human costs of immigration detention

Australia's mandatory detention policy has been widely criticized on multiple grounds. The policy itself has been condemned as a breach of the International Covenant on Civil and Political Rights and the Convention on the Rights of Persons with Disabilities, both of which prohibit arbitrary detention (AHRC, 2017a). The fact that the policy disproportionately affects maritime asylum seekers has been denounced a breach of the Convention relating to the Status of Refugees, which prohibits governments from discriminating against asylum seekers based on their means of arrival (Spinks and McCluskey, 2013). Further, Australia's policy of detaining children has been decried as a breach of the Convention on the Rights of the Child (AHRC, 2014).

Australia's detention policies have also been criticized for their impacts on people embroiled in this system. A growing body of research shows that Australia's detention system contributes to a range of physical and psychological illnesses and impairments, including depression, anxiety and PTSD, among other ailments (Steel et al,, 2006; Hadgkiss et al, 2012; Mares and Jureidini, 2004; Procter et al, 2013; Rivas and Bull, 2018). Children incarcerated in this system are also at heightened risk of physical, psychological and developmental problems (AHRC, 2014; Mares and Jureidini, 2004).

This book has made two key contributions to this body of scholarship. First, it has provided a new window into Australia's onshore immigration detention facilities, revealing the mechanisms through which harm is imposed within them. It has highlighted the plethora of micro-level deprivations and frustrations that shape detainees' lives in detention, asserting a debilitating asymmetry of power. It has also illuminated larger disruptions – such as the forced relocation of detainees between detention facilities – and shown how these practices intensify the vulnerability, isolation and desperation of detention spaces. The role of visitors within this regime has been a key concern for this book, as the study has drawn attention to a range of subtle but systematic attacks on detainees' sustaining relationships.

Second, this book has offered an expanded understanding of the human costs of detention by documenting the visitation experiences of detainees' friends and loved ones and exposing their impacts vis-à-vis visitor well-being. What is clear from these testimonies is that the difficulties associated with supporting people in detention extend beyond the anguish associated with witnessing trauma. The participants in this study – unlike the counsellors and care professionals evoked in most discussions of 'secondary trauma' (Dass-Brailsford and Thomley, 2012) – were not physically or temporally removed from the site of their friends' suffering. Neither were they emotionally distanced from the suffering they encountered. They visited within, contributed to and were affected by the very environments that have been shown to produce trauma in detainees. They were positioned within detention as quasi-inmates and experienced a diluted form of the pains of imprisonment as they tried, in the face of mounting institutional impediments, to support their friends in their everyday survival and resistance.

The emotional impacts of this disempowerment in the face of preventable suffering were considerable.

In presenting these findings, this book has also made a theoretical claim. By grounding this study in foundational social science research of carceral environments (see Chapter Two), it has framed detainee and visitor suffering as *intended* elements of the system's design. This concluding chapter returns to the question of intentionality, making the case for a bolder recognition of the *intentional* harms embedded in detention regimes.

Plain and tacit intentionality

In documenting the suffering caused by immigration detention, scholars have often avoided claiming that these harms are deliberate. It is common for researchers and even human rights organizations to frame the deleterious impacts of detention not as functions of these systems but as evidence of a need for reform. In the absence of physical evidence connecting detainees' suffering with explicit central directives, of course, intentionality is difficult to prove. Yet the question of intentionality is an important one as framing harms as unintended means obscuring lines of responsibility, culpability and vested interest, potentially depoliticizing harm and understating the obstacles to reform.

In some instances, harmful intent is plain to see, and it is difficult to conceptualize certain actions as anything other than deliberate attacks or reprisals. In these cases, the causal chain between a specific action and its adverse effects is so short – the relationship between a deed and its negative impacts so predictable – that any claim of 'unintended consequences' seems disingenuous at best. Instances of *plain intent*, as I term them, do occur in detention, and were regularly highlighted by participants in this study.

Interviewees used the language of intentionality to describe a number of *specific* cruelties they had witnessed in detention. Claims of this nature were particularly common with respect to forced relocations, where many visitors could point to particular transfer operations that appeared to have been carried out with punishment in mind. As Beth at BITA explained,

'If someone's giving too much trouble, they send them on a detention centre "holiday" where they get transferred to all the detention centres around and move them every couple of months. [...] [I]t really ends up breaking them.'

In these cases, visitors and detainees alike read plain intentionality into the actions of decision-makers.

Visitors evidenced this plain malintent with accounts of detainees being openly threatened with relocation if they did not comply with institutional directives. Often these threats surrounded detainees' everyday acts of resistance – for example, their participation in protests or their efforts to share their stories with the media.

> 'They're told – some of the ones who are more outspoken – "you better be careful what you say and how often you say it because we'll move you". Part of the punishment is people get moved from detention centre to detention centre to detention centre. So, some of them have been in three, four, more detention centres.' (Oliver, Melbourne)

The threatened transfers were generally to more remote or high-security facilities; threats of transfer to Christmas Island or Yongah Hill IDC were particularly insidious. The reprisal being threatened was thus greater isolation, as well as the comparative harshness that was possible in facilities with less visitor accountability than those on Australia's (highly populated) east coast.

A number of cases in the public domain provide further substantiation of these claims, suggesting that threats of this kind are far from hollow. In the first year of this study, for example, 21-year-old detainee Mojgan Shamsalipoor was moved from Brisbane to Darwin after completing an interview with Australia's national broadcaster, the Australian Broadcasting Corporation (ABC). At the time, Mojgan was in the final stages of completing her high school education through a local Brisbane school, and had special permission to leave BITA during the day to attend classes. Her relocation to Darwin took her away from both her Brisbane husband and her school community, triggering public outcry. As her young husband told the media at the time, "[t]hey were dragging her on the ground and [...] telling her she's going to be deported and separated from the husband and she's not going to be able to study anymore" (in Tlozek, 2015: np).

Another example from later in the study speaks to the ongoing use of the transfer process as a form of reprisal. In 2020, Iranian refugee and detainee Farhad Rahmati was transferred between detention facilities on two separate occasions. Both transfers occurred shortly after he spoke with the media. "I had an ABC interview on 11 June, and on the same day they removed me from Kangaroo Point [APOD to BITA]", Rahmati told Sydney Criminal Lawyers (in Gregoire, 2020: np). Several months later, Rahmati again spoke to the media. "I had another interview with the ABC and I was removed from BITA [to Villawood]". The timing of these relocations makes it difficult not to conclude that they were carried out with punishment in mind.

As Chapter Six documented, visitors also shared stories of friends being transferred at critical points in their legal cases. A Melbourne-based migration agent recalled an asylum seeker client being moved just weeks before a major legal hearing. Other visitors described friends being moved after their cases had been heard, when it became clear to the Department that their friends had strong support networks in the community and were gaining momentum surrounding their claims. As one Villawood IDC visitor explained regarding a friend who was relocated immediately after a "legal win", "[y]ou get the sense that they [moved him] because they saw how much support he had and wanted to move him away from that" (Frannie, Sydney). In these instances, relocations served not only to punish 'troublesome' detainees, but also to disadvantage specific asylum seekers in their protection claims.

Instances of this kind are notable because they make visible what I will refer to here as the *tacit intentionality* that underlies the detention system. By tacit intentionality, I mean the unstated aims that shape the structures, cultures and practices of this system, causing harms that are *simultaneously predictable and officially deniable*. Obvious acts of reprisal are not isolated incidents, but are entirely consistent with the more subtle, diffuse and relentless programme of cruelty that pervades this system. Tacit intentionality means that even when explicit directives are not issued, the detention system functions to impose politically expedient harm.

In the context of Australia's detention system, the evidence of tacit intent lies in the constellation of policies and practices mapped in this book. If considered individually, these examples might appear merely arbitrary or capricious. When examined as a whole, however, they exhibit a clear thematic coherence and functional unity with respect to the overarching objective of deterrence.

Deterrence, as conceptualized in this book, can take two forms. *General deterrence* involves efforts to discourage prospective asylum seekers from travelling to a country to claim protection. *Specific deterrence* involves pressuring asylum seekers who have already arrived in a country to abandon their refugee claims and return home. Political leaders on both sides of politics have been open in framing Australia's detention policies as an aspect of the country's programme of general deterrence. What has received less attention and less public acknowledgement, however, is the fact that the detention system also functions as a specific deterrent – working to coerce detainees to leave the country of their own volition. This function of the detention system cannot be openly acknowledged as Australia has obligations under international law to consider asylum seekers' protection claims and not return them to danger. Nonetheless, this book has demonstrated that Australia's detention regime exerts a constant coercive pressure on people who are detained, encouraging so-called voluntary repatriations by breeding despair.

This implicit goal of the detention system pervades its culture and operation. The use of prison contractor, Serco, to run Australia's detention system, for example, together with the embedding of detention policies within a discourse of national security, means that staff at these facilities are encouraged to view detainees as deserving of punishment. As one Serco guard (in The Global Mail, 2014: np) described his training experience in 2014,

'This guy came in and introduced himself as our trainer. His last job was in the prison system. He told us, "the only thing that's different is the clothes we let them wear". [...] That's the thing about this place. Serco is a company that runs prisons. That's what they do. [The trainer told us,] "Detention is part of Australia's border protection. If we didn't protect our borders we'd have a massive flow of people into the country and our quality of life would decline". It was clear from the first day of training what kind of culture they were trying to foster among their employees.'

For their part, the guard observed, Serco staff are highly invested in this portrayal of detainees as criminals and Others.

'My co-workers were good people but to be able to sleep at night they had to convince themselves that the people they were guarding were dangerous. None of the Serco staff had any understanding of what the people had been through before they arrived in Australia.'

Even when individual actions are not calculated to cause pain, this prevalent view of detainees as dangerous and undeserving influences behaviour. As long-term MITA visitors Claire reflected, "[t]hey're people that we're trying to dissuade from even coming here in the first place. In a culture of that kind anything gets past".

Statements from the Department of Immigration add to this picture, revealing an acceptance of human suffering as a necessary by-product of the detention system. Responding to AHRC concerns regarding forced relocations, for example, the Department insisted in 2019 that these transfers were necessary to manage cohort numbers and ensure individual detainees were placed in facilities with appropriate security features (Department of Home Affairs, 2019b: 2). The Department has acknowledged concerns regarding the deleterious impact of relocations on detainees' access to social, emotional, legal and medical support, but has dismissed these problems as unavoidable.

In making placement decisions, medical needs are given priority, and family and community links are carefully considered. In considering the placement of an individual, the broader immigration detention network (IDN) is also considered. There is finite capacity across the national network and there is often an operational need to transfer detainees to rebalance the network and ensure detention facility stability. This means that detainees cannot always be placed close to family links. (Department of Home Affairs, 2019a: 2)

As is often the case with bureaucratic language, the justificatory claims made here are difficult to interpret and even more difficult to challenge. The claim about 'rebalancing' a network with finite capacity appeals to resource limitations but seems particularly strained given the high cost of relocations. Yet what is perhaps most significant about statements of this kind is that the Immigration Department acknowledges awareness of the human costs of detention practices but justifies them as an 'operational necessity'. In other words, harm is *sanctioned*, here, as a tolerable cost of achieving the system's objectives (see Broom et al, Forthcoming).

The practices documented in this book are part of Australia's asylum seeker deterrence policy. They are key, if subtle, mechanisms through which isolation and desperation are produced and weaponized among unwanted immigrants. In practice, specific deterrence involves the production of hopelessness and despair, so that people fleeing violence and persecution in their countries of origin will elect to abandon their refugee claims and return to danger.

It is said that to will the end is to will the means. To will deterrence is to will and excuse immeasurable cruelty.

Notes

Introduction

[1] Australia is not the only country to hold asylum seekers outside or at the outskirts of its territory in order to limit their access to legal rights. The US's Guantanamo Bay has been used for similar purposes, with detainees held for years in harsh conditions while their asylum claims are assessed and 'third country' resettlement options explored (Dastyari, 2015; Hirsh and Bell, 2017). Navy and customs vessels in the US, Europe and Australia similarly intercept asylum seeker boats in international waters and prevent them from entering their territories (Schloenhardt and Craig, 2015; Dastyari, 2015; Fitzgerald, 2020); physical barriers, including border walls, block equivalent entrance via land routes (Hirsch and Bell, 2017). Legal strategies are also used to keep asylum seekers at bay. 'Destination' countries have at times forged agreements with the governments of transit countries, incentivizing them to ensure that the asylum seekers on route to their borders are not permitted to proceed (Hirsch and Bell, 2017; Nethery et al, 2013; Gammeltoft-Hansen and Hathaway, 2014). 'Remote control' strategies of this kind function to prevent forced migrants from accessing rights in the Global North and have become a cornerstone of many governments' efforts to filter and exclude undesired migrants (Fitzgerald, 2020).

[2] Non-refoulment is a fundamental principle of international human rights law. It forbids countries from returning asylum seekers to countries where they are likely to face persecution. It applies to all asylum seekers, irrespective of visa status or means of arrival.

[3] The majority of interviews took place in person in the interviewees' home cities; a small number occurred via phone. Most interviews lasted between 45 and 90 minutes. Interviews were semi-structured. Most questions were open in nature and designed to elicit narrative responses. Pseudonyms are used in this book to protect participants' privacy and that of the people they visit in detention.

[4] There are two main types of secure or 'closed' detention facilities in Australia's onshore system: Immigration Detention Centres (IDCs) and Immigration Transit Accommodations (ITAs). These labels denote different security conditions. IDCs 'are used for adults deemed to be "medium to high risk"', while ITAs 'have less intrusive security measures than IDCs' (AHRC, 2017a: 11) and are typically used to accommodate more vulnerable or 'low risk' individuals. In practice, IDCs and ITAs are very similar. In this book, the terms 'immigration detention centre' and 'immigration detention facility' are used interchangeably to refer to all closed detention facilities in the onshore network. Where individual detention facilities are discussed, their names are provided.

[5] In addition to these formal facilities, Australia at times uses APODs or 'flexible placement options' (Department of Home Affairs, 2018c) for detention purposes. Community locations such as aged care facilities, schools and hospitals have at times been used as APODs. During the study period, several commercial hotels were designated as APODs and used to hold dozens of detainees for extended durations.

Chapter 1

[1] While located on an Island, the Christmas Island facility is part of Australia's 'onshore' detention system, as it operates on an Australian territory, within the jurisdiction of Australia's courts.

[2] Under Howard's Pacific Solution, 1,637 asylum seekers were sent offshore for processing on PNG or Nauru. 70 per cent of these people were ultimately found to be refugees; of these, 705 (around 61 per cent) were quietly resettled in Australia (Phillips, 2015).

[3] In the interests of consistency, this book uses the term 'Immigration Department' – and, at times 'the Department' – to refer to the Australian Federal government department responsible for immigration. In reality, the name of this department has changed regularly over the years.

[4] Australia's *Migration Act* requires the detention of all unauthorised non-citizens. This includes people arriving without visas in search of asylum, as well as other immigrants who do not have permission to be in the country. Among this second cohort of detainees are people facing deportation under Section 501 of the *Migration Act* – that is, people whose visas have been cancelled on character grounds, including because of criminal misconduct. People whose visas have expired and those caught fishing illegally in Australian waters are at times also incarcerated.

Chapter 2

[1] Global inequalities also contribute to the production of refugees to begin with. Building on a long legacy of colonial domination, the global economic system facilitates the extraction of wealth from the Global South to the Global North and – to at least some extent – incentivises 'corrupt and oppressive national regimes' by delivering gains to leaders who facilitate economic exploitation (Pogge, 2005: 49). Yet as those fleeing social degradation in the wake of this wealth extraction come to realise, borders that are permeable to resources and financial assets are largely impenetrable for the human beings left behind. For scholars like Slavoj Zizek (2016: 45–6), this global system and the gross inequalities it perpetuates are not accidental:

> most refugees come from 'failed states', states where public authority is more or less inoperative, at least in large parts of the countries in question (Syria, Lebanon, Iraq, Libya, Somalia, Congo, and so on). In all these instances, this disintegration of state power is not purely a local phenomenon but the result of international economics and politics; in some cases, such as in Libya and Iraq, it is even a direct outcome of Western intervention. It is clear that this rise of 'failed states' in the late twentieth and twenty-first centuries is not an unintended misfortune; rather, it is one of the ways in which the great powers practise their economic colonialism.

This is a system where profit is routinely valued over (certain) human lives (Badiou, 2015; Smith, 2016).

Chapter 3

[1] Documents secured under Freedom of Information suggest that an application form did exist at this time, but it was seemingly being used primarily to record who was visiting detention, rather than to screen prospective visitors. The form asked only for basic details including the visitor's name, the person or people they were visiting, and the time and

purpose of their visit (GSL, 2003). There was no indication that it needed to be filled out in advance.

2   In Australia, points are allocated to different forms of identification. For example, passports and birth certificates are worth 70 points each; driving licences and tertiary student identification cards are worth 40 points each; utility bills, change of name certificates and marriage certificates are 25 points each. 100 point identification checks are usually only conducted when there is a perceived risk of identity theft or fraud, for example, when opening a bank account or applying for a driving licence.

3   While these new food rules were restrictive in themselves, they were at times enforced in legalistic ways. As John (Sydney) put it, "I wouldn't say some [officers] are flexible, but I would say that some are extremely rigid". John had himself argued with a guard regarding whether a protein drink (specifically requested by a health-conscious detainee) constituted 'milk' and should thus be rejected. The requirement to bring only commercially sealed items into the facilities was also escalated by some personnel, who asked visitors to open individually wrapped chocolate bars at reception and place them in clear zip-lock bags. The varying ways that rules were enforced made it difficult for visitors to know when officers were enforcing "legitimate rules" and when they were "just people asserting their power" (Chrissy, Melbourne). Feelings of frustration, humiliation and powerlessness – which would continue throughout the visitation experience – were common.

Chapter 4

1   The use of handcuffs in detention is a serious issue. The AHRC (2020: 65) notes that '[r]estraints can cause significant distress for some people in immigration detention, with some people reporting that they had refused to attend appointments (including medical appointments) due to advice from Serco that they would be restrained'. Being physically restrained can be particularly upsetting for people who have experienced trauma and torture in their country of origin.

Chapter 6

1   In February 2017, lawyers representing people in detention launched a federal court challenge to Australian Border Force's policy of confiscating detainees' mobile phones. The court ruled in the detainees' favour (Guardian, 2018). The Minister subsequently introduced legislation to parliament to reinstate the ban. The Bill passed the House of Representatives in February 2018 but lapsed before passing the Senate. In 2020, a revised version of the Bill was introduced to parliament but again failed to pass.

References

Abbott, T. (2013) 'Transcript of the Hon Tony Abbott MHR joint press conference with Mr Scott Morrison MHR Shadow Minister for Immigration and Citizenship, Melbourne', *Parliament of Australia, Parlinfo*, [online] 16 August, Available from: https://parlinfo.aph.gov.au/parlInfo/download/media/pressrel/2672160/upload_binary/2672160.pdf;fileType=application%2Fpdf#search=%22we%20determine%20who%20comes%20here%20abbott,%20tony,%20(former%20pm)%22 [Accessed 8 March, 2021].

Al Hussein, Z. R. (2014) 'Opening Statement by Zeid Ra'ad Al Hussein United Nations Human Rights Commissioner for Human Rights at the Human Rights Council 27th session', *Office of the High Commissioner for Human Rights*, (online) 8 September, Available from: OHCHR | Opening Statement by Zeid Ra'ad Al Hussein United Nations High Commissioner for Human Rights at the Human Rights Council 27th Session [Accessed 27 March 2021].

Albanese, A. (2005) 'Anti-terrorism bill no 2 2005: second reading speech', *Parliament of Australia, Parlinfo*, [online] 28 November, Available from: https://parlinfo.aph.gov.au/parlInfo/genpdf/chamber/hansardr/2005-11-28/0140/hansard_frag.pdf;fileType=application%2Fpdf [Accessed 8 March 2021].

Ali, M. (2021a) [Twitter] 30 July, Available from: https://twitter.com/MehdiAli98/status/1420921250335969282 [Accessed 7 December 2021].

Ali, M. (2021b) [Twitter] 7 October, Available from: https://twitter.com/MehdiAli98/status/1445770829476753423 [Accessed 7 December 2021].

Ali, M. (2021c) [Twitter] 2 October, Available from: https://twitter.com/MehdiAli98/status/1444185495940993030 [Accessed 7 December 2021].

Ali, M. (2021d) 22 November, Available from: https://twitter.com/MehdiAli98/status/1462637868967333891 [Accessed 11 December 2021].

Amnesty International Australia (2017) 'Submission to the Legal and Constitutional Affairs Legislation Committee Inquiry into the Migration Amendment (Prohibiting Items in Immigration Detention Facilities) Bill 2017', *Amnesty International Australia*, [online] 13 October, Available from: https://www.amnesty.org.au/wp-content/uploads/2017/11/Senate-Committee-Migration-Amendment-Items-in-Detention-facilities-submission-1.pdf [Accessed 8 March 2021].

Anderson, T. (2002) 'Solidarity activism, identity politics and popular education', *The Koori History Website*, [online] Available from: http://www.kooriweb.org/foley/resources/story18.html [Accessed 8 March 2021].

Arendt, H. (1963) *Eichmann in Jerusalem: A Report on the Banality of Evil*, New York: The Viking Press.

Asylum Seeker Resource Centre, Save the Children and GetUp (2019) 'At what cost? The human and economic costs of Australia's offshore detention policies 2019', *Asylum Seeker Resource Centre*, [online] Available from: https://www.asrc.org.au/wp-content/uploads/2013/04/1912-At-What-Cost-report.pdf [Accessed 27 March 2021].

Augoustinos, M. and Quinn, C. (2003) 'Social categorization and attitudinal evaluations: illegal immigrants, refugees, or asylum seekers?' *Nouvelle Revue de Psychologie* 2(1): 29–37.

Auslander, L. and Zahra, T. (2018) 'The things they carried: war, mobility, and material culture', in L. Auslander and T. Zahra (eds) *Objects of War: The Material Culture of Conflict and Displacement*, Ithaca: Cornell University Press, pp. 1–22.

Australian Bureau of Statistics (ABS) (2021) 'Corrective Services Australia', *Australian Bureau of Statistics*, [online] March, Available at https://www.abs.gov.au/statistics/people/crime-and-justice/corrective-services-australia/latest-release [Accessed 4 June 2021].

Australian Border Force (ABF) (2016) 'Changes to the food policies in immigration detention facilities', *Department of Home Affairs*, [Released under the *Freedom of Information Act* 1982] May.

Australian Border Force (ABF) (2018a) 'Immigration detention facility visiting multiple detainees request form', *Australian Border Force*, [online] February, Available at https://www.abf.gov.au/what-we-do-subsite/files/visiting-multiple-detainees-request-form.pdf [Accessed 8 March 2021].

Australian Border Force (ABF) (2018b) 'Immigration detention facility conditions of entry form', *Department of Home Affairs*, [Released under the *Freedom of Information Act* 1982] January.

Australian Border Force (ABF) (2020) 'Visit detention: apply to visit', *Australian Border Force*, [online] 17 March, Available from: https://www.abf.gov.au/about-us/what-we-do/border-protection/immigration-detention/visit-detention/apply-to-visit [Accessed 8 March 2021].

Australian Greens (2020) 'Australian Greens dissenting report: Migration Amendment (Prohibiting Items in Immigration Detention Facilities) Bill 2020', *Parliament of Australia*, [online] Available from: https://www.aph.gov.au/Parliamentary_Business/Committees/Senate/Legal_and_Constitutional_Affairs/ProhibitedItems/Report/section?id=committees%2freportsen%2f024483%2f73521#footnote33target [Accessed 27 March 2021].

Australian Human Rights Commission (AHRC) (2008) 'Immigration detention report: summary of observations following visits to Australia's immigration detention facilities', *Australian Human Rights Commission*, [online] December, Available from: https://www.refworld.org/docid/4a2e34692.html [Accessed 8 March 2021].

Australian Human Rights Commission (AHRC) (2014) 'The forgotten children: national inquiry into children in immigration detention', *Australian Human Rights Commission*, [online] November, Available from: https://www.humanrights.gov.au/our-work/asylum-seekers-and-refugees/publications/forgotten-children-national-inquiry-children [Accessed 8 March 2021].

Australian Human Rights Commission (AHRC) (2017a) 'Asylum seekers, refugees and human rights: snapshot report', *Australian Human Rights Commission*, [online] 30 March, Available from: https://www.humanrights.gov.au/our-work/asylum-seekers-and-refugees/publications/asylum-seekers-refugees-and-human-rights-0 [Accessed 8 March 2021].

Australian Human Rights Commission (AHRC) (2019a) 'Risk management in immigration detention', *Australian Human Rights Commission*, [online] May, Available from: https://www.humanrights.gov.au/our-work/asylum-seekers-and-refugees/publications/risk-management-immigration-detention-2019 [Accessed 8 March 2021].

Australian Human Rights Commission (AHRC) (2019b) 'Use of force in immigration detention', *Australian Human Rights Commission*, [online] May, Available from: https://www.humanrights.gov.au/our-work/asylum-seekers-and-refugees/publications/use-force-immigration-detention [Accessed 8 March 2021].

Australian Human Rights Commission (AHRC) (2020) 'Inspections of Australia's immigration detention facilities 2019 report', *Australian Human Rights Commission,* [online] December, Available from: https://humanrights.gov.au/our-work/asylum-seekers-and-refugees/publications/inspections-australias-immigration-detention [Accessed 8 March 2021].

Australian Law Reform Commission (2017) 'Pathways to justice: an inquiry into the incarceration rate of Aboriginal and Torres Strait Islander peoples', *Australian Government*, [online] Available from: https://www.alrc.gov.au/wp-content/uploads/2019/08/final_report_133_amended1.pdf [Accessed 14 March 2022].

Baaz, M., Heikkinen, S. and Lilja, M. (2017) 'Editorial', *Journal of Political Power* 10(2): 127–32.

Badiou, A. (2015) *Our Wound is Not So Recent: Thinking the Paris Killings of 13 November*. London: Polity Press.

Bailey, A. (2017) 'The migrant suitcase: food, belonging and commensality among Indian migrants in the Netherlands', *Appetite* 110: 51–60.

Banks, G. and McGregor, A. (2011) 'Pacific "solutions" and imaginaries: reshaping Pacific relations or re-colonising the "Sea of Islands"', *Asia Pacific Viewpoint* 52(3): 233–5.

Bashford, A. and Strange, C. (2002) 'Asylum-seekers and national histories of detention', *Australian Journal of Politics and History* 48(4): 509–27.

Beaugrand, C. (2011) 'Statelessness and administrative violence: *Biduns'* survival strategies in Kuwait', *The Muslim World* 101(April): 228–50.

Baumer, E. P., O'Donnell, I. and Hughes, N. (2009) 'The porous prison: A note on the rehabilitative potential of visits home', *The Prison Journal* 89(1): 119–26.

Benisty, M., Bensimon, M. and Ronel, N. (2020) 'Familial pains of imprisonment: the experience of parents and siblings of incarcerated men', *Victims and Offenders*, 16(2): 247–65.

Berger, R. (2015) *Stress, Trauma, and Posttraumatic Growth: Social Context, Environment, and Identities*, Florence: Taylor and Francis.

Berlant, L. (2004) 'Introduction: compassion (and withholding)', in L. Berlant (ed) *Compassion: The Culture and Politics of an Emotion*, New York: Routledge, pp. 1–15.

Billings, P. (2019) *Crimmigration in Australia: Law, Politics and Society*, Singapore: Springer.

Bloomfield, A. (2016) 'Alternatives to detention at the crossroads: humanisation or criminalisation?' *Refugee Survey Quarterly* 35(1): 29–46.

Boochani, B. (2017) 'A message from Behrouz Boochani – Kurdish refugee and independent journalist', *Asylum Seeker Resource Centre*, [online] 28 November, Available from: https://asrc.org.au/2017/11/28/message-behrouz-boochani-kurdish-refugee-independent-journalist/ [Accessed 8 November 2021].

Boochani, B. (2018a) *No Friend but the Mountains: Writing from Manus Prison*, Sydney: Pan Macmillan Australia.

Boochani, B. (2018b) 'Manus prison poetics/our voice: revisiting 'A Letter From Manus Island', a reply to Anne Surma', *Continuum*, 32(4): 527–31.

Boochani, B., Doherty, B. and Evershed, N. (2017) 'Revealed: year-long campaign to make conditions harsher for Manus refugees', *The Guardian*, [online] 17 May, Available from: https://www.theguardian.com/austra lia-news/2017/may/17/revealed-year-long-campaign-to-make-conditi ons-harsher-for-manus-refugees?CMP=Share_iOSApp_Other [Accessed 8 March 2021].

Bosworth, M. (2014) *Inside Immigration Detention*, Oxford: Oxford University Press.

Bosworth, M. and Turnbull, S. (2014) 'Immigration detention, punishment and the criminalization of migration', in S. Pickering and J. Ham (Eds) *The Routledge Handbook on Crime and International Migration*, London: Routledge, pp. 91–106.

Braman, D. (2007) *Doing Time on the Outside: Incarceration and Family Life in Urban America*, Ann Arbor, MI: University of Michigan Press.

Briskman, L. (2013) 'Technology, control, and surveillance in Australia's immigration detention centres', *Refuge* 29(1): 9–19.

Briskman, L., Latham, S. and Goddard, C. (2008) *Human Rights Overboard: Seeking Asylum in Australia*, Australia: Scribe.

Brod, H. (1987) 'A case for men's studies', in M.S. Kimmel (Ed) *Changing Men: New Directions in Research on Men and Masculinity*, Beverly Hills: Sage Publications, pp. 263–77.

Brodkin, E. Z. and Majmundar, M. (2010) 'Administrative exclusion: organizations and the hidden costs of welfare claiming', *Journal of Public Administration Research and Theory* 20(4): 827–48.

Broom, A., Peterie, M., Kenny, K., Ramia, G. and Ehlers, N. (2022) 'The administration of harm: From unintended consequences to harm by design', *Critical Social Policy*, [online] Available from: https://doi.org/10.1177/02610183221087333 [Accessed 19 April 2022].

Bull, M., Schindeler, E., Berkman, D. and Ransley, J. (2012) 'Sickness in the system of long-term immigration detention', *Journal of Refugee Studies* 26(1): 47–68.

Byrne, J., Kras, K. R. and Marmolejo, L. M. (2019) 'International perspectives on the privatization of corrections', *Criminology and Public Policy* 18: 477–503.

Canning, V. (2019) 'Degradation by design: women and asylum in northern Europe', *Race and Class* 61(1): 46–63.

Chauka, Please Tell Us the Time (2017) [Film] Sarvastani, A. K. and Boochani, B. (dir.) Netherlands, Australia and Papua New Guinea: Sarvin Productions.

Chee-Beng, T. (2015) 'Commensality and the organization of social relations', in S. Kerner, C. Chou and M. Warmind (eds) *Commensality: From Everyday Food to Feast*, London: Bloomsbury, pp. 18–31.

Christian, J. (2005) 'Riding the bus: barriers to prison visitation and family management strategies', *Journal of Contemporary Criminal Justice* 21(1): 31–48.

Christian, J., Mellow, J. and Thomas, S. (2006) 'Social and economic implications of family connections to prisoners', *Journal of Criminal Justice* 34(4): 443–52.

Clyne, M. (2005) 'The use of exclusionary language to manipulate opinion: John Howard, asylum seekers and the reemergence of political incorrectness in Australia', *Journal of Language and Politics* 4(2): 173–96.

Coalition (2013) 'The Coalition's policy for a regional deterrence framework to combat people smuggling', *Parliament of Australia, Parlinfo*, [online] August, Available from: https://parlinfo.aph.gov.au/parlInfo/search/display/display.w3p;query=Id:%22library/partypol/2686733%22 [Accessed 25 March 2021].

Coffey, G. J., Kaplan, I., Sampson, R. C. and Montagna Tucci, M. (2010) 'The meaning and mental health consequences of long-term immigration detention for people seeking asylum', *Social Science and Medicine* 70(12): 2070–9.

Cohen, K. and Collens, P. (2013) 'The impact of trauma work on trauma workers: a metasynthesis on vicarious trauma and vicarious posttraumatic growth', *Psychological Trauma: Theory, Research, Practice, and Policy* 5(6): 570–80.

Cohen, S. and Taylor, L. (1972) *Psychological Survival: The Experience of Long-Term Imprisonment*, Baltimore: Penguin Books.

Comfort, M. (2003) 'In the tube at San Quentin: the "secondary prisonization" of women visiting inmates', *Journal of Contemporary Ethnography* 32(1): 77–107.

Comfort, M. (2008) *Doing Time Together: Love and Family in the Shadow of the Prison*, Chicago and London: The University of Chicago Press.

Commonwealth of Australia (2019) 'Senate legal and constitutional affairs legislation committee migration amendment (repairing medical transfers) bill 2019 [provisions] report', *Commonwealth of Australia*, [online] October, Available from: https://www.aph.gov.au/Parliamentary_Business/Committees/Senate/Legal_and_Constitutional_Affairs/RepairMedicaltransfers/Report [Accessed 20 December 2021].

Commonwealth Ombudsman (2020a) 'Monitoring immigration detention: review of the Ombudsman's activities in overseeing immigration detention July–December 2019', *Commonwealth Ombudsman*, [online] Available from https://www.ombudsman.gov.au/__data/assets/pdf_file/0015/111390/Six-monthly-immigration-detention-report-Jul-Dec-2019.pdf [Accessed 8 March 2021].

Commonwealth Ombudsman (2020b) 'Immigration detention oversight: review of the Ombudsman's activities in overseeing immigration detention – January to June 2019', *Commonwealth Ombudsman*, [online] Available from: https://www.ombudsman.gov.au/__data/assets/pdf_file/0017/109700/Immigration-Detention-Oversight-Report_January-to-June-2019.pdf [Accessed 8 March 2021].

Conlon, D. and Hiemstra, N. (eds) (2017a) *Intimate Economics of Immigration Detention: Critical Perspectives*, Abingdon and New York: Routledge.

Conlon, D. and Hiemstra, N. (2017b) 'Mobility and materialisation of the carceral', in J. Turner and K. Peters (eds) *Carceral Mobilities: Interrogating Movement in Incarceration*, London and New York: Routledge, pp. 100–14.

Cox, A. (2011) 'Doing the programme or doing me? The pains of youth imprisonment', *Punishment and Society* 13(5): 592–610.

Crewe, B. (2011) 'Depth, weight, tightness: revisiting the pains of imprisonment', *Punishment and Society* 13(5): 509–29.

Crewe, B., Hulley, S. and Wright, S. (2017) 'The gendered pains of life imprisonment', *The British Journal of Criminology* 57(6): 1359–78.

Darling, J. (2011) 'Giving space: care, generosity and belonging in a UK asylum drop-in centre', *Geoforum* 42(4): 408–17.

Dass-Brailsford, P. and Thomley, R. (2012) 'An investigation of secondary trauma among health volunteers after Hurricane Katrina', *Journal of Systematic Therapies* 31(3): 36–52.

Dastyari, A. (2015) *United States Migrant Interdiction and the Detention of Refugees in Guantanamo Bay*, New York: Cambridge University Press.

Deci, E. L. and Ryan, R. M. (2014) 'The importance of universal psychological needs for understanding motivation in the workplace', in M. Gagne (ed) *The Oxford Handbook of Work Engagement, Motivation and Self-Determination Theory*, Oxford: Oxford University Press, 13–32.

Department of Home Affairs (2018a) 'Immigration detention and community statistics summary', *Australian Government*, [online] 31 January, Available from: https://www.homeaffairs.gov.au/research-and-stats/files/immigrat ion-detention-statistics-31-january-2018.pdf [Accessed 26 March 2021].

Department of Home Affairs (2018b) 'Detention services manual: visitor management, procedural instruction', *Department of Home Affairs*, [Released under the *Freedom of Information Act* 1982] 12 January.

Department of Home Affairs (2018c) 'Detention services manual: detainee placement – Alternative Places of Detention', *Department of Home Affairs*, [Released under the *Freedom of Information Act* 1982] 3 October.

Department of Home Affairs (2019a) 'Answer to question on notice 221: 2019–2020 supplementary budget estimates', *Parliament of Australia*, [online] 21 October, Available from https://www.aph.gov.au/Parliamenta ry_Business/Senate_estimates/legcon/2019-20_Supplementary_Budget_ Estimates [Accessed 25 March 2021].

Department of Home Affairs (2019b) 'Home Affairs response to the Australian Human Rights Commission (AHRC) risk management in detention report, 2019', *Australian Government*, [online] Available from: https://www.humanrights.gov.au/sites/default/files/home_affairs_ response_ahrc_risk_report2019.pdf [Accessed 8 March 2021].

Department of Home Affairs (2020) 'Transfers to Australia for medical treatment or as accompanying family', *Department of Home Affairs*, [Released under the *Freedom of Information Act* 1982] 23 October.

Department of Home Affairs (2021a) 'Immigration detention and community statistics summary', *Australian Government*, [online] 31 August, Available from: https://www.homeaffairs.gov.au/research-and-stats/files/immigrat ion-detention-statistics-31-august-2021.pdf [Accessed 4 January 2022].

Department of Home Affairs (2021b) 'Immigration detention and community statistics summary', *Australian Government*, [online] 31 January, Available from: https://www.homeaffairs.gov.au/research-and-stats/files/immigrat ion-detention-statistics-31-january-2021.pdf [Accessed 25 March 2021].

Department of Immigration and Border Protection (2015a) 'Detention services manual', *Department of Home Affairs*, [Released under the *Freedom of Information Act* 1982] 1 September.

Department of Immigration and Border Protection (2015b) 'Immigration detention and community detention statistics', *Australian Government*, [online] 31 January, Available from: https://www.homeaffairs.gov.au/resea rch-and-stats/files/immigration-detention-statistics-jan2015.pdf [Accessed 8 March 2021].

Department of Immigration and Citizenship (2013) 'Immigration detention statistics summary', *Australian Government*, [online] 31 January, Available from: https://www.homeaffairs.gov.au/research-and-stats/files/immigrat ion-detention-statistics-20130131.pdf [Accessed 8 March 2021].

Dilts, A. (2012) 'Revisiting Johan Galtung's concept of structural violence', *New Political Science* 34(2): 191–4.

Disney, T. (2017) 'The orphanage as an institution of coercive mobility', *Environment and Planning A: Economy and Space* 49(8): 1905–21.

Doherty, B. (2016) 'Doctors refuse to discharge "baby Asha" because of fears for safety on Nauru', *The Guardian* [online] 12 February, Available from: https://www.theguardian.com/australia-news/2016/feb/12/doct ors-refuse-to-discharge-baby-asha-because-of-fears-for-safety-on-nauru [Accessed 8 March 2021].

Doherty, B. (2018a) 'Hamid Kehazaei: Australia responsible for "preventable" death of asylum seeker', *The Guardian*, [online] 30 July, Available from: https://www.theguardian.com/australia-news/2018/jul/30/death-asylum-seeker-hamid-kehazaei-preventable-coroner-says [Accessed 8 March 2021].

Doherty, B. (2018b) 'Coroners examine deaths in Australian immigration detention', *The Guardian*, [online] 30 July, Available from: https://www. theguardian.com/australia-news/2018/jul/30/coroners-examine-deaths-in-australian-immigration-detention [Accessed 8 March 2021].

Doherty, B. (2020) 'The Iranian refugee writing songs of love from his "luxury torture cell"', *The Guardian*, [online] 28 May, Available from: https://www.theguardian.com/news/2020/may/28/the-iranian-refugee-writing-songs-of-love-from-his-luxury-torture-cell [Accessed 7 June 2021].

Doherty, B. (2021) '"Time can break your heart": The harsh toll of eight years in Australian immigration detention', *The Guardian*, [online] 1 November, Available from: https://www.theguardian.com/australia-news/2021/nov/01/time-can-break-your-heart-the-harsh-toll-of-eight-years-in-australian-immigration-detention

Doherty, B. and Davidson, H. (2016) 'Somali refugee in critical condition after setting herself alight on Nauru', *The Guardian*, [online] 3 May, Available from: https://www.theguardian.com/australia-news/2016/may/03/somali-refugee-in-critical-condition-after-setting-herself-alight-on-nauru [Accessed 8 March 2021].

Dreby, J. (2012) 'The burden of deportation on children in Mexican immigrant families', *Journal of Marriage and Family* 74(4): 829–45.

Dunn, K. M., Klocker, N. and Salabay, T. (2007) 'Contemporary racism and Islamaphobia in Australia: racializing religion', *Ethnicities* 7(4): 564–89.

Edgemon, T. G. and Clay-Warner, J. (2019) 'Inmate mental health and the pains of imprisonment', *Society and Mental Health* 9(1): 33–50.

Edwards, K. (2006) 'Aspiring social justice ally identity development: a conceptual model', *NASPA Journal* 43(4): 36–60.

Edwards, S. (2020) 'Building solidarity with religious minorities: a reflective practice for aspiring allies, accomplices, and coconspirators', *Religion and Education*.

Eisenkraft Klein, D. and Madureira Lima, J. (2021) 'The prison industrial complex as a commercial determinant of health', *American Journal of Public Health* 111(10): 1750–2.

Eldridge, E. and Reinke, A. (2018) 'Introduction: ethnographic engagement with bureaucratic violence', *Conflict and Society* 4(1): 94–98.

Elliott, J. (2005) *Using Narrative in Social Research: Qualitative and Quantitative Approaches*, London: SAGE Publications.

Erickson, J. (2012) 'Volunteering with refugees: neoliberalism, hegemony, and (senior) citizenship', *Human Organization* 71(2): 167–75.

Essex, R. (2019) 'Should clinicians boycott Australian immigration detention', *Journal of Medical Ethics* 45(2): 79–83.

Essex, R. (2020) *The Healthcare Community and Australian Immigration Detention*, Singapore: Palgrave Macmillan.

Evans, C. (2008) 'Refugee policy under the Rudd Government – the first year: address to the Refugee Council of Australia', *Parliament of Australia, Parlinfo*, [online] 17 November, Available from: https://parlinfo.aph.gov.au/parlInfo/download/media/pressrel/QNAW6/upload_binary/qnaw60.pdf;fileType=application%2Fpdf#search=%22media/pressrel/QNAW6%22 [Accessed 25 March 2021].

Evershed, N., Liu, R., Farrell, P. and Davidson, H. (2016) '*The Nauru files: the lives of asylum seekers in detention detailed in a unique database*', The Guardian, [online] 10 August, Available from https://www.theguardian.com/australia-news/ng-interactive/2016/aug/10/the-nauru-files-the-lives-of-asylum-seekers-in-detention-detailed-in-a-unique-database-interactive [Accessed 8 March 2021].

Every, D. and Augoustinos, M. (2007) 'Constructions of racism in the Australian parliamentary debates on asylum seekers', *Discourse and Society* 18(4): 411–36.

Every, D. and Augoustinos, M. (2008) '"Taking advantage" or fleeing persecution? Opposing accounts of asylum seeking', *Journal of Sociolinguistics* 12(5): 648–67.

Farrell, P., Evershed, N. and Davidson, H. (2016) 'The Nauru files: cache of 2,000 leaked reports reveal scale of abuse on children in Australian offshore detention', *The Guardian,* [online] 10 August, Available from https://www.theguardian.com/australia-news/2016/aug/10/the-nauru-files-2000-leaked-reports-reveal-scale-of-abuse-of-children-in-australian-offshore-detention [Accessed 8 March 2021].

Farrington, K. (1992) 'The modern prison as total institution? Public perception versus objective reality', *Crime and Delinquency* 38(1): 6–26.

Figley, C. R. (2012) *Encyclopedia of Trauma: An Interdisciplinary Guide*, Los Angeles: SAGE Reference.

Figley, C. R., and Kleber, R. J. (1995) 'Beyond the "victim": secondary traumatic stress', in R. J. Kleber, C. R. Figley and P. R. Berthold Gersons (eds) *Beyond Trauma: Cultural and Societal Dynamics*, New York: Plenum Press, 75–98.

Fischler, C. (2011) 'Commensality and the organization of social relations', in S. Kerner, C. Chou and M. Warmind (eds.) *Commensality: From Everyday Food to Feast*, London: Bloomsbury, pp. 18–31.

Fiske, L. (2016) *Human Rights, Refugee Protest and Immigration Detention*, London: Springer.

Fitzgerald, D. S. (2020) 'Remote control of migration: theorising territoriality, shared coercion, and deterrence', *Journal of Ethnic and Migration Studies* 46(1): 4–22.

Flanagan, T. (1980) 'The pains of long term imprisonment: a comparison of British and American perspectives', *British Journal of Criminology* 20(2): 148–156.

Fleay, C. (2015) 'The limitations of monitoring immigration detention in Australia', *Australian Journal of Human Rights* 21(1): 21–46.

Fleay, C. and Briskman, L. (2013) 'Hidden men: bearing witness to mandatory detention in Australia', *Refugee Survey Quarterly* 32(3): 112–29.

Flynn, C. (2014) 'Getting there and being there: visits to prisons in Victoria – the experiences of women prisoners and their children', *Probation Journal* 61(2): 176–191.

Follis, L. (2015) 'Power in motion: tracking time, space, and movement in the British penal estate', *Environment and Planning D: Society and Space*, 33(5): 945–62.

Foster, C. (2021) [Twitter] 1 December, Available from: https://twitter.com/Craig_Foster/status/1465784652589789184 [Accessed 11 December 2021.

Foucault, M. (1975) 'Michel Foucault, on the role of prisons', *The New York Times*, [online] 5 August, Available from: https://www.nytimes.com/1975/08/05/archives/michel-foucault-on-the-role-of-prisons.html [Accessed 20 April 2021].

Foucault, M. (1980) *Power/Knowledge: Selected Interviews and Other Writings 1972–1977*, New York: Panetheon Books.

Foucault, M. (1995 [1975]) *Discipline and Punish: The Birth of the Prison*, New York: Vintage Books.

Galtung, J. (1969) 'Violence, peace, and peace research', *Journal of Peace Research* 6(3): 167–91.

Gammeltoft-Hansen, T. and Hathaway, J. C. (2014) 'Non-refoulement in a world of cooperative deterrence', *Columbia Journal of Transnational Law* 53(2): 235–84.

Gammeltoft-Hansen, T. and Tan, N. F. (2017) 'The end of the deterrence paradigm? Future directions for global refugee policy', *Journal on Migration and Human Security* 5(1): 28–56.

Garcia Hernandez, C. C. (2011) 'Due process and immigrant detainee prison transfers: moving LPRs to isolated prisons violates their right to counsel', *Berkeley La Raza Law Journal* 21: 17–60.

Gelber, K. (2003) 'A fair queue? Australian public discourse on refugees and immigration', *Journal of Australian Studies* 27(77): 23–30.

Gerver, M. (2017) 'Paying refugees to leave', *Political Studies* 65(3): 631–645.

Ghezelbash, D. (2020) '*How refugees succeed in visa reviews: new research reveals the factors that matter*', *The Conversation*, [online] 10 March, Available from: https://theconversation.com/how-refugees-succeed-in-visa-reviews-new-research-reveals-the-factors-that-matter-131763 [Accessed 8 March 2021].

Giddens, A. (1991) *Modernity and Self-Identity: Self and Society in the Late Modern Age*, Stanford, CA: Stanford University Press.

Gill, N. (2009) 'Governmental mobility: the power effects of the movement of detained asylum seekers around Britain's detention estate', *Political Geography* 28(3): 186–96.

Gill, N. (2013) 'Mobility versus liberty? The punitive uses of movement within and outside carceral environments', in D. Moran, N. Gill and D. Conlon (eds) *Carceral Spaces: Mobility and Agency in Imprisonment and Migrant Detention*, London and New York: Routledge, pp. 19–35.

Gillard, J. (2010) 'Moving Australia forward: Lowy Institute, Sydney', *Parliament of Australia, Parlinfo*, [online] 6 July, Available from: https://parlinfo.aph.gov.au/parlInfo/download/media/pressrel/IE8X6/upload_binary/ie8x60.pdf;fileType=application%2Fpdf#search=%22media/pressrel/IE8X6%22 [Accessed 25 March 2021].

Gillespie, E. (2021) '"Like a new person": refugee Moz freed after eight years in detention', *SBS The Feed*, [online] Available from: https://www.sbs.com.au/news/the-feed/like-a-new-person-refugee-moz-freed-after-eight-years-in-detention [Accessed 7 June 2021].

Gleeson, M. (2016) *Offshore: Behind the Wire on Nauru and Manus*, Sydney: NewSouth Publishing.

Global Detention Project (2016) 'United States immigration detention', *Global Detention Project*, [online] Available from: https://www.globaldetentionproject.org/countries/americas/united-states [Accessed 22 April 2021].

Global Detention Project (2018) 'France immigration detention', *Global Detention Project*, [online] Available from: https://www.globaldetentionproject.org/countries/europe/france [Accessed 22 April 2021].

Goffman, E. (1961) *Asylums: Essays on the Social Situation of Mental Patients and Other Inmates*, London: Penguin Books.

Golash-Boza, T. (2019) 'Punishment beyond the deportee: the collateral consequences of deportation', *American Behavioral Scientist* 63(9): 1331–49.

Golash-Boza, T. and Hondagneu-Sotelo, P. (2013) 'Latino immigrant men and the deportation crisis: a gendered racial removal program', *Latino Studies* 11(3): 271–92.

Gonzalez, G. and Patler, C. (2020) 'The educational consequences of parental immigration detention', *Sociological Perspectives*.

Gosden, D. (2007) 'From humanitarianism to human rights and justice: a way to go', *Australian Journal of Human Rights* 13(1): 149–76.

Greenfield, E. A. and Marks, N. F. (2004) 'Formal volunteering as a protective factor for older adults' psychological well-being', *The Journals of Gerontology* 59(5): S258–S264.

Gregoire, P. (2020) 'Punishing, silencing and detaining the innocent: An interview with Refugee Farhad Rahmati', *Sydney Criminal Lawyers*, [online] 9 September, Available from: https://www.sydneycriminallawyers.com.au/blog/punishing-silencing-and-detaining-the-innocent-an-interview-with-refugee-farhad-rahmati/ [Accessed 11 December 2021].

Grimm, R., Spring, K. and Dietz, N. (2007) 'The health benefits of volunteering: a review of recent research', *Corporation for National and Community Service*, [online] April, Available from: https://www.nationalservice.gov/pdf/07_0506_hbr.pdf [Accessed 8 March 2021].

GSL (2003) *'Detention services visits application form', Department of Home Affairs*, [Released under the *Freedom of Information Act* 1982], 23 October.

Guardian (2018) 'Asylum seeker detainees can keep mobile phones, federal court rules', *The Guardian*, [Online] 22 June, Available from: https://www.theguardian.com/australia-news/2018/jun/22/asylum-seeker-detainees-can-keep-mobiles-phones-federal-court-rules [Accessed 12 December 2021].

Gustafsson, K. and Krickel-Choi, N. C. (2020) 'Returning to the roots of ontological security: insights from the existentialist anxiety literature', *European Journal of International Relations* 26(3): 875–95.

Gutierrez Rivera, L. (2017) 'The world of the "rondines": trust, waiting, and time in a Latin American prison', in J. Turner and K. Peters (eds) *Carceral Mobilities: Interrogating Movement in Incarceration*, London and New York: Routledge, pp. 178–90.

Hadgkiss, E., Lethborg, C., Al-Mousa, A. and Marck, C. (2012) 'Asylum seeker health and wellbeing: scoping study', *St Vincent's Health Australia*, [online] September, Available from: http://www.mhima.org.au/pdfs/asylum%20seeker%20health%20and%20wellbeing.pdf [Accessed 13 August 2018].

Hand, G. (1992) 'Second reading speech: Migration Amendment Bill 1992', *Parliament of Australia, Parlinfo*, [online] 5 May, Available from: https://parlinfo.aph.gov.au/parlInfo/search/display/display.w3p;page=0;query=%22The%20Government%20is%20determined%20that%20a%20clear%20signal%20be%20sent%20that%20migration%20to%20Australia%20may%20not%20be%20achieved%20by%20simply%20arriving%20in%20this%20country%20and%20expecting%20to%20be%20allowed%20into%20the%20community%22;rec=1;resCount=Default [Accessed 25 March 2021].

Harlow, R., and Cantor, N. (1996) 'Still participating after all these years: a study of life task participation in later life', *Journal of Personality and Social Psychology* 71(6): 1235–49.

Hashman, N. (2016) 'Detention centre workers suffering their own trauma dealing with asylum seekers', *The Sydney Morning Herald*, [online] 26 February. Available from: http://www.smh.com.au/federal-politics/political-news/detention-centre-workers--suffering-their-own-trauma-in-dealing-with-asylum-seekers-20160225-gn3buk.html [Accessed 8 March 2021].

Hashman, N., Ting, I., Muller, S. and Hall, B. (2016) 'Australia's harshest detention centre revealed', *The Sydney Morning Herald*, [online] 21 January, Available from: https://www.smh.com.au/politics/federal/australias-harshest-detention-centre-revealed-20160121-gmapbd.html [Accessed 8 March 2021].

Hassan, L. (2000) 'Deterrence measures and the preservation of asylum in the United Kingdom and United States', *Journal of Refugee Studies* 13(2): 184–204.

Hatton, T. and Lim, A. (2005) 'Australian asylum policy: the *Tampa* effect', *Agenda* 12(2): 115–30.

Heckert, C. (2020) 'The bureaucratic violence of the health care system for pregnant immigrants on the United States-Mexico border', *Human Organization* 79(1): 33–42.

Hedrick, K. (2017) 'Getting out of (self-) harm's way: a study of factors associated with self-harm among asylum seekers in Australian immigration detention', *Journal of Forensic and Legal Medicine* 49(July): 89–93.

Hedrick, K., Armstrong, G., Coffey, G. and Borschmann, R. (2019) 'Self-harm in the Australian asylum seeker population: a national records-based study', *Population Health* 8: 1–9.

Held, V. (2004) 'Care and justice in the global context', *Ratio Juris* 17(2): 141–55.

Herzog, A. R., Franks, M. M., Markus, H. R. and Holmberg, D. (1998) 'Activities and well-being in older age: effects of self-concept and educational attainment', *Psychology and Aging* 13(2): 179–85.

Hiemstra, N. (2013) '"You don't even know where you are": chaotic geographies of US migrant detention and deportation', in D. Moran, N. Gill and D. Conlon (eds) *Carceral Spaces: Mobility and Agency in Imprisonment and Migrant Detention*, London and New York: Routledge, pp. 58–75.

Hirsch, A. L. and Bell, N. (2017) 'The right to have rights as a right to enter: addressing a lacuna in the international refugee protection regime', *Human Rights Review* 18(4): 417–37.

Hoggett, P. (2006) 'Pity, compassion, solidarity', in S. Clarke, P. Hoggett and S. Thompson (eds) *Emotion, Politics and Society*, UK: Palgrave MacMillan, pp. 145–161.

Hughes, M. (2019) 'The social and cultural role of food for Myanmar refugees in regional Australia', *Journal of Sociology* 55(2): 290–305.

Holt, R. (2019) 'A horror week in Australian onshore detention', *Crikey*, [online] 19 July, Available from: https://www.crikey.com.au/2019/07/19/immigration-detention-centre-week/ [Accessed 8 March 2021].

Howard, J. (2001a) 'Interview with Jon Faine, Radio 3LO, Melbourne', *Australian Government Department of the Prime Minister and Cabinet*, [online] 9 October, Available from: https://pmtranscripts.pmc.gov.au/release/transcript-12120 [Accessed 8 March 2021].

Howard, J. (2001b) 'Campaign launch speeches: address at the Federal Liberal Party campaign launch, Sydney', *Parliament of Australia, Parlinfo*, [online] 28 October, Available from: https://parlinfo.aph.gov.au/parlInfo/download/library/partypol/1178395/upload_binary/1178395.pdf;fileType=application%2Fpdf#search=%22we%20will%20decide%20who%20comes%20to%20this%20country%20and%20the%20circumstances%20in%20which%20they%20come%202000s%202001%22 [Accessed 25 March 2021].

Howard, J. (2001c) 'Transcript of the prime minister the Hon. John Howard MP press conference, Melbourne', *Parliament of Australia, Parlinfo*, [online] 7 November, Available from: https://parlinfo.aph.gov.au/parlInfo/download/media/pressrel/SWC56/upload_binary/swc561.pdf;fileType=application%2Fpdf#search=%22no%20way%20howard%20terrorist%22 [Accessed 25 March 2021].

Human Rights and Equal Opportunity Commission (2004) 'A last resort: national inquiry into children in immigration detention', *Human Rights and Equal Opportunity Commission*, [online] April, Available from: https://humanrights.gov.au/our-work/asylum-seekers-and-refug ees/publications/last-resort-national-inquiry-children-immigration [Accessed 8 March 2021].

Hurst, D. (2014) 'Scott Morrison sees detaining children as a "consequence" of border protection', *The Guardian*, (Online) 22 August, Available from: https://www.theguardian.com/world/2014/aug/22/scott-morri son-sees-detaining-children-as-a-consequence-of-border-protection [Accessed 24 March 2021].

Hutchinson, E. (2014) 'A global politics of pity? Disaster imagery and the emotional construction of solidarity after the 2004 Asian tsunami', *International Political Sociology* 8(1): 1–19.

Hynes, M. (2013) 'Reconceptualizing resistance: sociology and the affective dimension of resistance', *The British Journal of Sociology* 64(4): 559–577.

Ibsen, A. (2013) 'Ruling by favors: prison guards' informal exercise of institutional control', *Law and Social Inquiry* 38(2): 342–63.

Ichikawa, M., Nakahara, S. and Wakai, S. (2006) 'Effect of post-migration detention on mental health among Afghan asylum seekers in Japan', *Australian and New Zealand Journal of Psychiatry* 40(4): 341–6.

Immigration National Office (2013) 'Detention services manual', *Department of Home Affairs*, [Released under the *Freedom of Information Act* 1982] 16 August.

Jupp, J. (2002) *From White Australia to Woomera: The Story of Australian Immigration*, New York: Cambridge University Press.

Kathrani, P. (2011) 'Asylum law or criminal law: blame, deterrence and the criminalisation of the asylum', *Jurisprudence* 18(4): 1543–54.

Keller, A. S., Rosenfeld, B., Trinh-Shvin, C., Meserve, C., Sachs, E. et al, (2003) 'The mental health of detained asylum seekers', *Lancet* 362(9397): 1721–3.

Kenny, M. A., Procter, N. and Grech, C. (2016) 'Mental health and legal representation for asylum seekers in the "legacy caseload"', *Cosmopolitan Civil Societies* 8(2): 84–103.

Khorana, S. (2018) *The Tastes and Politics of Inter-Cultural Food in Australia*. London: Rowman and Littlefield Publishers.

Kleber, R. J., Brom, D. and Defares, P. B. (1992) *Coping with Trauma: Theory, Prevention, and Treatment*, Amsterdam: Swets and Zeitlinger.

Klocker, N. and Dunn, K. M. (2003) 'Who's driving the asylum debate? Newspaper and government representations of asylum seekers', *Media International Australia* 109(1): 71–92.

Korf, B. (2007) 'Antinomies of generosity: moral geographies and post-tsunami aid in Southeast Asia', *Geoforum* 38(2): 366–78.

Kox, M., Boone, M. and Staring, R. (2020) 'The pains of being unauthorised in the Netherlands', *Punishment and Society* 22(4): 534–52.

Laing, R. D. (1990 [1960]) *The Divided Self: An Existential Study in Sanity and Madness*, London: Penguin Books.

Lange, C., Kamalkhani, Z. and Baldassar, L. (2007) 'Afghan Hazara refugees in Australia: constructing Australian citizens', *Social Identities* 13(1): 31–50.

Lanskey, C., Lösel, F., Markson, L. and Souza, K. (2018) 'Prisoners' families, penal power, and the referred pains of imprisonment', in R. Condry and P. Scharff Smith (eds) *Prisons, Punishment, and the Family: Towards a New Sociology of Punishment?* UK: Oxford University Press, pp. 181–95.

Leerkes, A. and Broeders, D. (2010) 'A case of mixed motives? Formal and informal function of administrative immigration detention', *The British Journal of Criminology* 50(5): 830–50.

Leerkes, A., van Os, R. and Boersema, E. (2017) 'What drives "soft deportation"? Understanding the rise of assisted voluntary return among rejected asylum seekers in the Netherlands', *Population, Space and Place* 23(8): 1–11.

Li, S., Liddell, B. and Nickerson, A. (2016) 'The relationship between post-migration stress and psychological disorders in refugees and asylum seekers', *Current Psychiatry Rep* 18(9): 82–91.

Lietaert, I., Broekaert, E. and Derluyn, I. (2015) 'The lived experiences of migrants in detention', *Population, Space and Place* 21: 568–79.

Loff, B., Snell, B., Creati, M. and Mohan, M. (2002) '"Inside" Australia's Woomera detention centre', *The Lancet* 359: 683.

Longazel, J., Bergman, J. and Fleury-Steiner, B. (2016) 'The pains of immigrant imprisonment', *Sociology Compass* 10(11): 989–98.

Lynch, P. and O'Brien, P. (2001) 'From dehumanisation to demonisation: the MV *Tampa* and the denial of humanity', *Alternative Law Journal* 26(5): 215–18.

MacKellar, M. (1977) 'News conference with the Minister for Immigration and Ethnic Affairs, the Hon. Michael J. R. Mackellar', *National Archives of Australia*, [M4452] 8 December.

Maglen, K. (2007) 'Inside truths: "truth" and mental illness in the Australian asylum seeker and detention debates', *The Mental Health of Detained Asylum Seekers* 26(4): 47–66.

Mahamede, J. (2021a) [Twitter] 27 July, Available from: https://twitter.com/jalal_mahamede/status/1419901464932065283 [Accessed 11 December 2021].

Mahamede, J. (2021b) [Twitter] 25 July, Available from: https://twitter.com/jalal_mahamede/status/1419233873431392259 [Accessed 11 December 2021].

Manne, R. (2013) 'Australia's shipwrecked refugee policy', *The Monthly*, [online] March, Available from: https://www.themonthly.com.au/australia-s-shipwrecked-refugee-policy-tragedy-errors-guest-7637#mtr [Accessed 8 March 2021].

Mares, P. (2002) *Borderline: Australia's Response to Refugees and Asylum Seekers in the Wake of the Tampa*. Sydney: University of New South Wales Press.

Mares, S. (2021) 'Mental health consequences of detaining children and families who seek asylum: a scoping review', *European child and Adolescent Psychiatry* 30: 1615–39.

Mares, S. and Jureidini, J. (2004) 'Psychiatric assessment of children and families in immigration detention: clinical, administrative and ethical issues', *Australian and New Zealand Journal of Public Health* 28(6): 520–6.

Marr, D. and Wilkinson, M. (2003) *Dark Victory: How A Government Lied its Way to Political Triumph*. Sydney: Allen and Unwin.

Martin, C. A (2020) 'Jumping the queue? The queue-jumping metaphor in Australian press discourse on asylum seekers', *Journal of Sociology*.

Martin, G. (2015) 'Stop the boats! Moral panic in Australia over asylum seekers', *Continuum* 29(3): 304–22.

Martin, L. (2019) 'Carceral mobility and flexible territoriality in immigration enforcement', in K. Mitchell, R. Jones and J. L. Fluri (eds) *Handbook on Critical Geographies of Migration*, Cheltenham and Northampton: Edward Edgar Publishing, pp. 244–54.

Martin, L. L. and Mitchelson, M. L. (2009) 'Geographies of detention and imprisonment: interrogating spatial practices of confinement, discipline, law, and state power', *Geography Compass* 3(1): 459–77.

Martinez, L. M. and Ortega, D. M. (2019) 'Dreams deterred: the collateral consequences of localized immigration policies on undocumented Latinos in Colorado', *Law and Policy* 41(1): 120–41.

Masi, C. M., Hsi-Yuan Chen, H., Hawkley, L. and Cacioppo, J. T. (2011) 'The meta-analysis of interventions to reduce loneliness', *Personality and Social Psychology Review* 15(3): 219–66.

MC, A. (2021) 'Medically vulnerable refugees in Australia hotels finally freed', *Aljazeera*, [online] 22 January, Available from: https://www.aljazeera.com/news/2021/1/22/medically-vulnerable-refugees-in-australia-hotels-finally-freed [Accessed 7 June 2021].

McAdam, J. and Chong, F. (2014) *Refugees: Why Seeking Asylum is Legal and Australia's Policies Are Not*. Sydney: UNSW Press.

McHugh-Dillon, H. (2015) 'If they are genuine refugees, why? Public attitudes to unauthorised arrivals in Australia', *The Victorian Foundation for Survivors of Torture*, [online] 16 November, Available from: https://www.foundationhouse.org.au/wp-content/uploads/2015/07/Public-attitudes-tounauthorised-arrivals-in-Australia-Foundation-House-review-2015.pdf [Accessed 8 March 2021].

McKay, F. H., Thomas, S. L. and Kneebone, S. (2011) 'It would be okay if they came through the proper channels: community perceptions and attitudes towards asylum seekers in Australia', *Journal of Refugee Studies* 25(1): 113–33.

McLoughlin, P. and Warin, M. (2008) 'Corrosive places, inhuman spaces: mental health in Australian immigration detention', *Health and Place* 14(2): 254–64.

McMaster, D. (2002a) *Asylum Seekers: Australia's Response to Refugees.* Melbourne: Melbourne University Press.

McMaster, D. (2002b) 'Asylum-seekers and the insecurity of a nation', *Australian Journal of International Affairs* 56(2): 279–90.

McPherson, M., Smith-Lovin, L. and Cook, J. M. (2001) 'Birds of a feather: homophily in social networks', *Annual Review of Sociology* 27(1): 415–4.

Michalon, B. (2013) 'Mobility and power in detention: the management of internal movement and governmental mobility in Romania', in D. Moran, N. Gill and D. Conlon (eds) *Carceral Spaces: Mobility and Agency in Imprisonment and Migrant Detention*, London and New York: Routledge, 37–55.

Mitzen, J. (2006) 'Ontological security in world politics: state identity and the security dilemma', *European Journal of International Relations* 12(3): 341–70.

Moran, D. (2013) 'Between inside and outside? Prison visiting rooms as liminal carceral spaces', *GeoJournal* 78(2): 339–51.

Moran, D. (2016) *Carceral Geography: Spaces and Practices of Incarceration*, London and New York: Routledge.

Moran, D. (2017) 'Foreword', in J. Turner and K. Peters (eds) *Carceral Mobilities: Interrogating Movement in Incarceration*, London and New York: Routledge, pp. xxi–xxii.

Moran, D., Conlon, D. and Gill, N. (eds) (2013) *Carceral Spaces: Mobility and Agency in Imprisonment and Migrant Detention*, London and New York: Routledge.

Moran, D., Piacentini, L. and Pallot, J. (2012) 'Disciplined mobility and carceral geography: prisoner transport in Russia', *Transactions of the Institute of British Geographers* 37(3): 446–60.

Morina, N., Kip, A., Hoppen, T. H., Priebe, S. and Meyer, T. (2021) 'Potential impact of physical distancing on physical and mental health: a rapid narrative umbrella review of meta-analyses on the link between social connection and health', *BMJ Open* 11(3): 1–11.

Morris, B. S., Chrysochou, P., Dalgaard Christensen, J., Orquin, J. L., Barraza, J., Zak, P. J. and Mitkidis, P. (2019) 'Stories vs facts: triggering emotion and action-taking on climate change', *Climate Change* 154: 19–36.

Morrison, S. (2019) 'Transcript radio interview with Oliver Peterson, 6PR', *Parliament of Australia*, [online] 22 October, Available from: https://parli nfo.aph.gov.au/parlInfo/download/media/pressrel/6983402/upload_bin ary/6983402.pdf;fileType=application%2Fpdf#search=%22medivac%20 faking%20morrison%22 [Accessed 25 March 2021].

Moss, P. (2015) 'Review into recent allegations relating to conditions and circumstances at the Regional Processing Centre in Nauru: final report', *Department of Home Affairs*, [online] 6 February, Available from: https:// www.homeaffairs.gov.au/reports-and-publications/reviews-and-inquir ies/departmental-reviews/independent-reviews-regional-processing-cen tre-nauru#content-index-1 [Accessed 8 March 2021].

Mountz, A. (2013) 'On mobilities and migrations', in D. Moran, N. Gill and D. Conlon (eds) *Carceral Spaces: Mobility and Agency in Imprisonment and Migrant Detention*, London and New York: Routledge, pp. 13–18.

Mountz, A., Coddington, K., Catania, R. T. and Loyd, J. M. (2012) 'Conceptualizing detention: mobility, containment, bordering, and exclusion', *Progress in Human Georgraphy* 37(4): 522–41.

Murray, R. (2019) 'Exploring the banality of bureaucracy in carceral states', in C. V. Zanini and L. Bhuiyan (Eds) *This Thing of Darkness: Shedding Light on Evil*, Oxford: Inter-Disciplinary Press, pp. 72–82.

Nare, L. (2020) '"Finland kills with a pen": asylum seekers' protest against bureaucratic violence as politics of human rights', *Citizenship Studies* 24(8): 979–993.

Neil, D. and Peterie, M. (2018) 'Grey networks: the contradictory dimensions of Australia's immigration detention system', *Asia Pacific Viewpoint* 59(1): 132–44.

Neil, D. and Peterie, M. (Forthcoming) 'Asylum seekers, healthcare and the right to have rights: the political struggle over Australia's "medevac" laws', in P. Billings (Ed.) *Regulating Refugee Protection Through Social Welfare Provision*, Routledge.

Nethery, A. (2019) 'Australia's refugee detention regime: offshore and unaccountable', *Current History September*, 118(809): 221–8.

Nethery, A. and Holman, R. (2016) 'Secrecy and human rights abuses in Australia's offshore immigration detention centres', *The International Journal of Human Rights* 20(7): 1018–38.

Nethery, A., Rafferty-Brown, B. and Taylor, S. (2013) 'Exporting detention: Australia-funded immigration detention in Indonesia', *Journal of Refugee Studies* 26(1): 88–109.

Nethery, A. and Silverman, S. (eds) (2015) *Immigration Detention: The Migration of a Policy and its Human Impact*, London and New York: Routledge

Newman, L. K., Dudley, M. and Steel, Z. (2008) 'Asylum, detention, and mental health in Australia', *Refugee Survey Quarterly* 27(3): 110–27.

Newman, L. K. and Steel, Z. (2008) 'The child asylum seekers: psychological and developmental impact of immigration detention', *Child and Adolescent Psychiatric Clinics of North America* 17(3): 665–83.

Ntoumanis, N., Ng, J. Y. Y., Prestwich, A., Quested, E., Hancox, J. E., Thøgersen-Ntoumani, C., Deci, E. L., Ryan, R. M., Lonsdale, C. and Williams, G. C. (2020) 'A meta-analysis of self-determination theory-informed intervention studies in the health domain: effects on motivation, health behaviour, physical, and psychological health', *Health Psychology Review*.

O'Malley, N. (2019) 'The 8000 "forced movements" on Australian flights in two years', *The Sydney Morning Herald*, [online] 7 September, Available from: https://www.smh.com.au/politics/federal/the-8000-forced-movements-on-australian-flights-in-two-years-20190906-p52oq8.html [Accessed 8 March 2021].

Ortiz, J. M. and Jackey, H. (2019) 'The system is not broken, it is intentional: the prisoner re-entry industry as deliberate structural violence', *The Prison Journal* 99(4): 484–503.

Papastergiadis, N. (2004) 'The invasion complex in Australian political culture', *Thesis Eleven* 78(8): 8–27.

Patler, C. and Branic, N. (2017) 'Patterns of family visitation during immigration detention', *The Russell Sage Foundation Journal of the Social Sciences* 3(4): 18–36.

Pedersen, A., Watt, S. and Hansen, S. (2006) 'The role of false beliefs in the community's and the federal government's attitudes towards Australian asylum seekers', *Australian Journal of Social Issues* 41(1): 105–24.

Peters, K. and Turner, J. (2017) 'Carceral mobilities: a manifesto for mobilities, an agenda for carceral studies', in J. Turner and K. Peters (eds) *Carceral Mobilities: Interrogating Movement in Incarceration*, London and New York: Routledge, pp. 1–14.

Peterie, M. (2017) 'Docility and desert: government discourses of compassion in Australia's asylum seeker debate', *Journal of Sociology* 53(2): 351–66.

Peterie, M. (2018a) 'Technologies of control: asylum seeker and volunteer experiences in Australian immigration detention facilities', *Journal of Sociology* 55(2): 181–98.

Peterie, M. (2018b) 'Deprivation, frustration, and trauma: immigration detention centres as prisons', *Refugee Survey Quarterly* 37(3): 279–306.

Peterie, M. and Neil, D. (2020) 'Xenophobia towards asylum seekers: a survey of social theories', *The Journal of Sociology* 56(1): 23–35.

Phillips, J. (2015) 'Asylum seekers and refugees: what are the facts?', *Parliament of Australia*, [online] 2 March, Available from: https://www.aph.gov.au/about_parliament/parliamentary_departments/parliamentary_library/pubs/rp/rp1415/asylumfacts [Accessed 8 March 2021].

Phillips, J. (2017) 'Boat arrivals and boat 'turnbacks' in Australia since 1976: a quick guide to the statistics', *Parliament of Australia*, [online] 17 January, Available from: https://www.aph.gov.au/About_Parliament/Parliament ary_Departments/Parliamentary_Library/pubs/rp/rp1617/Quick_Gui des/BoatTurnbacks [Accessed 8 March 2021].

Phillips, J. and Spinks, H. (2013) 'Immigration detention in Australia', *Parliament of Australia* [online] 20 March, Available from: https://www. aph.gov.au/About_Parliament/Parliamentary_Departments/Parliament ary_Library/pubs/BN/2012-2013/Detention [Accessed 8 March 2021].

Pickering, S. (2001) 'Common sense and original deviancy: news discourses and asylum seekers in Australia', *Journal of Refugee Studies* 14(2): 169–86.

Poertner, E. (2017) 'Governing asylum through configurations of productivity and deterrence: effects on the spatiotemporal trajectories of cases in Switzerland', *Geoforum* 78: 12–21.

Pogge, T. (2005) 'Real world justice', *The Journal of Ethics* 9(1/2): 29–53.

Poynting, S. (2002) ' "Bin Laden in the suburbs": attacks on Arab and Muslim Australians before and after 11 September', *Current Issues in Criminal Justice* 14(1): 43–64.

Poynting, S., Noble, G., Tabar, P. and Collins, J. (2004) *Bin Laden in the Suburbs: Criminalising the Arab Other*, Sydney: Sydney Institute of Criminology.

Procter, N. G., De Leo, D. and Newman, L. (2013) 'Suicide and self-harm prevention for people in immigration detention', *Medical Journal of Australia* 199(11): 730–1.

Procter, N. G., Kenny, M.A., Eaton, H. and Grech, C. (2018) 'Lethal hopelessness: Understanding and responding to asylum seeker distress and mental deterioration', *International Journal of Mental Health Nursing* 27: 448–454.

Public Interest Advocacy Centre (2021) 'Healthcare denied: Medevac and the long wait for essential medical treatment in Australian immigration detention', *Public Interest Advocacy Centre* [online] December, Available from: https://piac.asn.au/wp-content/uploads/2021/12/PIAC_Medevac-Report_2021_IssueE_03122150-1-1.pdf [Accessed 9 December 2021].

Pugliese, J. (2008) 'The tutelary architecture of immigration detention prisons and the spectacle of "necessary suffering"', *Architectural Theory Review* 13(2): 206–221.

Puthoopparambil, S.J., Maina Ahhlberg, B. and Bjerneld, M. (2015) ' "It is a thin line to walk on": challenges of staff working at Swedish immigration detention centres', *International Journal of Qualitative Studies in Health and Well-being* 10(1): 1–11.

Rackley, E.B. (2002) *Solidarity and the Limits of Humanitarianism: A Critique of Humanitarian Reason* [Dissertation], New School for Social Research.

Rae, M., Holman, R. and Nethery, A. (2018) 'Self-represented witnessing: the use of social media by asylum seekers in Australia's offshore immigration detention centres', *Media, Culture and Society* 40(4): 479–95.

Rae, M., Holman, R. and Nethery, A. (2019) 'Earwitnessing detention: carceral secrecy, affecting voices, and political listening in *The Messenger* podcast', *International Journal of Communication* 13: 1036–55.

Refugee Council of Australia (RCOA) (2017) 'Unwelcome visitors: challenges faced by people visiting immigration detention', *Refugee Council of Australia*, [online] 2 August, Available from: https://www.refugeecouncil.org.au/publications/reports/detention-visitors/ [Accessed 8 March 2021].

Refugee Council of Australia (RCOA) (2019) 'Submission to the Inquiry on the Migration Amendment (Repairing Medical Transfers) Bill 2019 [Provisions], Submission 43', *Senate Standing Committees on Legal and Constitutional Affairs*, [online] Available from: https://www.aph.gov.au/Parliamentary_Business/Committees/Senate/Legal_and_Constitutional_Affairs/RepairMedicaltransfers/Submissions [Accessed 8 March 2021].

Refugees, Survivors and Ex-Detainees (RISE) (2020) 'Ex-detainees' demands', *Refugees, Survivors and Ex-Detainees*, [online] 9 January, Available from: http://riserefugee.org/exdetaineesdemands/ [Accessed 8 March 2021].

Reinke, A. (2018) 'The bureaucratic violence of alternative justice', *Conflict and Society* 4(1): 135–50.

Richards, B. (1978) 'The experience of long-term imprisonment: an exploratory investigation', *British Journal of Criminology* 18(2): 162–9.

Rivas, L. and Bull, M. (2018) 'Gender and risk: an empirical examination of the experiences of women held in long-term immigration detention in Australia', *Refugee Survey Quarterly* 37: 307–27.

Robjant, K., Hassan, R. and Katona, C. (2009) 'Mental health implications of detaining asylum seekers: systematic review', *The British Journal of Psychiatry* 194(4): 306–12.

Roguski, M. and Chauvel, F. (2009) *The Effects of Imprisonment on Inmates' and their Families Health and Wellbeing*, Wellington: National Health Committee.

Rowe, R. and O'Brien, E. (2016) '"Genuine" refugees or illegitimate "boat people": political constructions of asylum seekers and refugees in the Malaysia Deal debate', *Australian Journal of Social Issues* 49(1): 171–93.

Rudd, K. (2006) 'Faith in Politics', *The Monthly*, [online] October, Available from: https://www.themonthly.com.au/monthly-essays-kevin-rudd-faith-politics--300 [Accessed 8 March 2021].

Rundle, G. (2001) 'The opportunist: John Howard and the triumph of reaction', *Quarterly Essay* 3(October): 1–65.

Ryan, H. (2020) 'Australian Government to reopen Christmas Island Detention Centre during COVID-19 crisis', *The Guardian*, [online] 5 August, Available from: https://www.theguardian.com/australia-news/2020/aug/04/australian-government-to-reopen-christmas-island-detention-centre-during-covid-19-crisis [Accessed 8 March 2021].

Sands, V., O'Neill, D. and Hodge, G. (2019) 'Cheaper, better, and more accountable? Twenty-five years of prison privatisation in Victoria', *Australian Journal of Public Administration* 78: 577–95.

Scheper-Hughes, N. and Bourgois, P. (2004) 'Introduction: making sense of violence', *The Violence in War and Peace: An Anthology*, Oxford: Wiley-Blackwell.

Schermuly, A. and Forbes-Mewett. H. (2016) 'Food, identity and belonging: a case study of South African-Australians', *British Food Journal* 118(10): 2434–43.

Schloenhardt, A. and Craig, C. (2015) '"Turning back the boats": Australia's interdiction of irregular migrants at sea', *International Journal of Refugee Law* 27(4): 536–72.

Schlosser, E. (1998) 'The prison-industrial complex', *The Atlantic*, [online] December, Available from: https://www.theatlantic.com/magazine/archive/1998/12/the-prison-industrial-complex/304669/ [Accessed 6 June 2021].

Scott, J. C. (1986) 'Everyday forms of peasant resistance', *The Journal of Peasant Studies* 13(2): 5–35.

Scott, J. C. (1989) 'Everyday forms of resistance', *The Copenhagen Journal of Asian Studies* 4(1): 33–62.

Scott, J. C. (1990) *Domination and the Arts of Resistance: Hidden Transcripts*, New Haven: Yale University Press.

Senate Legal and Constitutional Affairs Legislation Committee (2019) 'Migration Amendment (Repairing Medical Transfers) Bill 2019 [Provisions]', *Commonwealth of Australia*, [online] October, Available from: https://parlinfo.aph.gov.au/parlInfo/download/committees/report sen/024304/toc_pdf/MigrationAmendment(RepairingMedicalTransf ers)Bill2019[Provisions].pdf;fileType=application%2Fpdf [Accessed 22 April 2021].

Silverman, S. J. and Massa, E. (2012) 'Why immigration detention is unique', *Population, Space and Place* 18(6): 677–86.

Silverstein, J. (2020) 'Refugee children, boats and drownings: a history of an Australian 'humanitarian' discourse', *History Australia* 17(4): 728–42.

Sirriyeh, A. (2018) *The Politics of Compassion*, United Kingdom: Bristol University Press.

Smith, J. (2016) *Imperialism in the Twenty-First Century: Globalization, Super-Exploitation, and Capitalism's Final Crisis*, New York: Monthly Review Press.

Snyder, J. A. (2009) *A Sociology of Trauma: Violence and Self-Identity* [Dissertation] University of Virginia.

Spinks, H. and McCluskey, I. (2013) 'Asylum seekers and the Refugee Convention', *Parliamentary Library*, [online] December, Available from: https://parlinfo.aph.gov.au/parlInfo/download/library/prspub/2902 997/upload_binary/2902997.pdf;fileType=application%2Fpdf#search= %22library/prspub/2902997%22 [Accessed 22 April 2021].

Spinks, H. and Phillips, J. (2011) '*Tampa*: ten years on', *Flagpost*, [online] 22 August, Available from: https://www.aph.gov.au/About_Parliament/ Parliamentary_Departments/Parliamentary_Library/FlagPost/2011/Aug ust/Tampa_ten_years_on [Accessed 27 March 2021].

St Guillaume, L. and Finlay, E. (2018) 'Disabled mobility and the production of impairment: the case of Australia's migration policy framework', *Asia Pacific Viewpoint* 59(1): 119–31.

Stateless (2020) ABC Television, March–April.

Stayner, T. (2020) 'The International Criminal Court has found conditions asylum seekers are held in on Nauru and Papua New Guinea may constitute a breach of international law', *SBS News*, (online) 14 February, Available from: https://www.sbs.com.au/news/offshore-detention-conditions-may- constitute-a-breach-of-international-law-but-australia-won-t-be-prosecu ted [Accessed 27 March 2021].

Steel, Z., Silove, D., Brooks, R., Momartin, S., Alzuhairi, B. and Susljik, I. (2006) 'Impact of immigration detention and temporary protection on the mental health of refugees', *British Journal of Psychiatry* 188(January): 58–64.

Stevens, R. (2012) 'Political debates on asylum seekers during the Fraser Government, 1977–1982', *Australian Journal of Politics and History* 58(4): 526–41.

Stoller, N. (2003) 'Space, place and movement as aspects of health care in three women's prisons', *Social Science and Medicine* 56: 2263–75.

Surawski, N., Pedersen, A. and Briskman, L. (2008) 'Resisting refugee policy: stress and coping of refugee advocates', *The Australian Community Psychologist* 20(2): 16–29.

Svensson, B. and Svensson, K. (2006) *Inmates in Motion: Metamorphosis as Governmentality – A Case of Social Logistics, Working Paper 2006, 5*, Lund: Lund Universite.

Sykes, G. (2007 [1958]) *The Society of Captives: A Study of a Maximum Security Prison*, Princeton and Oxford: Princeton University Press.

Tasca, M. (2018) 'The (dis)continuity of parenthood among incarcerated fathers: an analysis of caregivers' accounts', *Child Care in Practice* 24(2): 131–47.

Tazreiter, C. (2020) 'The emotional confluence of borders, refugees and visual culture: the case of Behrouz Boochani, Held in Australia's Offshore Detention Regime', *Critical Criminology* 28: 193–207.

Tazreiter, C. (2010) 'Local to global activism: The movement to protect the rights of refugees and asylum seekers', *Social Movement Studies* 9(2): 201–214.

Tewksbury, R. and DeMichele, M. (2005) 'Going to prison: a prison visitation program', *The Prison Journal* 85(3): 292–310.

The Global Mail (2014) 'At work inside our detention centres: A guard's story', *The Global Mail*, [online] Available from: http://tgm-serco.patar mstrong.net.au/ [Accessed 21 December 2021].

The Migration Observatory (2020) 'Immigration detention in the UK', *The Migration Observatory,* [online] 20 May, Available from: https://migra tionobservatory.ox.ac.uk/resources/briefings/immigration-detention-in-the-uk/ [Accessed 22 April 2021].

The Sydney Morning Herald (2001) 'Credibility overboard', *The Sydney Morning Herald*, [online] 8 November, Available from: https://www.smh.com.au/national/credibility-overboard-20011108-gdf9oq.html [Accessed 22 April 2021].

Tilbury, F. (2007) ' "We are family": the use of family tropes in refugee/advocate talk', *Social Identities: Journal for the Study of Race, Nation and Culture* 13(5): 627–49.

Tlozek, E. (2015) 'Asylum seeker school student "dragged on ground", put in detention in lieu of deal to return Iranian citizens, husband says', *ABC News*, [online] 20 December, Available from: https://www.abc.net.au/news/2015-08-08/iranian-asylum-seekers-devastated-by-return-to-detent ion/6682210 (Accessed 19 December 2021).

Tlozek, E. (2016) 'Reza Barati death: two men jailed over 2014 murder of asylum seeker at Manus Island detention centre', *ABC News*, [online] 19 April, Available from: https://www.abc.net.au/news/2016-04-19/reza-barati-death-two-men-sentenced-to-10-years-over-murder/7338928 (Accessed 27 March 2021).

Tofighian, O. (2020) 'Introducing Manus Prison theory: knowing border violence', *Globalizations* 17(7): 1138–1156.

Turner, J. and Peters, K. (2017) 'Rethinking mobility in criminology: beyond horizontal mobilities of prisoner transportation', *Punishment and Society* 19(1): 96–114.

Ugelvik, T. (2011) 'The hidden food: mealtime resistance and identity work in a Norwegian prison', *Punishment and Society* 13(1): 47–63.

Ugelvik, T. and Damsa, D. (2018) 'The pains of crimmigration imprisonment: perspectives from a Norwegian all-foreign prison', *British Journal of Criminology* 58(5): 1025–43.

United Nations Committee against Torture (2014) 'Concluding observations on the combined fourth and fifth periodic reports of Australia', *United Nations*, (online) Available from: http://docstore.ohchr.org/SelfServices/FilesHandler.ashx?enc=6QkG1d%2FPPRiCAqhKb7yhsoQ6oVJgGLf6YX4ROs1VbzHbjPhQXE%2B0WWmIrYFRkrdSVDi646tTx7wQu2ScGTgf%2BJVP%2Bu4P9Ry9gI0FCCIcBVuKEcWc%2Fk%2FXTL4sM%2BWHda%2Fd [Accessed 27 March 2021].

United Nations Human Rights Committee (2017) 'Concluding observations on the sixth periodic report of Australia', *United Nations Human Rights Committee*, [online] 1 December, Available from: http://docstore.ohchr.org/SelfServices/FilesHandler.ashx?enc=6QkG1d%2FPPRiCAqhKb7yhsoAl3%2FFsniSQx2VAmWrPA0uA3KW0KkpmSGOue15UG42EodNm2j%2FnCTyghc1kM8Y%2FLQ4n6KZBdggHt5qPmUYCI8eCslXZmnVlMq%2FoYCNPyKpq [Accessed 8 March 2021].

United Nations Human Rights Council (2016) 'Report of the working group on the universal periodic review: Australia', *United Nations General Assembly*, (online) 13 January, Available from: https://documents-dds-ny.un.org/doc/UNDOC/GEN/G16/004/89/PDF/G1600489.pdf?OpenElement [Accessed 27 March 2021].

van der Veen, G. (1995) 'Psychotherapeutic work with refugees', in R. J. Kebler, C. R. Figley and B. P. R. Gersons (eds) *Beyond Trauma: Cultural and Societal Dynamics*, New Jersey: Transaction Books, pp. 151–70.

van Kooy, J., Magee, L. and Robertson, S. (2021) '"Boat people" and discursive bordering: Australian parliamentary discourse on asylum seekers, 1977–2013', *Refuge* 37(1): 13–26.

Vandervoordt, R. (2017) 'The politics of food and hospitality: how Syrian refugees in Belgium create a home in hostile environments', *Journal of Refugee Studies* 30(4): 605–21.

Vinthagen, S. and Johansson, A. (2013) '"Everyday resistance": explorations of a concept and its theories', *Resistance Studies Magazine* 1: 1–46.

von Werthern, M., Robjant, K., Chui, Z., Schon, R., Ottisova, L., Mason, C. and Katona, C. (2018) 'The impact of immigration detention on mental health: a systematic review', *BMC Psychiatry* 18(382): 1–19.

Vujkovic, M. (2019) 'His burns were "very survivable" but Omid Masoumali died slowly over two days', *ABC News*, [online] 1 March, Available from: https://www.abc.net.au/news/2019-03-01/inquest-death-iranian-refugee-omid-masoumali-burns/10854742 [Accessed 8 March 2021].

Warr, J. (2016) 'The deprivation of certitude, legitimacy and hope: foreign national prisoners and the pains of imprisonment', *Criminology and Criminal Justice* 16(3): 301–18.

Webber, F. (2011) 'How voluntary are voluntary returns', *Race and Class* 52(4): 98–107.

Whyte, S. (2014) 'Abbott offers asylum seekers $10k to go home', *The Sydney Morning Herald* [online] 21 June, Available from: https://www.smh.com.au/politics/federal/abbott-offers-asylum-seekers-10k-to-go-home-20140620-3ajr6.html [Accessed 24 March 2021].

Yaxley, L. (2015) 'Gillian Triggs has a "completely partisan approach": Scott Morrison', *The World Today*, [online] 9 June, Available from: https://www.abc.net.au/worldtoday/content/2015/s4251480.htm [Accessed 20 December 2021].

Zhou, N. (2020) 'Kurdish refuge "shocked" by Australia's decision to free him after seven years in detention', *The Guardian*, [online] 12 December, Available from: https://www.theguardian.com/australia-news/2020/dec/12/kurdish-refugee-shocked-by-australias-decision-to-free-him-after-seven-years-in-detention [Accessed 7 June 2021].

Zion, D., Briskman, L. and Loff, B. (2010) 'Returning to history: the ethics of researching asylum seeker health in Australia', *The American Journal of Bioethics* 10(2): 48–56.

Zizek, S. (2016) *Against the Double Blackmail: Refugees, Terror and Other Troubles with the Neighbours*, United Kingdom: Allen Lane.

Index

References to endnotes show both the page
number and the note number (141n5).

and personhood recognition 82, 83, 84
and relocations 102, 103–4, 137–8
response to harm 72–3, 76
visitor attrition 128, 129–30
visitor entrance procedure 46, 49, 50–1
visiting room, inside of
  communal celebrations 61–2
  everyday visits 58–61
  purpose-built visiting rooms 59, 65
visitor application processes 39–42
visitor attrition 128–30
visitor endurance 130–2
visitor entrance procedures
  admission of food 36–7, 50–3, 59
  admission of gifts 37, 48–50, 62
  approaching of facilities 43–4
  submitting to security screening 44–7
visitor–detainee relationships *see* friendships
  between visitors and detainees
volunteering benefits 115–16

W

Westbridge Migrant Centre (Sydney) 13
White Australian policy 11–12

whiteness, and detention system 30, 85–7,
  94, 116
Whitlam, G. 12
Wickham Point facility 22, 100
  see also Darwin facility
witness bearing 91–4
Woomera facility 14

X

Xenophobia 11

Y

Yongah Hill facility (Western Australia) 22
  and advocacy 90
  disruption and disorientation 107
  and relocations 101–2, 108, 109
  and intentionality 137
  visitor entrance procedures 43, 45, 47
  see also Perth and Western Australian
    facilities

Z

Zahra, T. 103
Zizek, S. 142n1